THEORY IN PRACTICE SERIES

General Editor: Nigel Wood, School of English, University of Birmingham

Associate Editors: Tony Davies and Barbara Rasmussen, University of Birmingham

Current titles:

Forthcoming titles include:

THE PRELUDE

EDITED BY
NIGEL WOOD

OPEN UNIVERSITY PRESS
BUCKINGHAM · PHILADELPHIA

Open University Press
Celtic Court
22 Ballmoor
Buckingham
MK18 1XW

and
1900 Frost Road, Suite 101
Bristol, PA 19007, USA

First Published 1993

A catalogue record of this book is available from the British Library

ISBN 0 335 09626 3 (pb)

Library of Congress Cataloging-in-Publication Data

The Prelude / Jon Cook . . . [et al.]; edited by Nigel Wood.
    p.   cm. — (Theory in practice series)
    Includes bibliographical references and index.
    ISBN 0-335-09626-3 (pb)
    1. Wordsworth, William, 1770–1850. Prelude.   I. Cook, Jon.
II. Wood, Nigel, 1953–   . III. Series.
PR5864.P74   1993
821'.7 — dc20   92–32420
                                               CIP

Typeset by Colset Pte Ltd, Singapore
Printed in Great Britain by St Edmundsbury Press Ltd,
Bury St Edmunds, Suffolk

Contents

The Editor and Contributors

JON COOK is Director of the Centre for Creative and Performing Arts at the University of East Anglia. He is co-author and editor (with David Aers and David Punter) of *Romanticism and Ideology: Studies in English Writing, 1765–1830* (1981), and editor of *The Selected Writings of William Hazlitt* for Oxford University Press (1991). He has also written numerous essays on the writing and cultural theory of the Romantic period.

PHILIP SHAW is lecturer in English at the University of Leicester. He is editor (with Peter Stockwell) of *Subjectivity and Literature from the Romantics to the Present Day: Creating the Self* (1991). His research interests include the writings of Byron and the interaction of aesthetics and perception in the period.

CLIFFORD SISKIN, a member of the English Department at the State University of New York at Stony Brook, works on problems of literary and social change in the eighteenth and early nineteenth centuries and on current issues in literary theory and cultural studies. He published *The Historicity of Romantic Discourse* with Oxford University Press in 1988 and is an advisory editor for *Literature and History* and *Reconstructing Romanticism*. At present, he is completing a book on the literary construction of professional behaviour.

SUSAN WOLFSON, professor of English at Princeton University, is the author of *The Questioning Presence: Wordsworth, Keats and the Interrogative Mode in Romantic Poetry* (1986), as well as numerous reviews and articles on various issues in English Romanticism. She is completing a book entitled *Formal Changes*, which is concerned with various crises in Romantic poetic theory and practice as they bear on the management of poetic forms. In development is *Figures on the Margin*, a study of the language of gender in the Romantic period, with special attention to texts, by both men and women, casting critical attention on gender stereotyping and contesting such discriminations.

NIGEL WOOD is a lecturer in the School of English at the University of Birmingham. He is the author of studies on Gay and Swift and of several essays on literary theory. He is also editor of Fanny Burney's diaries.

Editors' Preface

The object of this series is to help bridge the divide between the understanding of theory and the interpretation of individual texts. Students are therefore introduced to theory in practice. Although contemporary critical theory is now taught in many colleges and universities, it is often separated from the day-to-day consideration of literary texts that is the staple ingredient of most tuition in English. A thorough dialogue between theoretical and literary texts is thus avoided.

Each of these specially commissioned volumes of essays seeks by contrast to involve students of literature in the questions and debates that emerge when a variety of theoretical perspectives are brought to bear on a selection of 'canonical' literary texts. Contributors were not asked to provide a comprehensive survey of the arguments involved in a particular theoretical position, but rather to discuss in detail the implications for interpretation found in particular essays or studies, and then, taking these into account, to offer a reading of the literary text.

This rubric was designed to avoid two major difficulties which commonly arise in the interaction between literary and theoretical texts: the temptation to treat a theory as a bloc of formulaic rules that could be brought to bear on any text with roughly predictable results; and the circular argument that texts are constructed as such merely by the theoretical perspective from which we choose to regard them. The former usually leads to studies that are really just footnotes to the adopted theorists, whereas the latter is effortlessly self-fulfilling.

It would be disingenuous to claim that our interests in the teaching of theory were somehow neutral and not open to debate. The idea for this series arose from the teaching of theory in relation to specific texts. It is inevitable, however, that the practice of theory poses significant questions as to just what 'texts' might be and where the dividing lines between text and context may be drawn. Our hope is that this series will provide a forum for debate on just such issues as these which are continually posed when students of literature try to engage with theory in practice.

Tony Davies
Barbara Rasmussen
Nigel Wood

Preface

The idea for this series arose from the teaching of a course on Methods and Contexts at the University of Birmingham. I would like to express my gratitude to all who supported the idea in the first place, especially Tony Davies, Tom Davis, Lynne Pearce, Martin Pumphrey and Barbara Rasmussen who supplied many essential and timely suggestions, as did Ray Cunningham and John Skelton at the Open University Press. The challenge set by the work of the late (and much missed) Raman Selden in this area will be obvious to all those versed in the difficulties and rewards of practising theory. My enthusiasm for Wordsworth was first fostered by Roy Park some time ago; the decision to take *The Prelude* on in this format is some form of redress for not building on it sooner.

My greatest debt is to the contributors who have made this a genuinely collaborative project, and who have often reminded me of the remarkable Wordsworth, the radical in the midst of constraint.

Nigel Wood

How to Use
this Book

Each of these essays is composed of a theoretical and a practical element. Contributors were asked to identify the main features of their perspective on the text (exemplified by a single theoretical essay or book) and then to illustrate their own attempts to put this into practice.

We realize that many readers new to recent theory will find its specific vocabulary and leading concepts strange and difficult to relate to current critical traditions in most English courses.

The format of this book has been designed to help if this is your situation, and we would advise the following:

(i) Before reading the essays, glance at the editor's introduction where the literary text's critical history is discussed, and

(ii) also at the prefatory information immediately before the essays, where the editor attempts to supply a context for the adopted theoretical position.

(iii) If you would like to develop your reading in any of these areas, turn to the annotated further reading section at the end of the volume, where you will find brief descriptions of those texts that each contributor has considered of more advanced interest. There are also full citations of the texts to which the contributors have referred in the references. It is also possible that more local information will be contained in notes to the essays.

(iv) The contributors have often regarded the chosen theoretical texts
      as points of departure and it is also in the nature of theoretical
      discussion to apply and test ideas on a variety of texts. Turn,
      therefore, to question and answer sections that follow each essay
      which are designed to allow contributors to comment and expand
      on their views in more general terms.

A Note on
the Text

Unless otherwise indicated, quotations from *The Prelude* are from Wordsworth *et al.* (1979) (full publication details supplied in the references), and are abbreviated in the text to the version, book and line numbers. Where reference has been made to the non-poetic material, the citation is to *P* and then page number.

References to other works are to the edition of *William Wordsworth: The Poems*, ed. John O. Hayden (1977).

Introduction

NIGEL WOOD

In 1818, Wordsworth's stay in London was enlivened by several visits
from admirers both to his Mortimer Street lodgings and, in the case of
John Keats, to the house of his wife's cousin, Thomas Monkhouse. The
meeting had been arranged by the painter, Benjamin Robert Haydon,
to whom, a year earlier, Keats had confessed how the mere fact of
his poetry in Wordsworth's hands 'put [him] out of breath' with
'Reverence'. About this time, indeed, Keats sent the great man a copy
of his 1817 *Poems*, inscribed 'To W. Wordsworth with the Author's
sincere Reverence', and so, with Haydon by his side, Keats strode to
Queen Anne Street, expressing 'the purest, the most unalloyed pleasure
at the prospect' of the meeting. What is known of what then occurred
is coloured by Haydon's determination to scoop others with inside
knowledge. His version has it that Keats was prevailed upon to recite
his *Hymn to Pan* from *Endymion*, whereupon Wordsworth 'drily said,
"a Very pretty piece of Paganism" '. According to Haydon, Keats was
offended and 'felt it *deeply*' (letter from Haydon to Edward Moxon, 29
November 1845, in Rollins 1948, II: 143–4). There is doubt as to
whether this actually took place quite as reported,[1] but what is clear is
that Keats's enthusiasm for Wordsworthian romanticism no longer
surfaces in poetic allusion or journal confession from near this date.
Parodied by Keats's great friend, J.H. Reynolds, in *Peter Bell: A Lyrical
Ballad* (1819) and recently criticized even by Coleridge in his *Biographia
Literaria* (1817),[2] Wordsworth's 'simplicity', his rush to describe

spiritual drama rather than its manifest cause, or, worse, to confuse them, was gradually opened up to parody and poetic alternatives. For Keats, the 'camelion poet' (the true 'poetical Character') was to stand quite distinct from 'the wordsworthian or egotistical sublime which [was] a thing per se and stands alone' (letter to Richard Woodhouse, 27 October 1818; Keats 1970: 157).

Keats's opinion would not be quite so resonant if it did not also illustrate some of the constant critical distrust of the grander claims of Wordsworth as Seer, whose 'philosophical' strain could also come to be regarded as a departure from genuine poetry. Better to be the creator of 'Tintern Abbey' with its desire to take away 'the heat and fever' and so ease 'the Burden of the Mystery' than to dabble in the philosophical 'axioms' of an *Excursion* (1814).[3] If it seemed obvious to Keats that poetic philosophy was a contradiction in terms, then it might not be so clearly the case with more recent readers – and, in any case, Keats could not have known of *The Prelude*, which was first published (posthumously) in 1850, and which could have been more of a test case for this taste for 'pure' poetry.

Does *The Prelude* Exist?

The subtitle to the 1850 *Prelude* (so called by Mary Wordsworth), is 'Growth of a Poet's Mind/An Autobiographical Poem'. This is an apt assessment as it describes not just the enlarged fourteen-book edition, but a whole process of revision and redirection that lasted from the first jottings in a small notebook carried by Wordsworth and his sister Dorothy during the 1798 isolation in Goslar, Germany (MS JJ; DC MS 19 held at Dove Cottage) to what was largely the result of perhaps expedient decisions by Wordsworth's executors in 1850. We can never be sure that Wordsworth ever regarded even his fair manuscript drafts as printer's copy; although we know of his work on such a copy for the 1850 version, what we have of the verse *as an integrated item* is still an unauthorized construction by others.[4] In the most commonsensical way, this does not mean that the poem does not exist, for most libraries stock a reassuringly hardback *Prelude*, doubtless with a critical apparatus (that is easy to ignore). Wordsworth, however, always saw the poem in its various forms as a prelude to a long 'philosophical' poem, tentatively entitled *The Recluse*. As a 'finished' product, therefore, in whatever version we choose, the poem's self-sufficiency and even relation back to Wordsworth's authority and sanction gives an impression that is foreign to the known biographical and bibliographical facts.

There are several 'Preludes': the 'Two-Part Prelude' of 1799, regarded for the first time by Helen Darbishire in 1959 as 'one vital and self-contained whole',[5] the so-called 'Five Book' *Prelude*, dating from January to March 1804[6] suddenly abandoned and left in a fragmentary state by Wordsworth when he abruptly considered it suitable for extension, the thirteen-book 1805 version, copied out in a fair draft between November 1805 and February 1806 (clearing the way for renewed emphasis on the main philosophical sections that he thought would lead to the completion of *The Recluse*), an intermediate version on which Mark Reed gives full information in his Cornell edition of the thirteen-book poem (see Reed 1991), and the first published edition of 1850. It is therefore crucial to realize the difference between the chronology of composition and the actual availability of the earlier printed texts for critical evaluation. It was perhaps not possible before Ernest de Selincourt's 1926 variorum edition, where the 1805 text was first published, to appreciate the full scale of the multi-part *Prelude*. As the editor then phrased it:

> *The Prelude* is the essential living document for the interpretation
> of Wordsworth's life and poetry; any details, therefore, that can
> be gathered of the manner and circumstances of its composition
> must be of interest alike to biographer and critic. But of more
> vital importance than these is a knowledge of its original text.
>
> (de Selincourt 1926: xv)

Where, then, can we find the poem's point of origin? Or, to anticipate a further line of critical enquiry, what would we make of it when found? There would surely be a counterargument to the effect that what we could discover of the author's *final* intentions should weigh more heavily in the balance, presumably when Wordsworth had had longer to digest matters. For the purposes of critical assessment and interpretation this possible contention as to which *Prelude* is to be preferred is perhaps of less impact than the fact of the textual uncertainty itself. Even if scholarship were to unearth an unequivocal directive from Wordsworth as to what form of the poem best suited him, this, while of no little interest in itself, would not prevent some readers identifying this hypothetical pronouncement as 'true' only of the 'Wordsworth' at the date of its utterance. Similarly, the various forms of the poetry need not take their chronological position in some smooth gradient of development, emanating in the highly evolved 1850 lines. In its several manuscript forms, *The Prelude* is composed by several 'Wordsworths' – and more: Dorothy, who transcribed the verse, and Coleridge, who supplied not just inspiration but also careful advice, to say nothing of Mary and the executors who prepared the 1850 edition. Given that there are few clear indicators as to where *Wordsworth* exists in relation to the hardback copy (however variorum) we find in the library, the roll-call of contributors to the 'meaning' derived from *The Prelude* should include Helen Darbishire, Ernest de Selincourt, M.H. Abrams, Jonathan Wordsworth, Stephen Gill, Stephen Parrish, W.J.B. Owen and Mark L. Reed. 'Exit author' means enter reader and most certainly editor.

This 'deconstruction' of the author-figure has at least two significant results. First, it could allow (authorize?) readerly adventures in the text. If the printed words on the page are the product of necessary editorial intervention as well as the spread of the identifiable 'Wordsworths' who penned the manuscripts, then we might feel ourselves free to draw a basic distinction, following Roland Barthes's influential wording, between two forms of critical discourse: that interested in *The Prelude*'s existence as a 'work', an object of consumption, knowledge, library classification and integrity, and its existence as a 'text', something '*experienced only in an activity of production*' and thus a 'methodological field' that is plural and which is produced in the process of reading: 'The Text can be approached, experienced, in reaction to the sign. The work closes on a signified' (Barthes 1977: 158–9). *The Prelude* is only, therefore, an exaggerated example of what could be postulated of all writing.

But, if we are not reading Wordsworth, we are consequently left with the conclusion that, ultimately, we are reading ourselves, noting merely the modes of how we 'displace' anxieties on to the text or, in, negotiating with the words we read (however disparate their provenance), how we transfer our own desires on to them. Even the most relativistic theory of the production of meaning makes use of the idea of 'text', if for no better reason than that it provides (although does not determine) differences in reading.

The second result of the fainter authorial outline is the recognition that, although it is a manifestly difficult task to pick one's way through the palimpsestuous writing that makes up the poem's full range of meanings, where revision obscures and subverts any original context for unitary meaning, this still remains an obligation for the analysis of each of its forms. Instead of hiving off the verifiable from the textual, E.D. Hirsch, in his *Validity of Interpretation* (1967) and *Aims of Inter-*

pretation (1976), promotes a norm for interpretation *based* on the author's meaning. He would thus avoid what he takes to be a confusion that 'mistakenly identifies meaning with mental processes rather than with an object of those processes' (Hirsch 1967: 32). Meaning can be shared between reader and author only by a rigorous process of reassessment and revision until there is identified a distinction between what an author 'does mean by a word sequence and what he could mean by it' (Hirsch 1967: 38).[7] This does not mean that we are tied to the empirical facts as to the writer's conscious intention in the work of criticism. In locating a work's 'intrinsic genre' and its communication of some sharable 'type idea', Hirsch is confident that, while initial notions of 'meaning' can often be corrected when further information about the writer's context and declared aims is gradually discovered, the validity of this critical aim is not undermined. A work's 'meaning' is thus not to be confused with the 'significance' it has for individuals or communities whose shared concepts or subsequent cultural situation establish a particularly binding relationship with the work in question. 'Meaning' exists (and can be phrased in several alternative ways given the variety of its interpreters) as much as a relationship to it: its 'significance'.

In practical interpretative terms, as the words of the poem seem always to be in process of revision, Wordsworthian 'intention' is a curiously qualified discovery. As its title suggests, the poem is designed to anticipate another state of existence, either *The Recluse*, the mature poetic career or his wider redemptive vocation, when, together with Coleridge, they may be

> United helpers forward of a day
> Of firmer trust, joint labourers in the work —
> Should Providence such grace to us vouchsafe —
> Of their redemption, surely yet to come.
> Prophets of Nature, we to them will speak
> A lasting inspiration, sanctified
> By reason and by truth; what we have loved
> Others will love, and we may teach them how:
> Instruct them how the mind of man becomes
> A thousand times more beautiful than the earth
> On which he dwells . . .
>
> (1805, XIII: 438–48)

This may seem direct enough, yet the provisional nature of this statement can be seen if we identify what happened to the 'lasting inspiration' by 1850: 'sanctified/By reason, blest by faith' (1850, XIV: 447–8). If the 1805 'truth' meant roughly the same as 'faith', why was it altered in 1832, the poem's last substantial change? We should also consider the provenance of the 'redemption' promised mankind (1805, XIII: 441; in 1850, 'deliverance', XIV: 445). This millenarian zeal first hoves into view as early as the two-part *Prelude*, where the wreck of Revolutionary ideals, the 'sneers/On visionary minds' (II: 485–6) and 'This melancholy waste of hopes o'erthrown' (II: 479), is historically specific and some way distant from an exercise of 'faith' as opposed to 'truth'-telling.

The evidence we have as to Wordsworth's conscious intentions in starting *The Recluse* points to a political motive.[8] Coleridge's advice around 10 September 1799 was to persevere with its grand idea, and address it to

> those, who in consequence of the complete failure of the French Revolution, have thrown up all hopes of the amelioration of mankind, and are sinking into an almost epicurean selfishness, disguising the same under the soft titles of domestic attachment and for visionary *philosophes*.
>
> (1956–71, I: 527)

If Coleridge is to be believed, especially at the turn of the century, Wordsworth's inspiration was a philosophical one, and yet, the emphasis in most of the latter's notes on the role of *The Prelude* in the project is subtly different. When, in March 1804, he considered the extension of *The Prelude* to a thirteen-book format in his letter to De Quincey, he stresses its autobiographical qualities ('a Poem on my own life') which is a 'tributary' to the more impressive conception, 'a moral and Philosophical Poem; the subject whatever I find most interesting in Nature, Man, Society, most adapted to Poetic illustration' (de Selincourt 1967– , I: 454). The triad of 'Nature, Man, Society' recurs in his 25 December 1804 letter to Sir George Beaumont ('Man, Nature, and society'; see 1967– , I: 517), and picks up the same theme as first announced to James Tobin on 6 March 1798. In the 'Preface' to *The Excursion* (1814) this survives, where the poem is related to *The Recluse* as 'the ante-chapel . . . to the body of a gothic church' (Owen and Smyser 1974, III: 5).

There are at least three points to be made about these testimonies and especially as regards *The Prelude*. First, Wordsworth often conceived it as a set of exercises to be kept back until time and his own inclination had provided the world with *The Recluse*. He certainly thought about publication, as the fair copy of the 1805 version and (incomplete) work on the 1850 printer's copy makes clear, but the poem kept growing at the expense of the larger (and more Coleridgean) idea.

Second, its lack of narrative structure, or rather, of dramatic plot with varied action, is often worthy of remark. The sanctioned informality of the biography locates the controlling centre in a single consciousness. Wordsworth is acutely aware of the possible egotism of the scheme. On 1 May 1805, he is almost shocked at his own temerity: such a long poem, 'a thing unprecedented in literary history that a man should talk so much about himself'. Nevertheless, this apparent self-regard is no 'self-conceit . . . but real humility' as it is pursued as the inferior task. This is a simpler option than the choice of the deeps of philosophy charted for *The Recluse*, 'as I had nothing to do but describe what I had felt and thought' (de Selincourt 1967– , II.i, 586–7).

Lastly, there is a persistent difficulty if we attempt to trace some clear, intended audience for the poem in any form, or some declaration that the poem had ever reached the status of a final, 'organic whole'. As late as 16 November 1842, Wordsworth, in mentioning 'my MS. poem on my own life' to Aubrey de Vere, discloses no intention to publish it or any enthusiasm about its eventual fate (1967– , V: 1386–7) – this, after the last revision stage of 1839. The audience for which it is most intended is a domestic one, as if its private scope might have disqualified it for publication. The 1805 fair copy did gain a hearing, on the other hand. Coleridge composed his ode, 'To W. Wordsworth. Lines Composed, For The Greater Part On The Night,/On Which He Finished The Recitation Of His Poem/(In Thirteen Books) Concerning The Growth/And History Of His Own Mind', in early January 1807, in circumstances described in the title. The poem is a rather breathless affair, and yet one salient detail is Coleridge's prizing of the 'truth' of the 1805 version, the way that his work

> Makes audible a linked Song of Truth.
> Of Truth profound a sweet continuous Song
> Not learnt, but native, her own natural notes!
>
> (*P*, 543, II: 51–3)

The work is not itself the 'Song of Truth', note, but it announces it in some way. This continuum is subtextual, an idea not amenable to direct representation. It is especially fitting for Coleridge to close the poem with a cameo scene, inclusive of the poem's first audience, the 'happy Vision of beloved Faces!/All, whom I deepliest love, in one room all!' (*P*, 545; II: 113–14).

Does it much matter, therefore, which version we choose to call *The Prelude*? If the verse was for a domestic readership, why not allow the free play of choice as to which form to read? This is no procedural pedantry. The example cited above of the closing exordium to both the 1805 and 1850 versions manifests wholesale revision, and the attention is not just to the tidying of the style. From 'truth' to 'faith' may seem a small step, but the greater devotional repose introduced by the later revisions amounts to a sea change in the poem's play of emphases. It is not that faith did not provide consolation in 1805 or that we have then the distillation of the radical Wordsworth, lost thereafter. It is just that there is enough evidence to suppose that there were several 'final intentions' and that this fact is obscured by the need for a unitary performance. As also illustrated by the above example, the later versions (especially) may be read from blind as continuous and loose, but eventually coherent, works. By 1850, however, there are frequent outcrops of several earlier formations, forming almost a geological cross-section of earlier authorial selves. Do the 1850 and 1805 versions simply provide successfully edited and newly formed units, where the memories of previous incarnations are effaced? Or does retrospective editorial tinkering manage to create fully original and new poems?

A close look at some textual variations puts this interpretative problem in perspective. (For a comprehensive account of the major structural changes in the life of the poem, see *P*, 512–24.) Most of the changes are not structural, but there are two significant inclusions for 1850: the praise of Edmund Burke at 1850, VII: 512–43, and the reverie on the desecration of the Grande Chartreuse monastery at 1850, VI: 420–88. By then the thinly veiled autobiographical account of Wordsworth's relationship with Annette Vallon, which is recounted in the Julia and Vaudracour passage at 1805, IX: 560–935, has been excised. These are not idle alterations for changing fashion's sake. Julia and Vaudracour are lifted out of the poem to conform with Wordsworth's new-found prominence as a man of letters – even if it is told in the third person. The other inclusions are more crucial, and often prejudice readers either for or against 1850. Edmund Burke would certainly have looked most out of place in 1805. As the author of *Reflections on the Revolution in France* (1790) he had stressed reform as an alternative to French innovation, and had done more than most to turn English opinion against the stirring events. Now, in 1850, the genius of Burke inspires a recantation, as Wordsworth asks his shade for forgiveness granted to 'the pen seduced/By specious wonders' (1850, VII: 512–13). Burke stands for the opposition to William

Godwin's almost anarchic individualism,[9] providing ridicule at 'all systems built on abstract rights' (1850, VII: 524). In their place, Burke is praised for reminding us of the 'vital power of social ties/Endeared by Custom' and the confounding of 'upstart Theory' (1850, VII: 527–9). Coleridge's enthusiasm at the 'philosophical Poem' Wordsworth had commenced in 1798 seems a long way away. The passage ends in the personified and reified 'Wisdom, like the Goddess from Jove's brain,/[Breaking] forth in armour of resplendent words' in Parliament (1850, VII: 538–9). Here 'Wisdom' is no achieved possession. The allusion to Athena's birth when fully formed from the head of Zeus treats it as a given, and the personification gives the illusion of its obvious qualities.

The Grande Chartreuse interpolation is more integral to the logic of 1805, in that it produces the kind of dramatic irony that pervades the account of Wordsworth's tour of France with Robert Jones in 1790–1. Written from the perspective of the 'mature' poet of 1816–19, this section has a proleptic quality, providing a knowledge of its eventual despoliation (in 1792) that the young travellers could not have predicted. The first account of the visit to the monastery can be found in *Descriptive Sketches* (1793), which reads more like the most Parnassian passages from 1850. Travelling with such hope 'that prudence could not then approve', the companions encounter the Chartreuse in a theatrical set-piece that only occurs in the imagination: 'Whither is fled that Power whose frown severe/Awed sober reason till she crouched in fear?' (*Poems*, 43, 54–5). Overlaying the scene as then encountered, and thus removing its present and full visual impact, there is emblematic warfare that actually occurred almost two years earlier: 'A viewless flight of laughing Demons mock/The Cross, by angels planted on the aerial rock' (*Poems*, 69–70, cf. 1850, VI: 484–5). For *1850* the appearance of the monastery is as a beseiged citadel, although it is most unlikely that the 'military glare/Of riotous men' (1850, VI: 424–5) would be seen until at least eighteen months after Wordsworth and Jones had passed by. The solitude of the place is invaded by patriotic zeal. The passage combines the immediate narrative regret at the loss of 'soul-affecting *solitude*' (VI: 421), where the 'conquest over sense' (VI: 458) is ensured, with the more strident and politically motivated identification of the guilty transgressors, the 'unrestricted and unthinking' who ignore the 'great spirit of human knowledge' (VI: 478, 450). Here the proud individual is pitted against the 'State-whirlwind' (VI: 488) of Jacobin rapine. It is a drama which is not played out at the time reported but in 1816–19 when Wordsworth revised the structure of Book VI, and also touched up the ideological colouring of the whole work. Individualism is here an anti-Jacobin stance, the more so if the interpolated passage is considered in relation to the book as it was 'finished' for 1805, where, 'Unhoused beneath the evening star' he and Jones were permitted a view of the 'Dances of liberty' (1805, VI: 380–1).

This change in Book VI cannot be taken as a secure indication of how all the many changes between the editions were carried out, but it is no surprise if the passage of over forty years would have brought about a significant change of intention – or else why feel that the poem needed further attention? Herbert Lindenberger sums up a prevalent critical attitude: believing that 'the later Wordsworth had forgotten much that the younger poet was trying to do in *The Prelude*' (1964: 297–8). In the process of improving the prosody and tightening the narrative structure, Wordsworth erased the work's original delights, 'the conversational tone, the off-handedness, the struggle towards definition' that are embedded in the 1805 version's 'inner turmoil' and 'mystical passages'.[10] As M.H. Abrams has noted at length (1971: 451–3), the appearance of the passage in 1850 only accentuates the qualification of millennial enthusiasm that can be traced in the 'soulless image' of Mont Blanc (1805, VI: 454), the anti-climactic crossing of the Alps and the troubled night above Lake Como. Joseph F. Kishel is aware, too, of the larger adaptations Wordsworth had to undertake, not just to rework the passage from *Descriptive Sketches* but also that from *The Tuft of Primroses* (1808), where, in the midst of his elegy on changes at Grasmere, 'Nature' is allowed to address the reader directly 'from her Alpine throne' (539; see Kishel 1981: 84–7). Only four lines are allotted to Nature in 1850. The original tenor of the passage may be illustrated when it was used by Wordsworth in his still revolutionary 'Essay, Supplementary to the Preface', appended to the collected works in 1815 and still the sentiments of the manuscript *Tuft of Primroses* (Owen and Smyser 1974, III: 84). In order to educate the reader, the aspiring poet needs to break 'the bonds of custom . . . [overcome] the prejudices of false refinement . . . and [displace] the aversions of inexperience . . . [and, *N.B.*, divest] the reader of the pride that induces him to dwell upon those points wherein men differ from each other' (1974, III: 80). When the Chartreuse lines are placed in the 1850 version of *The Prelude* there is ideological work undertaken, the obscuring not just of an earlier text but also of an earlier self.

How, then, are we to regard the consequences of this for the task of criticism? The search for textual authority is usually undertaken to find biographical as well as procedural coherence. Susan Wolfson's detailed inspection of the revised 'Drowning Man' episodes concludes with the view that

> Wordsworthian revision sustains the illusion of mastery but steadily postpones that achievement as each review of the devised 'perfect view' yields 'A spectacle to which there is no end'. Revision is endlessly open, not simply because any field of vision is open to numerous, potentially infinite interpretations and organizations, but because each view discovers new motions, changes, and interchanges.
>
> (1984: 932)

What we are inevitably left with as an 'object' for interpretation is not just a poem, or even poems, but a process of making the poems that does not allow us to make easy generalizations about 'Wordsworth' or *The Prelude* without careful qualification.[11]

A Poetic Life

The conjunction of Wordsworth's death with the publication of *The Prelude* did much to condition the early reception of the poem. Although it was often conceded that the work was the fruit of much earlier enthusiasms, it was regarded as an anatomy of the poet's mind, allowing a view of the more unformed self. As Poet Laureate (since 1843), Wordsworth was an established and an Establishment figure, and, far from the failure it was once thought, the poem sold well. The first print-run of two thousand copies was bought by 1851 and a smaller, more compact edition followed.[12] *The Prelude*'s younger Wordsworth provided an image not quite consistent with the Victorian patriarch and Anglican sage (see Gill 1990: 416–19), and reminded his readers of his radical 1790s – and, by the mid-century, this was hardly a burning issue. In short, *The Prelude* was unassimilable material: published too late to play a part in forming his public image, and too potentially embarrassing to stand as canonical biographical witness. In his nephew, Christopher Wordsworth's, *Memoirs of William Wordsworth* (1851), the picture seemed more secure and so more acceptable. Thus, up to 1880, when *The Prelude* was still protected by copyright, it was often omitted from commemorative poetic selections.

What also threatened its general acceptance was its length. When *The Excursion* appeared in 1814, its reception was mixed, and, where resisted, it provoked dismissive and damaging comment. Francis Jeffrey reviewed it in November in the *Edinburgh Review*, and assured his readers that Wordsworth's case was 'manifestly hopeless', enough to persuade him that he ought to be given up altogether as 'beyond the power of criticism' (McMaster 1972: 123). This prolonged 'tissue of moral and devotional ravings' (McMaster 1972: 125) was indicative of the very worst of Wordsworth. This could account for the lack of a review on *The Prelude* from the *Edinburgh Review*, *Blackwood's* and *The Quarterly Review*.

On the other hand, the poem was noticed for its poetic as well as its documentary qualities. Frequently, the association of his personal and professional development with the deployment of his characteristic narrative style emphasized the egotistical Wordsworth. *The Eclectic Review* noticed its introversion, but then balanced that with the recognition that 'his object [was] not to weave an artful and amusing story, but sternly and elaborately to trace the "growth of a poet's mind" '. This was a 'metaphysical' rather than a biographical project (*P*, 549). Art arose from the most unpromising materials, anointed by his peculiar poetic eye for detail. Unfortunately, this could also appear clumsy: the reviewer noted 'the slow motion, as of a fleet leaving the harbour – the cumbrous manner in which he relates little things – the clumsiness of the connecting links in the history' (*P*, 550). The *Tait's Edinburgh Magazine* reviewer found him 'sometimes prolix, and some-times careless' and thus 'eminently artless' (*P*, 551). The *Gentlemen's Magazine* regretted the lack of drama in this 'speculative contempla-tion', the way the 'heat and glare' was transmitted 'through some less pervious and colder lens' (*P*, 552). Indeed, the lack of a social element in his imagination was a drawback, as the *Examiner* pointed out:

> He never seems to have passed through that erotic period out of which some poets have never emerged . . . He lives alone in a world of mountains, streams, and atmospheric phenomena, dealing with moral abstractions, and rarely encountered by even shadowy spectres of beings outwardly resembling himself.
>
> (*P*, 558)

This narcissistic impulse has become a Romantic attribute,[13] yet the Victorian determination to break free of the self (often unsuccessful) brought with it a distrust of too much symbol – especially where it led to a sacrifice of plot.

This foregoing might suggest that Wordsworth's reputation was on the decline, but the truth is more complex. The Poet Laureate had outlived the shock he had once caused the reading public in the *Lyrical Ballads*, and he had been absorbed into the traditional canon where poetic sensibilities are safe commodities. As such, he was 'The Lost Leader', according to Browning's poem (in *Dramatic Romances and Lyrics* (1845)), a prime example of the turncoat who could accept a civil-list pension (1842) in return for poetic quiescence: 'Just for a handful of silver he left us,/Just for a riband to stick in his coat' (Browning 1981: 1–2). Browning was hardly the most representative voice, for in 1850 Wordsworth passed into the ranks of the commemorated. It is in Matthew Arnold's work that Wordsworth's poetic reputation is significantly modified.

Fraser's Magazine for June 1850 carried Arnold's elegy for Wordsworth, *Memorial Verses, April, 1850*, in which he is compared to both Goethe and Byron. Goethe may have been a sage and Byron a fiery titan, but Wordsworth supplies other consolations:

> He too upon a wintry clime
> Had fallen – on this iron time
> Of doubts, disputes, distractions, fears.
> He found us when the age had bound
> Our souls in its benumbing round;
> He spoke, and loosed our heart in tears.
> He laid us as we lay at birth
> On the cool flowery lap of earth . . .
>
> (Arnold 1979a: 42–9)

This seems disarmingly simple, but works by the careful associations built around Wordsworth's memory. Nature is some *anima mundi*, to which he returns the reader by heart-loosening tears. Poetic emotion is therefore not just an aimless sentimental stroll, but a means of redemption from the 'iron time' of Victorian progress and Gradgrindery. The association between Victorian problems and turn-of-the-century revolutions of thought and politics should not be dwelt on too much, as Arnold provided a reason for admiring Wordsworth, one that bypassed the Victorian sage and rediscovered the more radical Lyrical Balladeer.

The Prelude was not part of this redemptive canon. When introducing his edition of the poetry in 1879, Arnold made it clear that the large-scale narratives, *The Excursion* and *The Prelude*, were 'by no means [his] best work' which could be found in 'his shorter pieces'. The reason could be found in the common lament that the greater length exposed Wordsworth's liking for prosaic description – the style 'more properly that of eloquent prose than the subtle heightening and change wrought by genuine poetic style' (*P*, 561–2). Describe reality with an attempt to be denotative and you are unpoetic; digress from the object at hand to exemplify or explain its effect and you philosophize where you should be direct. For both Arthur Hugh Clough and Walter Pater (not normally regarded as of one mind) Wordsworth's poetry was an example of the victory of spirit over matter, or of style over content. Clough's 'Lecture on the Poetry of Wordsworth' (published in 1869) showed no concern for his dismantling of poetic style and diction, as he is conceived to have assembled one in its place, which was 'his chief and special charm'. He is revered by Clough for his lyrical and didactic talents, so much that 'it is upon beauty of expression that by the very necessity of his position he has to depend' (McMaster 1972: 181–2). Pater, similarly, appreciated his poetic theories, but fixed on the *effect* of his style and perspective: 'Contemplation – impassioned contemplation – that is with Wordsworth the end-in-itself, the perfect end' (McMaster 1972: 197). One's being is stressed rather than what one does, and Pater read this as a protest against the machine.

The Prelude was thus marginalized by this Victorian requirement to find the poet of Retirement. There is so much of the radical Wordsworth that went against the grain of turn-of-the-century taste, and many twentieth-century views as well. Read alongside the *Salisbury Plain* poems, however, *The Prelude* is far from controversial material. Just as there was an editorial delay on the 1799 and 1805 versions, it could be argued that the earlier unrevised Wordsworth (of no authoritative 'final intention') could only have contributed to critical estimates of the last fifty or so years. For example, the 1793–4 *Salisbury Plain* and the 1795–9 *Adventures on Salisbury Plain*, both indictments of the French War and the social effects it visited on the rural population, have only been fully available since Stephen Gill's Cornell edition of 1975. Known only through the published *Guilt and Sorrow; or Incidents on Salisbury Plain* (1842), and the Victorian attempt at canonizing the emotive Wordsworth, it has proved difficult to recover a historical context for this outraged and crusading poetry (see Hamilton 1986: 33–6; Roe 1988: 118–44; Turner 1986: 39–59; and Gill 1975: 3–14). Without this material, estimates of Wordsworth's intention have been based on partial information and unduly open to Victorian appropriation.

It would be most partisan to claim that the 'modern' view of Wordsworth was a predominantly historicizing one. In Thomas McFarland's recent work, the relevance of contextual discoveries and 'the *decorum* of connections' are assessed critically (1992: 1). Taking issue with Marjorie Levinson's *Wordsworth's Great Period Poems* (1986) and the general tendencies of the New Historicism (see next section), McFarland finds this contextual approach overingenious and marginal, an intervention 'so broad that [Levinson] really has no right to exclude anything' (1992: 29). In this, it ceases to be relevant to 'the forms of culture' (1992: 33; see also 119–36). As is apparent from the unpublished and thus submerged 'Wordsworth', there is no clear consensus as to what our 'forms of culture' might be without access to all testimony and expression – suppressed, marginal and unofficial. Otherwise we derive our notions of the 'normal' or 'central' from received traditions, often constructed to satisfy predominant tastes and values or at least disseminated to earn by them. I similarly find the lack of definition of terms in the return to history a regrettable short-cut (see the Endpiece), but the discovery of 'period' interests in Wordsworth's work is to remedy the lack of critical attention (by accident or design) to his historically relative meanings. If, as David Simpson and Levinson point out, Wordsworth displaces contemporary anxieties into poetic form, then such anxieties will be marginal *inevitably*.[14]

The Prelude became more recognized as a central Romantic document once its 'philosophy' became acceptable as poetic material. For A.C. Bradley, in his lecture on the poet in his *Oxford Lectures on Poetry* (1909; 1920), the characteristic Wordsworthian rhetoric involved an indispensable sublimity, a quality found pre-eminently in *The Prelude*: 'He apprehended all things, natural or human, as the expression of something which, while manifested in them, immeasurably transcends them' (*P*, 563). If the transcendence is to be appreciated, then it would be as well if we knew what was to be transcended – and the reason for such poetic evasion.[15]

Imagination and History

In Book IV of *The Prelude*, after a day of 'strenuous idleness' at Hawkshead (1850, IV: 377) and a night spent 'in dancing, gaiety and mirth' (1805, IV: 320; cf. 1850, IV: 312), Wordsworth takes his route home in a careless yet responsive spirit. On vacation from Cambridge, he is enjoying the 'transient and loose' thoughts (1805, IV: 354) associated with the mind at ease with itself, and thus freed from formulaic responses. Unknown to the student Wordsworth, however, this was to be a sacred moment, for, even though he made no vows himself,

VOWS
Were then made for me: bond unknown to me
Was given, that I should be—else sinning greatly—
A dedicated spirit. On I walked
In blessedness, which even yet remains.

(1805, IV: 341–5)

Suddenly, he senses 'an uncouth shape' coming towards him that causes him to hide within the 'shade/Of a thick hawthorn' in order that he could 'mark him well' (1805, IV: 402–4). He turns out to be a discharged soldier, whose tale so moves Wordsworth that he leads the man to a bed for the night.

This is one of those 'remembrances not lifeless' (1805, IV: 362) that are the stuff of the whole poem, a 'spot of time' that can nourish the self even in the most adverse circumstances. This 'dedication' (probably to poetry) works by disarming the conscious mind, for it only crystallizes as a significant moment in recollection. As this anecdote progresses this dual time scheme, the narrative tense (simple past) and the self-reflexive present of the poet's maturity, operate in tandem for the reader. The narrative is simple and usually progresses at the level of knowledge and consciousness of the earlier Wordsworth, whereas the moments of present invocation or self-analysis that punctuate this reportage are evaluative and transformative and provide links that cohere the poem – and remain integral, even when there is a return to the narrative events.

When this episode was first written in January–February 1798 (as it turns out, one of the first *Prelude* passages to have been written), it was as a companion piece to *The Old Cumberland Beggar*[16] and was shorn of the retrospective dimension. Indeed, it could be read as a contribution to the poetry of social concern that characterizes many of the *Lyrical Ballads* (1798 – *The Beggar* was included in 1800). For instance, *The Beggar* is an emotive piece that indicates the savagery of the Poor Laws,[17] his very uselessness an index of his claim to individual rights:

But deem not this Man useless – Statesmen! ye
Who are so restless in your wisdom, ye
Who have a broom still ready in your hands
To rid the world of nuisances . . .

(*Poems*, 67–70)

'Nature's law' (73) convinces the percipient reformer that he should be kept by communal yet instinctive charity from the workhouse

and by enforced alms from the parish rate. There is little of this
context carried forward to the *Prelude* passage. Here, the focus is on
the effect of the charitable act on Wordsworth. Three extra lines are
added (here italicized) to the original poem:

> I returned
> The blessing of the poor unhappy man,
> And so we parted. *Back I cast a look,*
> *And lingered near the door a little space,*
> *Then sought with quiet heart my distant home.*

(1805, IV: 500–4)

By 1850 the 'poor unhappy man' becomes a 'patient' one (1850,
IV: 465).

There is therefore some distance travelled from *The Discharged Soldier*
of 1798. The labourer who will willingly supply accommodation for the
soldier retains some of that natural charity noted more obviously in *The
Beggar*. Within the larger and personalized scheme of *The Prelude*,
though, the soldier exists as he is perceived and helped by Wordsworth,
who is left with a 'quiet heart'. It is likely that, in 1798, the specification
of his arena of warfare as 'the tropic islands' (1805, IV: 446) was meant
to summon up a certain distaste for the conduct of the French wars in
the West Indies. In the attempt to take over French colonies there some
40,000 mainly novice troops, inadequately supported, had perished
from yellow fever by 1796 (see the soldier's wasted condition) – more
than in the European theatre of war.[18] It is not, it should also be
noted, that Wordsworth necessarily evades historical comment in
supplying an alternative centre of interest in the 1805 and 1850 versions;
he does, however, write a 'different' poem merely by framing it
differently.

This example helps illustrate two usually alternative forms of recent
Wordsworth criticism. Jerome McGann, in his *The Romantic Ideology*,
heralds an attempt to prise our critical assumptions away from the
Romantics' own self-representations (1983b: 21–31, 147–52). It is no
surprise that this deliberate dislocation of what may be an unwarran-
table continuity of interest runs counter to the conclusions of some of
the most influential and sensitive Wordsworthians. In the work of
M.H. Abrams, Geoffrey Hartman and Harold Bloom, for example,
there is a powerful evocation of the autonomous Imagination (see note
15). *The Prelude*, while it may have been composed out of identifiable
autobiographical events, underpinned a reading where, as Clough had
it in 1869, 'all that exists is the feeling, somehow generated in the

poet's sensibility' (McMaster 1972: 183–4). For psychoanalytic criticism, the 'poet's sensibility' needs explaining nowadays less as a secure quality of spirit than as a tension between the will and/or superego and the forces of repressed desire that inhabit the unconscious. As the poem is (ostensibly) about the growth of the poetic mind, there seems more pretext than is usually the case for the commonsensical reader to analyse the splits and contradictions that repression will cause. On the other hand, the critics more aware of historical conditions and their contribution to the text's full meaning stress the coded way that Wordsworth will use the Discharged Soldier and other episodes that purport to demonstrate Wordsworth's subjectivity to elicit the historical subtext that he may have been trying to erase. Emphasis will be less on the *mode* of perception than on the incomplete view formed by *what* the reader is permitted to understand.

Constructing a Self

According to most textbook accounts of Wordsworth's theory of the mind, the dominant early influence was David Hartley's *Observations on Man, His Frame, His Duty and His Expectations* (1749). In short, Hartley believed, influenced by John Locke, that the mind is passive in the face of ingrained associations implanted when we first experience a certain item. When repeated, some of the original context and supplementary feelings are necessarily called once again to consciousness, even though no object that provided that original cause remains. The passive mind is retained in, for example, *Expostulation and Reply* (1798):

> 'The eye – it cannot choose but see;
> We cannot bid the ear be still;
> Our bodies feel, where'er they be,
> Against or with our will.'

> (17–20)

and could be deduced from the organizing belief in the nourishing effects of valuable 'spots of time' (First Part, I: 288–94; 1805, XI: 257–78; 1850, XII: 208–25). The self is thus inexorably developed out of this interaction between experience and its instinctive memory. The emphasis in this poetic faith is supremely important. Coleridge weaned himself off Hartley earlier than Wordsworth. In his letter to Sotheby of 10 September 1802, he lays stress more on the creative and positive powers of the mind:

Nature has her proper interest; and he will know what it is, who believes and feels, that every Thing has a Life of it's own, and that we are all *one Life*. A Poet's Heart and Intellect should be *combined*, *intimately* combined and *unified*, with the great appearances in Nature – and not merely held in solution and loose mixture with them . . .

(Coleridge 1956–71, I: 864)

In *The Prelude* there is a counter-current to Hartley's passive associationism. While the experiential basis is always admitted, the extent to which the original experience actually determines what the mind will do with the perception is limited. The lines on 'Tintern Abbey' (1798) stress that we 'half create' as well as 'perceive' (106–7) and in Book XII (1805) there is the discovery of

A balance, an ennobling interchange
Of action from within and from without:
The excellence, pure spirit, and best power,
Both of the object seen, and eye that sees.

(1805, XII: 376–9; cf. 1850, XIII: 375–8)

This may be regarded as a 'balance' by Wordsworth, but there are certain aspects of how it has been achieved that have attracted the attention of recent critical analysis.

I have already noted how, in the lines on the Grande Chartreuse, the original experience was anything but determining for Wordsworth. The distinction between the instantaneous value of the narrative events and the revision demanded by the grown poet is more of a tussle than a balanced synthesis. For example, in Matthew Brennan's recent study of the Discharged Soldier passage, weight is placed on Wordsworth's initial sighting of the 'uncouth shape'. Far from being part of a range of being external to the poet Brennan notes how the Soldier is remembered, and so has a function within *The Prelude*, as a projection of the poet himself. There may well have been an originating experience much as is recorded here, but that does not account for the prominence that that particular episode then plays in the poem. Why value and/or be terrified by *this* event?

For Brennan, as explained through Jungian psychology, the Soldier is a shadow or alter ego of Wordsworth's unconscious. By suddenly being forced to confront this usually unacknowledged and repressed other self (as is more evident in the original poem) he immediately projects on to it unwelcome and threatening powers (see Brennan

1987: 19–20). In striving to overcome his 'heart's specious cowardise' (1805, IV: 435), there is performed a psychodrama where the growth of the poet's mind is aided not just by the assimilation of greater experiences or craft but also the psychological strength that accrues whenever we exorcise deep anxieties. It is consistent with this tendency that the Soldier is first encountered in moonlight, where the literal existence of the figure is overlaid by transforming lighting effects and associations derived from night. Just before we read of the figure, the younger Wordsworth is indulging himself in 'beauteous pictures' that rise in his mind 'in harmonious imagery' (1805, IV: 392–3):

> they rose
> As from some distant region of my soul
> And came along like dreams . . .
>
> (1805, IV: 393–5)

While Wordsworth discovers some historical reality about the Soldier there is still the association with 'dreamlike and nightmarish images' (Brennan 1987: 19). Gradually, in the revision process, Wordsworth comes to understand the full impact of the vision. Brennan notes in the 1798 version the brusque condescension shown towards the Soldier ('And told him, feeble as he was, 'twere fit/He asked relief or alms' (161–2)), which gives way to the more polite (and self-excusing) injunction that

> He would not linger in the public ways,
> But ask for timely furtherance, and help
> Such as his state required.
>
> (1805, IV: 490–2)

The softening of tone marks the acceptance of this Other without the need to evade it by a blustering rejection.

Psychoanalytic criticism thus regards the poetic text as composed of negotiations between the unconscious and the repressive forces of the drive to represent and so control it. For Freud this tension exists to a greater or lesser extent in every narrative, or, in terms more familiar to his own work, 'case history'. The identification between a patient's account of anxiety and a piece of writing is a common one and lends itself to adoption by any commentator on *The Prelude*. While the poet seems to give a faithful or sincere account of his formative years, the distinction between truth and falsehood in these matters is a fruitless one if we are to understand how he, in 1798, 1805 or 1850, is 'making sense' of his past and so of his present, that is, the adult he has become. For

David Ellis in his *Wordsworth, Freud and the Spots of Time* (1985) the efforts at transcendence and a visionary afflatus are a compensation for a genuine lack of knowledge about his past and a fear of mortality. Retrospection reorders the events that contribute to the present 'self', but there are no obvious connections that lend the 'spots of time' anything other than local significance. The mature poet has to reconstruct a context for these epiphanies, for what he is left with are, in Jonathan Bishop's words, 'fragments of a drama, moments in a single action which has retired beyond the reach of direct expression, leaving in our hands fragments of imagery' (1959: 41). *The Prelude* represents, therefore, a proposition about the past that emerges from this anxiety to construct it *in the present*.

'Anxiety' is an apt word for this reordering, as it involves a working through of the displaced fears and repressed desires, a full coming to terms (in a quite literal sense) with these shadows of authority or Otherness that cannot be faced directly, either because they only now exist in a language that is metaphorical (and so require extensive interpretation) or because they need to be reassembled out of their chronological order in order that they can emerge for the conscious mind.[19] This listening to the new grammar or language of the unconscious is what Wordsworth often associates with the 'sense of God' – either as an external power or one that is apprehended internally. After climbing Snowdon, Wordsworth reports how the original experience was transformed by his 'meditation' on the 'lonely mountain' (1805, XIII: 66–7), where there formed

> The perfect image of a mighty mind,
> Of one that feeds upon infinity,
> That is exalted by an under-presence,
> The sense of God, or whatsoe'er is dim
> Or vast in its own being—above all,
> One function of such mind had Nature there
> Exhibited by putting forth, and that
> With circumstance most awful and sublime . . .
>
> (1805, XIII: 69–76)

Here there is eventual unity, and yet there is some distinction drawn between the passive mind that 'cannot chuse but feel' (1805, XIII: 84) when this larger 'mind' acts upon nature and the potency of individual imaginations that

> . . . from their native selves can send abroad
> Like transformation, for themselves create

A like existence, and, whene'er it is
Created for them, catch it by an instinct.

(1805, XIII: 93–6)

This is not a new synthesis, for, as we have seen *vis-à-vis* Hartley, the dialogue with associationism bred an enhanced realization of imaginative power. This 'motion and a spirit, that impels/All thinking things, all objects of all thought' ('Tintern Abbey' (1798), 100–1) is not a recapturable object for analysis. It exists as an intuition, a firm persuasion that the numinous order of perception can bridle even the riotous elemental chaos of the Simplon Pass in Book VI. Here the apparent disconnection can be recuperated by the analogy that the stark natural forms 'were all like workings of one mind, the features/Of the same face, blossoms upon one tree' which can also become 'types and symbols of eternity'. This seems reassuring, for we could presumably simply produce an updated emblem book and allegorize (and so anthropomorphize) such notions. However, they are at the same time 'characters of the great apocalypse' and figures 'of first, and last, and midst, and without end' (1805, VI: 568–72). Here the alpha and omega of Godhead ensures no easy possession. The figures do not exist in some careful spacing ('first, and last') but in the 'midst' of perception – not the middle or centre – and also in some unceasing motion.

When there emerge the Discharged Soldier or the 'huge cliff' from Book I that strides after him 'like a living thing' (1805, I: 409, 411–12), the fear of the uncharted disturbs Wordsworth and forces its conceptualization as another of his 'spots of time' that will actually supply spiritual health. Often, using Freudian terminology, there is an Oedipal fear of the Father, where the uninterrupted enjoyment of mother nature (see his trouble-free walk in Book IV before the Soldier appears), with its promise of full identification and loss of individuation, is rudely dislocated.

The sublime powers of Book VI that were summoned only to be filed in the great divine sensorium have not been quite so neatly assimilated by several readers. In Thomas Weiskel's *The Romantic Sublime* (1976) what characterizes Wordsworth's own form of sublime experience is *loss* of direction and a perplexity that makes the scene 'unreadable', in that the signifier (image) overwhelms the signified (apparent content) to produce 'a saving resistance to the passage from image to symbol' (Weiskel 1976: 185). This freeing of the imagination from 'Fatherly' authority (in Lacan's sense, the Symbolic presided over by the name-of-the-father) encourages a delight in the play of signifiers or, given the apocalyptic potential of the 'emblems' of Book VI, a terrifying vulnerability in the solitude of subjectivity.[20] This limit to interpretation runs counter to Wordsworth's more obvious design: to account for the self. For Mary Jacobus, this clash between the desire to interpret the past and its gnomic distance is figured by a 'textuality' that inscribes 'Imagination'

> in the apocalyptic characters that spell its own death; passages in which interpretation has to turn from the Romantic self as origin to the always missed encounter, not simply with the meaning of Romantic autobiography, but with the meaning – the reality – of its metaphors.
>
> (Jacobus 1989: 31)

In the section on the Discharged Soldier passage I posed two alternative ways of reading the lines. In addressing form and its metaphorical freedoms psychoanalytic readings 'enter the frame' and educe a new 'unintended' order to construct the particular language of the unconscious. The temptation emerges, however, to rest content with this, to render the work as part of some complicated effusion of personality. The concentration on the specific identification of the 'uncouth shape' as a Soldier, and, what is more, to one who has served in a particular theatre of conflict, is not totally within the orbit of a formalist reading – unless this detail can be converted to form and thus robbed of its History.

Noting the New History

In the essays by Philip Shaw (pp. 64–5) and Clifford Siskin (pp. 103–8) there is a review of what has come to be called new history or New Historicism. What follows supplements their comments. The 'old' historicism can be defined in several varied ways, but, in outline, it involves certain working principles: a belief that the investigator can be empirically neutral if she/he is scrupulous about source materials by quoting contemporary or primary authorities for historiographical conclusions. This presupposes the removal of the self from one's investigations so that the evidence may have a chance of 'speaking for itself', and ensures the even-handedness of one's approach, yet it is also regarded as a historian's duty to trace a coherent account (with agents and reagents) of what happened, to instil causes and effects that supply a global explanation of why and how. Overall, historicism deals in structure and direction. What New Historicists point out is that this is narration and that History is inextricably bound up with textual effects: it is *written*. Following Hayden White's *Metahistory* (1973) literary criticism has looked at the plotting of historical writing, and questioned the validity of laying claim to the grand universal term of history (see also White's 'New Historicism: A Comment', in Veeser 1989: 293–302).

The danger of herding all those writers together who have tried to return to history with the insights gleaned from deconstructive, feminist or psychoanalytic studies is that, while the initial premise may be shared, the practice has been so various. At one pole there is the impulse to resist the appropriation of the past, more pervasively known as 'cultural materialism'. As early as 1981, Alan Sinfield warned against the elision of an interpretation of the past with its appropriation, as

> a prime function of critical discourse should be to resist and reduce
> appropriative tendencies in our reading . . . We must reconstruct
> the ideological specificity of the text in its original context, with
> all the historical work involved, because otherwise we will slide
> back into the self-indulgence of finding what we want to find.
>
> (Sinfield 1981: 193)

In finding the past strange we might understand why the present appears so 'natural' and accessible, but is in fact a construction for us to function as authoritative critics.

The contrary tendency of New History is to stress the textuality of all historical context. In the recent work of Jonathan Arac, Clifford Siskin and Don Bialostovsky, the centre of interest lies in *how* Wordsworth is *now* read. For these critics this account takes centre stage, and a new literary history emerges, based on Foucault's concept of genealogy (see my Headnote to Siskin's essay, pp. 98–100; Bialostovsky 1982: 1–22; Arac 1979: 11–56; and Siskin 1988: 3–14), where there is a more or less overt attempt to identify the enabling limits for criticism that help determine current definitions of what is relevant or not. This vigilance provides some defence against the drift in interpretation towards converting the 'generic and the historical to the natural and the transcendent, metamorphosing all analysis into claims for Imaginative vision' (Siskin 1988: 12). Here there is no leap of the historical imagination because that would blind us to the more immediate task – of knowing what we are *now* about as regards Wordsworthian studies, and how we make sense of the past and so narrate it. The very least that is needed is to emphasize how *distinct* our available ideologies are from those that can be traced in Wordsworth's writing. As Stephen Greenblatt has recently pointed out in his description of 'Social Energy' in Chapter 1 of *Shakespearean Negotiations* (1988b), 'textual traces' have no 'numinous authority' and are rather 'the signs of continent social practices'. We cannot find their 'untranslatable essence', as the motive forces are the particular manipulation of 'collective beliefs and experiences'. How these ideas were wedded to material social practices becomes the goal of most of our critical attention:

> We can examine how the boundaries were marked between cultural practices understood to be art forms and other, contiguous forms of expression. We can attempt to determine how these specially demarcated zones were invested with the power to confer pleasure or excite interest or generate anxiety. The idea is not to strip away and discard the enchanted impression of aesthetic autonomy but to inquire into the objective conditions of this enchantment, to discover how the traces of social circulation are effaced.
>
> (Greenblatt 1988b: 5)

Similarly, Alan Liu has provided a first account of what this might entail as regards Romanticism and the study of Wordsworth in particular in his 1989 essay in the *Journal of English Literary History* (1989a) and Chapter 1 of his *Wordsworth: The Sense of History* (1989b). To summarize his argument is to make it liable to simplification as it is highly qualified (with justification). Liu returns to the triad of the Self (or Imagination)–Nature–History to discount the mediating force of Nature, which is no constant or distinct third term (1989b: 3–31). The 'unnatural' *Prelude* affects the supposedly 'natural' descriptions, rather than vice versa, and the 'objectivity' lent us so that we can comment with authority on the poem is more a relic of the nineteenth century than some free, disinterested choice of rhetorical/discursive options.

This History has no villains or heroes because it does not allow for distinct agencies aside from the passages across our consciousnesses of 'power', both temporal/political and epistemological. Whether we choose to interrogate the structures of feeling from the (constructed) past or our own neck of the academic woods, there is this radical edge to the historical account: that history is traced by us in the forms by which we find it intelligible – individuality, motivation, change in certain realized directions (as opposed to those that eventually promote no achieved goal), and so those that 'make sense' to *us* (see Lehan 1990 and for a more Marxist view, Martin 1991). What, then, is a more or less valid assessment of the past? Is textuality then merely a rather pernicious academic ideology, excusing our powerlessness by reducing all we see to operations of a disembodied 'power'? I leave these questions unanswered here to allow the contributors (and, through them, the Wordsworth they discover) to introduce their own interests and perhaps suggest to you your own practice.

CHAPTER 1

Paul de Man and Imaginative Consolation in *The Prelude*

JON COOK

[The work of Paul de Man has challenged several of what have been recognized as the guiding definitions of Romanticism. In Kant's *Critique of Pure Reason* (1781) knowledge was regarded not as the result of experience but rather as the effect of the mind's set of categories by which experience is processed and made intelligible. Necessary, a priori, conditions of experience, such as those of space and time, as well as the phenomenal world of nature, were never apprehended with mathematical precision by the mind. Indeed, the consideration of sense perception only led to full knowledge through an act of *synthesis*, where the imagination helped fuse disparate elements of experience in a flash of knowledge. This cohering force is a property of 'understanding', and not 'reason' and does not depend on the identification of physical resemblances or temporal coincidence. On the contrary, true knowledge was produced by a consideration of the necessary and enduring mental categories that formed associations of value. Wordsworth depicts the visit to 'Tintern Abbey', for example, not as a historically (or geographically) faithful event; it registers so powerfully with the poet because of the role it plays in his own memory and the ensuing trains of association.

This impulse towards transcendence and subjectivity was regarded by de Man as a delusion. Romanticism's desire to heal the rift between words and ideas or between the perceiving subject and the perceived object necessarily emphasized the apolitical and non-historical, and did so because it regarded a specific context as contingent to the apprehension of the world. In a series of closely argued studies of Romantic thought, de Man refused to accept its premises and persistently read against the grain of his chosen texts by granting the metaphors of writing (either overt or concealed) an autonomy that called into question any clear reference back to a clearly represented content. Any proposition, even one located within philosophical discourse, is dependent on language's powers of figuration. Consequently, if words can never quite escape their rhetorical nature to gesture towards non-verbal objects, then the Romantic concentration on divorcing states of being from the means by which they are communicated, the pursuit of a disinterested aesthetics, displays a blindness to the contextual nature of all conceptualization.

Rhetoric suspends the powers of logic to decipher meaning clearly, if at all. Always hovering between the literal and the figurative, verbal expression does not offer a clear choice between these two alternatives in that the two meanings often collide (or collude), so that 'it is impossible to decide by grammatical or other linguistic devices which of the two meanings (that can be entirely incompatible) prevails'. De Man takes this to be the defining characteristic of literature itself. While we may be led to think that we can divide the intended literal meaning of a text from its supposedly subservient images, 'rhetoric suspends logic and opens up vertiginous possibilities of referential aberration. And although it would perhaps be somewhat more remote from common usage, I would not hesitate to equate the rhetorical, figural potentiality of language with literature itself' (de Man 1979a: 10). Literature pre-eminently possesses this power to reverse an intended meaning, to open it up to constant irony.

Therefore, de Man found Romantic attempts to find a suggestive refuge in the symbolic vulnerable to his philosophical scepticism. In *Blindness and Insight* (1971; 1983a) and *Allegories of Reading* (1979a), a variety of texts were allowed to demonstrate the way that more overt meanings were subverted or appropriated by the necessary recourse to rhetoric. The Romantics typically mistook an experience for the representation of that experience, and thus founded a belief in the power of the symbolic to elude textual expression altogether in a complex process of spiritual cognition. In the essay, 'The Rhetoric of Temporality', de Man posited two opposed modes of comprehending figurative writing: the *symbolic* and the *allegorical*. The symbolic promises an autonomy of the poetic imagination, freed from history and the accidents of local particulars, which promotes an 'expression of unity between the representative and the semantic function of language' (1983a: 175). Allegory, however, usually associated with much earlier poetic modes, is a preferred alternative. In traditional usage, the term indicates images which seem to refer directly to definite signifieds, for example Milton's personifications, Sin and Error, in *Paradise Lost* (Book IV), biblical parables, or Vanity Fair from Bunyan's *The Pilgrim's Progress*. In these cases there is no intention of providing a symbolic identity between the signifier and signified, as the reader has to work at decoding the allegorical image. There is a gap between the words and some existence presumably indicated due to the arbitrariness of the chosen signifier and the time-lag between the first registering of the allegorical image and the understanding of it after it has been read off against one's store of interpretative codes and conventions. Allegory 'prevents the self from an illusory identification with the non-self' and 'designates . . . a distance in relation to its own origin, and, renouncing the nostalgia and the desire to coincide, it establishes its language in the void of this temporal difference' (1983a: 207), for an accessible account of this difference, see Norris 1985: 80–3).

The Romantics might have striven for symbolic identity yet they are always fated to provide the reader with an allegorical experience. Coleridge believed, in his *The Statesman's Manual* (1816), that the symbol was

> characterized by a translucence of the Special in the Individual or of the General in the Especial or of the Universal in the General. Above all by the translucence of the Eternal through and in the Temporal. It always partakes of the Reality which it renders intelligible; and while it enunciates the whole, abides itself as a living part in that Unity, of which it is the representative.

The allegorical, on the other hand,

> is but a translation of abstract notions into a picture-language which is itself nothing but an abstraction from objects of the senses.
>
> (Coleridge 1972: 30)

De Man inverts this Romantic priority, by recognizing the *temporal* predicament, both historical and as experienced in the reading process, of critical understanding. Against a desire for some 'complete' understanding, the authentic response always tends to deconstruct, that is, search for the non-natural or evident bases for, its attempts at such comprehensive mastery. (For a thorough and, at times, critical estimate of de Man's impact on the study of Wordsworth, see Bialostovsky 1982: 152–99).

In Jon Cook's essay, this emphasis on the eventual failure of readerly (symbolic) identification is examined primarily with reference to the collection of essays in de Man's *The Rhetoric of Romanticism* (1984). The general rationale behind the volume is to gather together those essays that perform the task of demystifying a Romantic ideology of aesthetic transcendence, such as that met with in Kant's work, especially his *Critique of Judgement* (1790; 1989). There is the pervasive recognition that, in the process of expressing intended ideas we, too, are not exempt from the fall into rhetorical 'Error' when the recourse to writing out our notions always involves implications surplus to intention that can 'unpick' or be regarded as running counter to the avowed argument. Cook, however, does not accept de Man's overall view of Wordsworth's revisionary reflections (not just in the 1850 version but within the retrospective moments of the 1805 text) that sought to correct excesses of imagination. In place of these he discovers 'an open dialectic' where the sense of loss produced by the overabundant imagination at certain points in the poem can be regarded as modes of discovery at others.]

NIGEL WOOD

The Prelude, especially in its 1805 version, has come to be regarded by literary critics and historians as a canonical Romantic poem. For modern critics, an understanding of the poem is thought to be a key to an understanding of the more general phenomenon of Romanticism, and the crucial role poetry plays within it. This judgement raises problems of historical perspective and textual interpretation. A late twentieth-century picture of Wordsworth's reputation is crucially formed by a poem which was unknown to his contemporary readership. A much revised version of the 1805 text was not published until after Wordsworth's death in 1850. The priority that recent criticism gives to the 1805 version of the poem gives rise to another historical displacement. The poem that we name *The Prelude* was not known by that name to Wordsworth and the few others who knew of its existence. At the time of its completion, the 1805 text was named 'Poem, Title not yet fixed upon, by William Wordsworth Addressed to S.T. Coleridge', a poem provisionally defined by the relation between its author and its chosen addressee.[1]

Readers in the late twentieth century identify Wordsworth's reputation by a version of a poem untitled at the time it was completed, and unknown to a contemporary public. These circumstances are telling about the ironies of reputation and critical judgement. Wordsworth was probably best known in his own lifetime as the author of another long poem, *The Excursion*, published in 1814, and now largely unread. The subsequent critical identification of *The Prelude* as a key text in understanding Romanticism indicates the extent to which a period in literary history can come to be known by a name, Romanticism, which writers at the time did not own to, and by taking as culturally central texts which, at the time of their writing, were fugitive or elusive. From one point of view, Romanticism is a name given to a cultural ancestry and inheritance which some twentieth-century readers have created for themselves. Romanticism, in this sense, becomes a transvaluation of the past, a powerful but historically and culturally specific interpretation which may, in some future period, be replaced by another name and a different organization of texts and readings.[2] But, even if this relativity is acknowledged, there is still an obstinate sense that whatever its projective and interpretative features, Romanticism does name an important historical event and change, one which the 1805 text of *The Prelude* was particularly responsive to and helped identify.

This dilemma about the reality of Romanticism, at once historical event and interpretative projection, each producing the other, is pertinent to *The Prelude* because the relation between interpretation and understanding is one of the poem's major concerns. In Book IV of the 1805 text, the poet narrator pauses to make one of many interpretations of the work he is composing:

> As one who hangs down-bending from the side
> Of a slow-moving boat upon the breast
> Of a still water, solacing himself
> With such discoveries as his eye can make
> Beneath him in the bottom of the deeps,
> Sees many beauteous sights — weeds, fishes, flowers,
> Grots, pebbles, roots of trees — and fancies more,
> Yet often is perplexed, and cannot part
> The shadow from the substance, rocks and sky,
> Mountains and clouds, from that which is indeed
> The region, and the things which there abide
> In their true dwelling; now is crossed by gleam
> Of his own image, by a sunbeam now,
> And motions that are sent he knows not whence,
> Impediments that make his task more sweet;
> Such pleasant office have we long pursued
> Incumbent o'er the surface of past time —
> With like success . . .

(IV: 247–64)

This elaborate, epical analogy proposes that writing about the past is inevitably involved in the perplexities of reflection. What is beneath the water – 'weeds, fishes, flowers' and so on – is held in a medium which produces an uncertainty that combines pleasure with 'impediments'. The poet's naming of what is there coexists with 'fancies more'. Or, if the words are read as a verb phrase, the very act of observation is a stimulus to fantasy which blurs the distinction between fact and fiction, the objectively given and the subjectively projected. Nor does the passage move to any resolution of this uncertainty. It seems impelled by an elaborate layering of complication where what the poet sees in watery memory includes a glimpse of himself, of a world – 'rocks and sky,/Mountains and clouds' – and something more enigmatic still, the visible signs of an enigmatic power: 'motions that are sent he knows not whence'.

The analogy developed at this point in Book IV of *The Prelude* is tied to personal recollection rather than public history. Yet this does not stop it from being a model of the problems and pleasures involved in recovering the past. Its further interest is indicated by the use of the first person plural at line 262. This is not an attempt to summon an impersonal authority, especially in a poem which is so conscious of the intimacy of its address to the reader. It continues to blur distinctions which might ground a stable world. One such blurring occurs between poet and reader, so that each can substitute for another. The passage invites the reader to look into the depths alongside the poet/observer. The same rhetorical gesture identifies the autobiographical poet as a reader of his own life, deciphering a scene whose reality becomes a matter of speculation. This movement in the poem's language at once draws on and transforms a standard metaphor in eighteenth-century literature for both reading and writing, that of observation. By the time Wordsworth came to write *The Prelude*, there was a well-established subgenre of loco-descriptive poetry including Dyer's *Grongar Hill* (1727) and Thomson's *The Seasons* (1730). These were all concerned with the observation of nature and, often, of a rural economy. They were principally concerned with the itemization and classification of nature's variety and with a commentary on the appropriate forms of rural labour. In each case this requires a position of spectatorship for the poet, surveying the scene from outside rather than being absorbed into it. Although not a loco-descriptive poem, the metaphor of writing as observation plays a central role in the opening lines of Johnson's *Vanity of Human Wishes* (1749):

Let Observation with extensive view
Survey Mankind from China to Peru
Remark each anxious toil, each eager strife
And watch the busy scenes of crowded life;

(1–4)

Johnson's magisterial observation confirms the poem's central argument: that wherever you look you will find evidence for the vanity of human wishes, and that this should confirm our dependence on religion. The poem reads like an accumulation of evidence, and delivers a judgement based on that accumulation. Observation in Johnson's poem is allied to a command of a subject. It has nearly the reverse effect in Wordsworth's poem. The observer is drawn into the scene he observes, almost engulfed by it, caught up in the play of appearances of which he himself becomes a part. This situation recurs in the poem: an observer is observed, a scene turns into a mirror, either with the tranquillity described here or an apocalyptic suddenness, and carries with it a muted or startling sense of revelation.

Taken as a whole, the passage may be read as a typical example of the romantic preoccupation with unity, something Wordsworth himself described in the Preface to the *Lyrical Ballads* (1802) as the poet's impulse to consider 'man and nature as essentially adapted to each other, and the mind of man as naturally the mirror of the fairest and most interesting properties of nature' (Owen and Smyser 1974, I: 140). The passage from Book IV brings together different versions of unity: the microcosm reflects the macrocosm, one part of nature contains nature in its entirety, from the rocks on the river bed to the mountains and sky. The corresponding rhetorical figure is metonymy, where part of an entity is taken to stand for the whole. Accompanying the metonymic force of the passage is a proliferating structure of analogy, suggesting correspondences between different orders of reality: as the observer is to the river, so Wordsworth is to his past, so the poet is to the poem, so the reader is to both poet and poem.

But a linguistic analysis which simply describes these forms of patterning may not respond to a deeper claim made by this passage and the poem more generally. Displays of verbal inventiveness which create connections between unlike things were in the eighteenth century and still are familiar features of poetic language. Samuel Johnson disapprovingly referred to the tendency to yoke together dissimilar things in his discussion of seventeenth-century poetry. He felt that verbal extravagance, usually described as wit, diverted poetry from the task of delivering general truths in a language purged of rhetorical excess.[3] Wordsworth and Coleridge identified a similar problem, but identified it in terms of a difference between fancy and imagination. The poetry of fancy is like wit: its connections are merely verbal. The poetry of imagination establishes connections which are felt to correspond to an underlying structure of reality. Poetic figures, whether of analogy or metonymy, are forms of revelation, and, as in the example from Book IV, what they reveal is the characteristically Wordsworthian claim that all life is one, and that all things are, therefore, equally deserving of value.[4]

The problems of sustaining this belief are considerable, both for the poet and his readers. The fact that the poem has the shape that it does may derive from its attempt to maintain this belief against what threatens it, whether that takes the form of personal loss or political catastrophe. The pleasurable minglings and the simultaneous invocation and deferral of judgement in the passage from Book IV indicate at least one of the problems. Underlying equivalence and analogy is the attempt to transform temporal into spatial relations. By comparing recollection to observation, differences in time – between past and present, between both and eternity – are refigured as simultaneously existing in the same space, however uncertain the distinctions between surface and depth might be within it. By the same token, what is invisible, the passage of time, is opened to the pleasures of sight.

Wordsworth claimed that poetry could work like this, as in this celebrated passage from the Preface to *Lyrical Ballads*:

> I have said that poetry is the spontaneous overflow of power-ful feelings: it takes its origin from emotion recollected in tranquillity: the emotion is contemplated till, by a species of re-action the tranquillity gradually disappears, and an emotion, kindred to that which was before the subject of contemplation, is gradually produced, and does itself actually exist in the mind.
> (Owen and Smyser 1974, I: 149)

The analysis is delivered with scientific confidence, offering a causal account of what poetry does in and to the mind. Yet the process describ-ed is as much alchemical as chemical. Poetry brings past emotion into the present, and in a way which dissolves the fact of its pastness. Poetry acts as a midwife, giving birth to feelings in the present which are 'kindred' to those in the past.

Taken together, the passage from Book IV of *The Prelude* and the excerpt from the Preface to *Lyrical Ballads* show Wordsworth as a commentator on his own poetry, engaging in what he later described in the essay supplementary to his 1815 Preface as the task of any original poet, to create 'the taste by which he is to be enjoyed' (Owen and Smyser 1974, III: 180). Despite opposition, especially from some of his contemporaries, there is plenty of evidence to suggest that Wordsworth has been successful in this task. He has created a terminology and an image of poetry which has helped confirm his greatness. Subsequent criticism has borrowed terms from his own poetry to describe and judge it. So, when modern critics of *The Prelude* discuss, as they often do, 'spots of time' in the poem, they follow Wordsworth's phrase in Book XI, and his own high estimate of how his poetry works to 'enshrine the spirit of the past/For future restoration' (1805, XI: 341–2).

Wordsworth's apparent success in creating 'the taste by which he is to be enjoyed' raises a question for anybody coming to read his poetry for the first time. Are the terms which establish and elaborate that taste to be accepted on trust? Is the purpose of criticism to spell out and update Wordsworth's own high estimation of his work? Or should we adopt a more sceptical stance? The passage from Book IV of *The Prelude*, already quoted, may obscure as much as deepen our understanding of the poem. The basic terms of the comparison, between Wordsworth's composition of a poem about his past and a person gazing into a river, do not acknowledge that the poem is in language, a written text. The whole pull of the passage is to return us to a state prior to language, a trance-like, silent contemplation in which the activity of writing is replaced by tranquil and hypnotic reflection. A gap opens up between the language of the text and what it claims to represent, only to be bridged by analogy. The terms of the analogy act as a screen or filter as much as a mirror. The analogy becomes absorbed in its own subject, not in what it is supposed to be an analogy of. What started as a comparison becomes a digression.

Paul de Man was a critic who combined both sceptical and affirmative perspectives on Wordsworth's poetry. The interplay of these two perspectives is what made him a 'deconstructive' critic. He wrote extensively about Wordsworth, often in an attempt to develop a comparative understanding of Wordsworth's poetry within the context of European Romanticism. His interpretation made the further claim that the historical moment of Romanticism is still our moment in the sense that our efforts to interpret Romanticism find their anticipation within Romantic writing itself. These arguments are part of a larger project of work in de Man's criticism which had, as one of its purposes, the reversal of a belief about what makes literary language special, its particular power to realize meaning with a unique fullness. To understand the value of de Man's readings of Wordsworth it is necessary to have, at least in outline, an understanding of the terms of the larger project.

For de Man, literature was a sophisticated exercise in frustration. The forms of literary language return us to an understanding which we are likely to deny. One formulation of this position comes in an essay from 1967, 'Criticism and Crisis':

> the statement about language, that sign and meaning can never coincide, is what is precisely taken for granted in the kind of language called literary. Literature, unlike everyday language, begins on the far side of this knowledge; it is the only form of language free from the fallacy of unmediated expression.
>
> (de Man 1983a: 17)

Certain assumptions about the nature of language are at work in this quotation. One, following from the linguistics of Saussure, is that language is a relational system, in which the meaning of a term derives from its place in relation to other contrasting or similar terms. Thus, the meaning of a word is never directly given *with* the word, but only in a mediated form, from our largely tacit awareness of how one word relates to another. Another way of putting this is to agree that words do not take on meaning because they have a capacity to refer directly to something outside language, whether that 'something outside' is identified as a reality outside the mind, or, in the expressive variant of the same view, as naming or expressing a subjective substance which exists prior to language.

Hence de Man's notion of the 'fallacy of unmediated expression', the fallacy, in his view, that words and sentences can be transparent to the world or the self, that language can ever arrive at a point where it represents something perfectly. Instead, meaning is always just a shot away, eluding our grasp, emerging and disappearing in the complex process of differentiation which is a language. The meaning of one word is caught up or traced through the meanings of others *ad infinitum*.

In de Man's work this by now familiar belief about language is given a particular set of inflections. In relation to beliefs about literary language, his claim that literature lives in the understanding that 'sign and meaning' can never coincide bluntly contradicts the belief of earlier generations of critics that this is exactly what literature does at its best, that meaning is given to us with a unique fullness and immediacy. Coleridge's account of the symbol, for example, which 'partakes of what it describes', or the assertion by the American poet and critic, Archibald MacLeish, that poetry 'creates the things it sees', or the view that 'form enacts meaning', all indicate a belief that the speciality of literature consists in its capacity to jump over the gap between words and the world, including the interior world of the self.[5]

This view about literature, which de Man contradicts, parallels another set of beliefs which he, and fellow deconstructive critics, regard as central to the Western philosophical tradition. The critical formulation given to this set of beliefs is 'the metaphysics of presence'. One example is in the idea that the goal of knowledge is to deliver us to an understanding of an unchanging reality which exists beneath a world of shifting and unreliable appearances. Another is in the seventeenth-century French philsopher Descartes's claim that the certainty of his self-awareness as a thinking being, 'Cogito ergo sum', is a reality invulnerable to refutation or doubt. Or, in relation to beliefs about language, there is the stubborn dream of creating an exact language whose terms are so precise there can be no disagreement about them. A parallel, if somewhat different, belief aspires to a form of language which would be a guarantee of the truth it states, a language which makes the truth present to us in the very act of its formulation.

The drive of de Man's criticism is towards an acknowledgement of separation, whether it be of sign from meaning, form from content, sentences from truth, knowledge from certainty, the linguistic from the non-linguistic. His criticism does not work in relation to local histories or particular national traditions, but interprets the authors he selects in terms of the recurrent workings of what in his view are a set of mistaken beliefs about language. The burden of literature is to 'know' that these beliefs are mistaken, in the special sense that can be drawn out by a critic like de Man. This knowledge cannot be directly presented in the form of a logical demonstration. That would be to fall back into the 'fallacy of unmediated expression'. It is intimated in the structure of literary form, and, more especially in literature's intimacy with figural language, with all the ways, to put it at its simplest, that rhetoric presents one thing in terms of another. But, for de Man, this presenting is not presenting at all. To think otherwise would be to think that sign and meaning can coincide. It would also overlook another central aspect of de Man's general critical position: the non-coincidence of sign and meaning is one indication of how we are related to language by desire, described by De Man as 'a fundamental pattern of being that discards any possibility of satisfaction' (de Man 1983a: 17). The discarded satisfactions are more to do with the mind than the body. What de Man proposes is that our desire for knowledge, whether of self or the world, can never be satisfied. We can never arrive at a point where we feel our knowledge to be complete, although we may be diverted into fantasies of knowledge which offer an illusion of completeness. The literary text, as an exemplary form of language, acts out this 'fundamental pattern of being' over and over again.

These beliefs about language and representation inform de Man's specific studies of Wordsworth, most of which are focused on readings of passages from *The Prelude*. Although de Man's work has been identified as constituting a revolution in literary criticism – and, for some, including de Man himself, as much more than that – one feature of his method will be familiar to most students of literature: the close reading of texts. When de Man writes about *The Prelude* he writes about bits of the poem, and then uses these interpretations as the basis for generalizations about Wordsworth's rhetoric, and through comparison with various writers, including Hölderlin, Rousseau and Shelley, about Romanticism more generally. When he might be expected to write about the poem more extensively, as, for example, in his essay, 'Autobiography as Defacement', he makes some brief references to *The Prelude* focusing attention instead on Wordsworth's sequence of 'Essays upon Epitaphs' written in 1810. This displacement seems odd, and may have consequences in assessing the applicability of de Man's arguments about autobiographical writing to *The Prelude*, but, for the moment, my concern is simply to remark the familiarity of de Man's critical method rather than its oddity.

This sense of familiarity is deepened by the passages from *The Prelude* de Man selects for detailed interpretation. They are all well-known sites for criticism: the crossing of the Alps episode in Book VI of the poem; the curious elegy, 'There was a boy — ye knew him well, ye cliffs/And islands of Winander' in Book V; the celebration of the new-born child in Book II. All of these readings pursue a well-established theme in criticism of *The Prelude*, that the poem is about the relation between imagination or consciousness and nature. All introduce some cautionary or admonitory note to readings of the poem which stress themes of reconciliation and unity rather than separation and estrangement.

De Man's essay on Wordsworth and Hölderlin brings together a reading of two of these passages, from Books V and VI of the poem. His interpretation of 'There was a boy' (1805, V: 389–422) develops the idea that the sequence is about 'illusory analogy'. The correspondence between man and nature, represented here by the owls' response to the boy's 'mimic hootings' (398), is described by de Man as a 'unity filled with analogy'. It is replaced by a 'tone of uncertainty', and 'anxiety' when the owls suddenly fall silent and the boy's expectant awareness is filled by another dimension of the scene:

> Then sometimes in that silence, while he hung
> Listening, a gentle shock of mild surprize
> Has carried far into his heart the voice
> Of mountain torrents; or the visible scene
> Would enter unawares into the mind
> With all its solemn imagery, its rocks,
> Its woods, and that uncertain heaven, received
> Into the bosom of the steady lake.
>
> (1805, V: 406–13)

The verse paragraph which immediately follows these lines – announcing the boy's death and describing his burial place and its power over the poet – leads de Man to analyse the whole sequence in terms of a series of related transitions. The first of these is a change from unity to a separation of consciousness from nature. We are left 'hovering between heaven and earth' (de Man 1984: 52). The second consists of de Man's reworking of Coleridge and Wordsworth's own distinction between fancy and imagination. The first fifteen lines of the sequence are written in a language of fancy, a language that is 'imitatively and repetitively true to sense perception', an echo of nature (1984: 53). What follows is a movement into the language of imagination, characterized by increasing verbal inventiveness – *'uncertain* heaven', *'hung*/Listening' – and subdued paradox: 'a gentle shock of mild surprize'. These two transitions are themselves contained in a third which, de Man argues, explains the tone of anxiety and unsettlement in the passage. The loss of unity with nature is connected implicitly to mortality; hence the juxtaposition of the boy's new awareness of his relation to nature with the announcement of his death. The starkness of this transition, and the awareness of insecurity and exile that it brings, are softened by a poetic language which maintains the hope that the 'fall into death' will be every bit as gentle as that of the 'uncertain heaven, received/Into the bosom of the steady lake'.

In a characteristically brisk passage of argument, de Man goes on to assert that the transitions he discerns in 'There was a boy' are typical of 'Wordsworth's poetic world': 'This sequence – the transformation of an echo language into a language of the imagination by way of the poetic understanding of mutability – is a reappearing theme in this poet' (1984: 54).

De Man finds further confirmation of this theme in a brief reading of an earlier passage in the poem (1805, II: 170–80) and then projects the theme on a grand scale in an interpretation of Book VI that splices together passages from the 1805 and, in a slightly emended form, the 1850 texts of *The Prelude*. Again the methodological focus is on interpreting the significance of juxtaposed sequences: one which describes and warns against the intention of a group of revolutionaries to sack the monastery of the Grande Chartreuse; the other, an account of Wordsworth's crossing of the Alps, and his subsequent reflection on the nature of imagination. De Man finds in his recomposed version of the poem the topic which he believes is central to European Romanticism: an understanding of the temporal structure which governs the relationship between consciousness and action.

De Man's reading of Book VI is guided by two conceptual and rhetorical structures: paradox and hubris. His compressed and elliptical reading of the passage from the 1850 text about the revolutionary threat to the monastery of the Grande Chartreuse gives an intense edge to Wordsworth's conservatism. For de Man's Wordsworth, the monastery is not an emblem of priestly oppression, but the meeting point of time and eternity, both in a specifically religious sense – the monastery as a place where social distinctions fall away before a continuing tradition of religious contemplation – and in a sense that interests de Man: the monastery, and its mountain setting, as a symbol of 'nature as the principle in which time finds itself preserved, without losing the movement of passing away which makes it real for those who are submitted to it' (1984: 56).

In this claim, de Man gives renewed insistence to a central theme in his interpretation of Wordsworth, that to understand Wordsworth as a poet of nature, we must understand him as a poet of time; that to understand Wordsworth as a poet concerned with the relation of 'inward' consciousness to an 'external' world, we must understand both consciousness and world as subject to processes of decay and renewal. To support his interpretation of nature as time preserved and time passing away, a paradoxical holding together of stasis and transience, de Man quotes from both the 1805 texts and the subsequent emended version of it, which eventually emerged in public form in the 1850 text:

> . . . these majestic floods, yon shining cliffs,
> The untransmuted shapes of many worlds,
> . . .
> These forests unapproachable by death
>
> (1850, VI: 463–6)

and

> . . . The immeasureable height
> Of woods decaying, never to be decayed,
> The stationary blasts of waterfalls,
>
> (1805, VI: 556–8)

In these descriptions, Wordsworth finds a scenic equivalent for the paradoxical temporality of nature: 'decaying, never to be decayed', or the movement of water which appears still, stationary falls.

The revolutionaries' desire to take over and destroy the monastery is, according to de Man, a threat to 'the temporal nature of existence'. They have the hubristic impulse to create what cannot be created, and to control what cannot be controlled. They want to live simultaneously in the moment, like the boy in Book V immersed in an energetic exchange of sounds, and in the reflective awareness of duration that follows it. But this is to ignore the fact that such reflective awareness of what endures arises only in the negation of the moment of energetic action, that, as de Man puts it, 'nonetheless constitutes its origin' (1984: 56).

The understanding of history in Wordsworth's poetry is itself paradoxical: at once the compulsion to destructive and heedless action, and the basis for a reflective awareness of time. De Man develops this interpretation by establishing a parallel between revolutionary enthusiasm and poetic imagination. He finds support for this by claiming parallels between the revolutionary threat to the Grande Chartreuse and Wordsworth's account, also in Book VI of the 1805 text, of how he crossed the Alps without realizing it (488–572). This episode has been interpreted by Hartman and others as an occasion when the poet is compelled into a reflection on the excesses of his imagination (Hartman 1987b: 238–42). His imaginative anticipation of what it means to cross the Alps outstrips the anticlimactic reality of the action itself. De Man's own interpretation follows this, but inflects it towards his own melancholic understanding of history. He focuses upon five lines of Wordsworth's own reflection upon the nature of imagination:

Our destiny, our nature, and our home,
Is with infinitude—and only there;
With hope it is, hope that can never die,
Effort, and expectation, and desire,
And something evermore about to be.

(1805, VI: 538–42)

This, according to de Man, gives one aspect of the imagination: a power that directs us towards the future, projecting us out of a mundane present. But it is constitutive of this aspect of the imagination that it is excessive, 'conscious of neither its power nor its limits', and therefore always in violation of the law. The second aspect of imagination arises in response to this. It is, in de Man's description, the 'interpretive reflection' which arises from experiencing the excesses of the imagination, and retrospective rather than prospective in character (1984: 58).

The relation between anticipation and retrospection is the form of *The Prelude*'s relation to time. It looks back on future projects which have failed. This is its characteristic moment of interpretation. But, de Man insists, the authority of this interpretive consciousness 'can only be had by one who has very extensively partaken of the danger and failure' – the danger and failure, that is, of an excessive imagination. Time in the poem is not narrated according to the figures of progress or redemption:

The future is present in history only as the remembering of a failed project that has become a menace. For Wordsworth there is no historical eschatology, but rather only a never-ending reflection upon an eschatological moment that has failed through the excess of its interiority. The poetry partakes of the interiority as well as the reflection: it is an act of the mind which allows it to turn from one to the other.

(de Man 1984: 58–9)

This restates de Man's concern with the significance of transitional moments in the poem. The 'excess' of 'interiority' is represented by the boy hooting to the owls, or the exuberance of the revolutionaries. It is characterized by an unselfconscious living in the present, oblivious to death or the limit to existence and energy symbolized by death. It assumes a world shaped by desire and its satisfaction. De Man's argument is that Wordsworth's poetry at once inhabits this moment and turns towards a reflective awareness of its limitations and errors. *The Prelude* repeatedly rehearses the movement of consciousness from one state to another, and, according to de Man, this movement corresponds to a transition from ignorance to insight. But the insight depends upon the ignorance it chastens. It cannot be realized without it. As such, *The Prelude* can stand comparison with other texts of European Romanticism (de Man goes on to compare Wordsworth's poem to Hölderlin's *Mnemosyne*). The separation of act and understanding, projection and retrospection, which de Man finds repeated in Wordsworth, 'discloses a general structure of poetic temporality: it lends duration to a past that otherwise would immediately sink into the nonbeing of a future that withdraws itself from consciousness' (de Man 1984: 64).

What sense or use can be made of de Man's reading of *The Prelude* in his essay on Wordsworth and Hölderlin? The moves in de Man's interpretation can provide a model of what a thorough reading of the poem might be. His method can encompass the significance of key words in the poem – in the case of this example, the word is 'hangs', which is read by de Man as a reflexive term, having both its local contextual significance and acting as a condensation of the basic movement of the poem, the moment of suspension in which the mind turns in and across time from imaginative excess to interpretive reflection. It engages with the poem in its sentences, its verse paragraphs, and their juxtaposition. It shows, too, how the different episodes of recollection, the visionary anecdotes, can be read in relation to each other, and in a way that brings out the recursive structure of the poem, its return to a fundamental pattern or rhetorical figure of transition. This overlaps with another level of interpretation: de Man's identification of what for him makes *The Prelude* a Romantic poem, and with this the emergence of a new order of comparison, not internal to the poem itself, but between *The Prelude* and the work of other poets. Hence de Man's emphasis on the *rhetoric* of Romanticism, a movement which is defined for him by the recurrence of the kinds of pattern identified in *The Prelude* across a range of poems, patterns which are themselves not simply the repetition of earlier classical variants of rhetoric, but *sui generis*, the inventions of Romanticism.

No single one of these levels of interpretation has causal or logical priority over the others. De Man's readings move from context to text and back again. His interpretations of textual detail contribute to an understanding of historical questions about the nature of Romanticism. Equally his powerful theoretical commitments contribute to his detailed readings of texts. In this sense, his procedures are those of a hermeneutic critic, whose interpretations emerge out of a dialectical weaving together of the details of texts with the totalities of a whole work or a historical context.

But none of this means that de Man's readings are any freer from preconception or prejudice than anyone else's, however authoritative the tone of his writing may be. While his writing may be useful as a model of the range of things an interpretation of *The Prelude* might consider, the specific readings developed in that range beg as many questions as they answer. These arise from de Man's insistence on reading Wordsworth's poetry through a lexicon or specialized discourse, of separation and dislocation. This has consequences for his interpretations of particular passages in *The Prelude* and for his claims about the poem's larger project.

The counterpoint can begin by returning to de Man's interpretation of 'There was a boy', and his claim that what happens in this passage is an unravelling of the boy's interrelationship with nature which, in turn, becomes suffused with an acknowledgement of mortality. Many critics, including de Man, have argued that this passage, like other 'spots of time' in the poem, turns on a transition which may also be the condition for the emergence of a new kind of consciousness in the poet or his surrogates. But this change need not be read in terms of the boy's – or the poet's – separation from nature. The boy's relation to nature changes when the owls cease to respond to his cries, but the ensuing silence precipitates a deepening awareness of what is around him, a new sensing of what is there:

> Then sometimes in that silence, while he hung
> Listening, a gentle shock of mild surprize
> Has carried far into his heart the voice
> Of mountain torrents; or the visible scene
> Would enter unawares into his mind
> With all its solemn imagery . . .
>
> (1805, V: 406–11)

In a way that is again characteristic of these moments in the poem, what was in the background – the sound of rivers, 'the visible scene' – comes into the foreground. As it does, what had seemed passive setting becomes active presence: the 'mountain torrents' take on a 'voice'; the 'visible scene' becomes the subject of a sentence. This change is itself the sign of another: a moment of internalization, indicated by the parallel phrases, 'into his heart', 'into his mind'. What the poem records at this point is the moment when a scene becomes memorable. This happens within a dormant structure of recollection. The poem recalls the creation of a memory, the means of its own making.

This heightens a sense of time in its passing away. De Man contributes to our understanding of the poem by emphasizing the importance within it of a form of consciousness whose condition is subject to transience. The awareness of passing time, without which memory is impossible, is also connected in this passage, and elsewhere in the poem, with an acknowledgement of mortality. But it does not follow from any of this, at least in Wordsworth's text, that the correspondence between the mind and nature is undone. The sentences from the Preface to the *Lyrical Ballads* which de Man cites in his discussion of the passage can be read in a sense he does not intend: the poet 'considers man and nature as essentially adapted to each other, and the mind of man as naturally the mirror of the fairest and most interesting properties of nature' (Owen and Smyser 1974, I: 140). De Man thinks this relevant to the opening of the passage – the exchange of sounds between the boy and the owls – but displaced if not contradicted by what follows. In my reading, the whole passage illustrates how the adaptation between 'man' and 'nature' occurs. The boy's connection to nature is deepened, not dissolved, when the owls cease to respond to his calls. In a typically Wordsworthian dialectic, as he absorbs the natural scene, as it becomes a content of his consciousness, so the natural scene absorbs him in return.

This is underlined by the passage that follows: the report of the boy's death and the poet's trance-like attention at his burial place:

. . . the churchyard hangs
Upon a slope above the village school,
And there, along that bank, when I have passed
At evening, I believe that oftentimes
A full half-hour together I have stood
Mute, looking at the grave in which he lies.

(1805, V: 417–22)

The boy's death absorbs him more fully into nature, without obliter-
ating his particular identity or distinction. That nature can sustain
identity beyond death, can turn death into a transition rather than a
separation, may be what holds the poet in silent wonder. We may, of
course, want to dismiss this as Wordsworth's fantasy. Coleridge could
find Wordsworth's attitude to death both blasphemous and perverse.[6]
The point here is that, whatever our final judgement on the imaginative
claim the passage makes, the relationship between nature and consciousness is presented in terms of an increasing complexity and depth
of connection, not the other way round.

What is at issue, and what de Man's criticism can bring compellingly
to our attention, is the nature and significance of transitions in *The
Prelude*. De Man's discussion of Book VI of the poem gives a political
edge to this issue in the connections he draws between revolutionary
and poetic excess. This presents difficulties of a new kind. De Man, like
many other critics, believes the 1805 text of *The Prelude* superior to the
1850 version. But his reading of Book VI relies heavily on a passage
about the revolutionary threat to the Chartreuse monastery which was
included by Wordsworth in the 1850 text, and does not figure in de
Selincourt's edition of the 1805 text. De Man claims an 1802 date for
the composition of the passage, which seems to have been added into
an 1805 version of the poem written out by Wordsworth's sister,
Dorothy. De Selincourt does not include the passage in his edition of
the 1805 text because he argues for a later date of composition, some-
time in 1806 or 1807. Other scholars put it later still, although the
subject had been knocking around in Wordsworth's imagination for a
long time.[7] It occurs in an abbreviated form in one of Wordsworth's
earliest published poems, the *Descriptive Sketches* of 1793. The formal
manner of that poem may have appealed to Wordsworth when he
returned to the subject after 1805, concerned to include something of
the publicly self-conscious voice which is more in evidence in the
1850 than the 1805 version of *The Prelude*.

Scholarly disputes of this kind can be notoriously difficult to resolve.

They do, however, raise serious questions about the identity, tone and authority of *The Prelude*. They remind us that the poem itself is uncertain in its identity and perhaps the radicalism of de Man's critical approach is to make use of that uncertainty by composing a version of the poem that answers to his own interpretive priorities. But if we accept the authority of de Selincourt's edition of the 1805 text, then one of the correspondences which sustains de Man's interpretation historically, simply disappears. In the 1805 version, according to de Selincourt, what precedes the crossing of the Alps is a general narration of the poet's southward trip through revolutionary France:

> All hearts were open, every tongue was loud
> With amity and glee. We bore a name
> Honoured in France, the name of Englishmen,
> And hospitably did they give us hail
> As their forerunners in a glorious course;
>
> > (1805, VI: 408–12)

Wordsworth briefly mentions a stay at the convent of Chartreuse, but there is no description or dramatization of any revolutionary threat to what it symbolizes.

The detail is important because it conditions the mood of the poem before Wordsworth's account of the crossing of the Alps. The location of the poem's narrative moves from the sociable plains to the solitary mountains, and this carries with it a resonance from a mythical topography which locates divinity in high places. Wordsworth's reference to the convent of Chartreuse marks this transition. What follows in the poem is some 60 lines describing the mountain society of the Swiss and Wordsworth's reactions to it. The passage anticipates the issue of the relation between the imaginary and the real which is played out more fully when Wordsworth describes his experience of crossing the Alps. The first sight of Mont Blanc is a disappointment:

> . . . a soulless image on the eye
> Which had usurped upon a living thought
> That never more could be . . .
>
> > (1805, VI: 454–6)

The 'living thought', the anticipation of what the mountain would be, is destroyed by the actual sight of Mont Blanc. But that disappointment is replaced by a new satisfaction, 'the wondrous Vale/of Chamouny', which made 'rich amends,/And reconciled us to realities' (1805, VI: 456–7, 460–1). Wordsworth maps the movement of his imagination from disappointment to unexpected satisfaction.

The same movement is played out but more intensely in crossing the Alps. The discrepancy between the moment conceived in imagination and the disappointing actuality baffles the poet. For a moment he loses his relation to the world outside him: 'I was lost as in a cloud,/Halted without a struggle to break through' (1805, VI: 529–30). But as the context of the passage makes clear, this is a temporary state of affairs. The whole address to the imagination, beginning at line 525 of Book VI, transforms the poet's loss of bearing into a revelation of the mind's power. The thwarting of the poet's expectations about crossing the Alps does not lead him to abandon his faith in the possible truths of imagination. Imagination stands for that aspect of consciousness which constantly moves beyond given circumstances, and creates an awareness of time as a medium of possibility: 'something evermore about to be'. The poet's refusal of disillusionment is rewarded in the passage that immediately follows. He comes across a scene which unexpectedly gives him the sublimity he had hoped for in crossing the Alps.

> The rocks that muttered close upon our ears —
> Black drizzling crags that spake by the wayside
> As if a voice were in them — the sick sight
> And giddy prospect of the raving stream,
> The unfettered clouds and region of the heavens,
> Tumult and peace, the darkness and the light
> Were all like workings of one mind, the features
> Of the same face, blossoms upon one tree . . .
>
> (1805, VI: 562–9)

The animation in the scene, the coexistence of contradictory qualities with what is none the less felt to be a totality, are the opposite of the 'soulless image' of Mont Blanc. The poet again discovers an equivalence between mind and nature, and one that fulfils the desires of imagination.

Where de Man's reading finds a transgressive excess of imagination corrected by subsequent interpretative reflection, my reading finds an open dialectic in which the imagination's capacity to imagine more than is offered by the world at one moment enables it to discover more in the world at another. As a whole *The Prelude* may be understood as a persistent testing of the validity of this structure. Wordsworth looks back in time to discover those moments in the past when the mind's relation to nature was lost and then deepened. The moment of loss arises both when nature appears to exceed what the mind conceives (as in the spots of time in the early books of the poem) and when the mind appears to exceed what nature can offer. But in each case loss is followed by restoration, as though moments of excess are themselves productive of an awareness on the poet's part of more complex forms of order.

The rhetorical equivalent of this movement is parataxis, the characteristic sequencing of phrases which both complement and absorb each other:

> . . . like workings of one mind, the features
> Of the same face, blossoms upon one tree,
> Characters of the great apocalypse,
> The types and symbols of eternity,
> Of first, and last, and midst, and without end.
>
> (1805, VI: 568–72)

This example of parataxis from Book VI develops as an effort of the making of similes. We can think of it as a banal frenzy of language or as a poetic form which is testing the possibilities of language, in which each of the phrases in the sequence is both equally apt and equally limited. The poem at this point appears to verge on a name which cannot finally be uttered. As such, it could be taken as an exemplary case of what de Man means by literature, a language drawn to a recognition that sign and meaning can never coincide. But the melancholy inflection which de Man gives to this situation may fall short of the significance of Wordsworth's poetic style. Coleridge, in a discussion of the superiority of poetry to painting, provides a different perspective:

> As soon as [the mind] is fixed on one image it becomes understanding; but while it is unfixed and wavering between them, attaching itself permanently to none, it is imagination . . . The grandest efforts of poetry are where the imagination is called forth, not to produce a distinct form, but a strong working of the mind, still offering what is still repelled, and again creating what is again rejected; the result being what the poet wishes to impress, namely the substitution of a sublime feeling of the unimaginable for a mere image.
>
> (1969: 149–50)

De Man has rephrased the Romantic fascination with the sublime – that which exceeds the images of the understanding – in terms of post-Saussurean linguistics. In the process he has leeched out the kinds of concerns represented by Coleridge's account: a poetics of energy, an equivalence between imagination and 'a strong working of the mind'.

The immediate reference for Coleridge's discussion is Milton's *Paradise Lost*, but its terms are peculiarly apt for *The Prelude*. The poem is crucially concerned with the circumstances which do or do not call forth the imagination. This, as Coleridge emphasizes, depends upon the unsettling of images and not the mind's attachment to them. In so far as the image is connected with a specular structure, based upon a fantasy of looking or over-looking, the poem arrives at specular moments only to move beyond them. In so far as this has to do with an account of poetic language, the failure of language in *The Prelude* is a token of the mind's success, its movement into 'strong working'.

Such movements in the poem are not necessarily accompanied by pleasure. The moods produced by the unsettling of a given image world can be fearful or terrified, involved, too, with a sense of punishment for some failure or transgression. But in every case, they heighten the poet's awareness of his relation to a world which is suddenly experienced as beyond the horizon established by his own preoccupations or his simple self-absorption. One example of this comes in a passage, not discussed by de Man, at the end of Book IV of the poem: Wordsworth's encounter with a discharged soldier. The episode is one of many that occur at night and under moonlight in the poem, indicating the poem's affiliation with that rhetoric of Romanticism which connects moon and night to moments of revelation. The poet is walking alone, immersed in the pleasures of his own imagination, pleasures that are not simply condemned:

O happy state! what beauteous pictures now
Rose in harmonious imagery; they rose
As from some distant region of my soul
And came along like dreams—yet such as left
Obscurely mingled with their passing forms
A consciousness of animal delight . . .

(1805, IV: 392–7)

This erotic solitude is disturbed by 'an uncouth shape' whose status is for a moment uncertain, wavering between the human and the super-natural. The poet hides himself, becomes a voyeur of the scene:

His arms were long, and bare his hands; his mouth
Shewed ghastly in the moonlight; from behind,
A milestone propped him, and his figure seemed
Half sitting, and half standing . . .

(1805, IV: 410–13)

The episode hinges on the complex relation between observation and recognition. The poet overcomes his fear and allows himself to be recognized by the man he observes. Voyeurism is replaced by acknowledgement. But none of this diminishes the strangeness of the soldier. The rhythm of perception is delicately nuanced, moving from an understanding that the soldier is the poet's fellow human being to a baffled sense that he is beyond Wordsworth's powers of observation or comprehension. Successive acts of observation are not converted into certainty about who or what the soldier is. Instead, they lead to a dawning recognition of the soldier's otherness. His imaginative autonomy is quite as powerful and as commanding as the poet's own.

The soldier calls forth Wordsworth's imagination in the way described by Coleridge in his contrast between poetry and painting. 'Beauteous pictures', 'harmonious imagery' are replaced by something else, not exactly the absence of imagery – the passage repeatedly attempts to give the appearance of the soldier – but a sense of its insufficiency, of a form of being beyond the image, and hence 'that substitution of a sublime feeling of the unimagineable for a mere image'. Transposed into the language of semiotics, the passage shows us the non-coincidence of sign and meaning, in that the soldier hovers outside the poet's desire to find out what he means, what he stands for. If we connect this to the subtitle given to the poem in its 1850 edition, 'Growth of a Poet's Mind', Wordsworth's encounter with the soldier becomes another example of the conditions of growth in the unsettling of image or sign.

The poem's identity as an autobiography raises a parallel set of questions about the compatability between Wordsworth's conception of literature and de Man's. In his essay 'Autobiography as De-Facement', de Man briskly demolishes various attempts within literary criticism to establish the rules governing autobiographical writing. The description of autobiography as a genre cannot resolve historical problems: is autobiography a Romantic or pre-Romantic phenomenon; is there a coherent account which can link together Augustine's *Confessions* to Rousseau's, and then on to Bertrand Russell's autobiography? Assertions by critics that autobiography is essentially a prose form are obviously inadequate in the face of the evidence of Wordsworth's *Prelude*. The claim to establish the identity of autobiography by distinguishing it from fiction cannot be decided. Whether autobiographical writing invents a life or a life invents autobiographical writing is a causal question which can be endlessly debated but never resolved.

De Man's solution to this is to have none. He offers a new description of autobiography as 'a figure of reading or understanding that occurs, to some degree, in all texts':

> The autobiographical moment happens as an alignment between the two subjects involved in the process of reading in which they determine each other by mutual reflexive substitution. The structure implies differentiation as well as similarity, since both depend on a substitutive exchange that constitutes the subject.
>
> (1984: 70)

The argument is that the sense of an identity, a subject, or a life produced by autobiography is a rhetorical effect. The rhetorical figure which creates autobiography is in the 'alignment between the two subjects', the one who writes, and the one who is written about, each determining the other in an endless and unresolvable play of difference and identity. In autobiography the writer claims identity with the subject he or she writes about. When Wordsworth writes: 'In summer among distant nooks I roved' (1805, VI: 208), we assume the 'I' in this sentence and the writer are the same person. Yet the writer is never simply identical with this 'I' because the act of writing itself necessarily creates a difference between the 'I' who writes and the 'I' who 'roved'. The rhetorical structure of autobiography divides the self in the act of composing it. This doubleness and division creates what de Man describes as 'a specular structure' (1984: 70): autobiography is the equivalent of a mirror, but a mirror in which it becomes increasingly difficult to distinguish between reflection and reality. The writer looks back or looks at him- or herself in pursuit of finding or knowing a self. But this self is composed in writing. According to de Man, autobiographical writing turns around this moment. It is tropological, in a way that recalls the root meaning of 'trope' in the Greek word for 'turn'. To read autobiography is to be caught up in this turning of the self in language.

But, in a move characteristic of de Man's deconstructive interpretation, autobiography's basis in rhetoric makes autobiography impossible. According to de Man, autobiography takes the form of a desire that cannot be fulfilled. It contains within it a reflection on its own rhetorical structure and a craving to break through to an identity in writing which will be outside rhetoric. De Man typically defines our relation to language this way. We want language to be or do something that it cannot be or do. Both autobiography, and the rhetoric of Romanticism, more generally exemplify this desire and its inevitable frustration.

De Man builds the metaphor of autobiography as 'de-facement' upon this double movement of escape from and reconfinement within rhetoric. The illustration for this argument is Wordsworth's *Essays upon Epitaphs*, although de Man approaches these by way of a brief detour into *The Prelude*. In a discussion which echoes the arguments of the essay on Wordsworth and Hölderlin, de Man identifies another pattern in the text, 'a discourse that is sustained beyond and in spite of deprivation'. De Man cites various examples: the account in Book II of the death of Wordsworth's mother; the story of the drowned man in Book V. These characters, including the boy of Winander, de Man interprets as 'figures of deprivation, maimed men, drowned corpses, blind beggars', who are all 'figures of Wordsworth's own poetic self' (1984: 73).

My argument has been that these 'figures of deprivation' can be equally well interpreted as revelations of some power or strength either new to the poet or forgotten by him. De Man's, in the essay on auto-biography, is to put in question the trustworthiness of the claim he finds in *The Prelude*, and Wordsworth's poetry more generally, that after moments of deprivation there can be compensation and restoration. His means of doing this is to disclose the 'consistent system of thought, of metaphors, and of diction' (1984: 74) at work in the *Essays upon Epitaphs*. One of the key terms in this system, relevant to *The Prelude* and an analysis of de Man's argument alike, is prosopopeia, a rhetorical figure which he glosses as:

> the fiction of an apostrophe to an absent, deceased, or voiceless entity which posits the possibility of the latter's reply and confers upon it the power of speech. Voice assumes mouth, eye, and finally face, a chain that is manifest in the etymology of the trope's name, *prosopon poien*, to confer a mask or a face . . . Prosopopeia is the trope of autobiography, by which one's name . . . is made as intelligible and memorable as a face.
>
> (1984: 75–6)

Prosopopeia is linked through Wordsworth's *Essays* to a poetic style based upon the transformation of contrasts into connections and transitions. It becomes further stylistic evidence of Wordsworth's attempt to break from the style of Pope and other Augustan poets, a style based upon antithesis. It also provides de Man with the pun which gives his essay its title: autobiography as de-facement, not the conferring of 'a mask or face'. De Man makes this move by tracing a number of inconsistencies in Wordsworth's *Essays Upon Epitaphs*. The poet recommends prosopopeia but then shies away from the full use of a figure which would give a voice to the dead, preferring a mode 'in which the survivors speak in their own persons' (Owen and Smyser 1974, II: 61). He sees this as an unconscious manifestation of an anxiety in Wordsworth's writing that the power of prosopopeia to give voice to the dead will, by the same token, deprive the living of speech. The rhetorical figure taps a deep fear that the living and the dead may change places.

Wordsworth's anxiety about the power of a rhetorical fiction is emphasized, according to de Man, by the poet's anger at the improper use of language. Words must be, according to Wordsworth, 'an incarnation of the thought', not 'a clothing for it'. The language advocated by the poet should be 'not what the garb is to the body but what the body is to the soul' (Owen and Smyser 1974, II: 84–5) But, for de Man, this attempts to establish a difference where there is only an analogy: as clothes stand to body, so body to soul, and language to what it represents. Wordsworth's distinction between the language which incarnates and the language which clothes cannot be sustained: 'To the extent that language is figure (or metaphor, or prosopopeia) it is indeed not the thing itself but the representation, the picture of the thing and, as such, it is silent, mute as pictures are mute' (de Man 1984: 80).

The very act of giving voice in writing, whether to the dead or the living, returns us to the absence or the silence of that voice, its merely textual not living presence. The attempt in autobiography to restore what transience and mortality have taken away, constantly repeats the deprivations it wants to overcome.

'Autobiography as De-Facement' repeats de Man's by now familiar insistence on the necessary failure of language, impelled by desires that cannot be fulfilled. Yet the absence of any sustained discussion of The Prelude in an essay that takes Wordsworth as exemplary is remarkable. He appears to want to read The Prelude as an autobiographical text by way of his interpretation of the Essays on Epitaphs. The rhetorical structure of The Prelude is, both explicitly and by implication, aligned with the rhetorical structure of the epitaph. As elsewhere in de Man's criticism, the poem is given a deathly cast.

If, for a moment, we accept the title of the 1850 text, we might notice a tension between names: Prelude and Epitaph, one indicating the anticipation of a future, the other commemorating a past life. To describe The Prelude as a poem of remembering and commemoration does not simply entail either the rhetoric or the anxieties of the epitaph. One sign of this is the theoretical feature which de Man claims as central to autobiography, prosopopeia. Stylistically The Prelude is marked by the frequency with which some person or aspect of nature is addressed in the poem. These can take the form of acknowledgements of indebtedness or guilt, of hymns of praise or gratitude, or the marking in the poem of its address to Wordsworth's friend and fellow poet, Coleridge. He is introduced as the poem's crucial audience early on: 'Thus far, O friend, did I, not used to make/A present joy the matter of my song' (1805, I: 55–6). Wordsworth turns to him repeatedly in the books that follow, most notably, perhaps, at the poem's conclusion which anticipates Coleridge's homecoming and the renewal of their collaboration. By this stage in the poem Wordsworth identifies the poem as a gift which he has designed for Coleridge.

Coleridge is the poem's ideal auditor. The poem is dedicated to him neither as its patron – *The Prelude* is set apart from a literary economy where praise of the powerful brings with it the possibility of financial security for the poet – nor as one of the great dead, the poetic predecessors whom Wordsworth must match if he is to qualify for the title of poet. Wordsworth's anticipation that his poem will be heard and understood by Coleridge gives him the confidence to write. It helps him negotiate his own uncertainties about what it is exactly that he is writing and whether it will make sense. This reminds us that *The Prelude* is an experimental poem. The subject of the poet's life, as the subject of a poem, occurs to him as if by accident, the solution to a dilemma set out in the first book of *The Prelude*. Wordsworth finds himself unable or unwilling to write a long poem of a traditional kind, a national epic, a poem of event and action. But he also finds himself unprepared to write 'some philosophic song/Of truth that cherishes our daily life' (1805, I: 230–1). Caught between a tradition whose terms he cannot follow and an aspiration he cannot fulfil, Wordsworth writes about himself. He is writing a poem without a genre, without the rules which establish a contract of meaning between a writer and a reader. His subject has no obvious claim on public attention. When Wordsworth began to write the poem, and when the 1805 text was completed, he was little known as a poet. *The Prelude* is not written in the confidence of an established reputation which can assume the curiosity of a readership about its author's life. The poem negotiates an anxiety about choice: in writing it Wordsworth wants to discover that he is what he is, that his life has been tending towards poetry in ways that are more than the product of his will to become a poet.

As the ideal auditor, Coleridge is figured in the poem as a listener who will understand the experimental and improvised quality of the poem. As a text, *The Prelude* discovers its compositional principles after and not before it is written. Its concern with writing a history of how the world changes with transitions of mood runs the risk that Wordsworth himself defined in the 1800 Preface to the *Lyrical Ballads*:

> I may have written upon unworthy subjects; but I am less apprehensive on this account, than that my language may frequently have suffered from these arbitrary connections of feelings and ideas with particular words, from which no man can altogether protect himself . . .
>
> (Owen and Smyser 1974, I: 152)

The risk of Wordsworth's poetry is that his reader will fail to catch the special inflexion the poem gives to its ordinary words: 'hangs', 'friend', 'sense', 'naked', 'breath', 'gleam', and so on. Coleridge is presented as a potential reader who is already within the linguistic orbit of the poem. The poet can have confidence in his own words because of his confidence in Coleridge's ability to interpret them rightly in the absence of any codifiable rules about how they are to be understood:

> To thee, in memory of that happiness,
> It will be known—by thee at least, my friend,
> Felt—that the history of a poet's mind
> Is labour not unworthy of regard:
> To thee the work shall justify itself.
>
> (1805, XIII: 406–10)

The danger is that these lines become the early nineteenth-century equivalent of showing holiday snapshots, full of significant associations only if you were there. The poem becomes esoteric not because it contains arcane knowledge but because of the highly particularized nature of the associations it deals with, accessible only to that intimate circle of readers who already know the poet's life history before it is written down. But this may be to read these lines too literally, or to take a very restricted view of the experience they summon. Coleridge occupies a double position in the poem. The lines address him directly, but, on the reader's side, he comes to stand for, not the *only* reader, but the *kind* of reader who will understand the poem, one who can find analogies for 'memory of that happiness'.

This consideration of Coleridge as the principal addressee of the poem has a bearing on the function of prosopopeia within it. De Man suggests that a particular imaginative constellation forms around this mode of address, one which shapes a face out of an ordering of features and the senses; 'Voice assumes mouth, eye, and finally face'. This is valuable for the way it indicates how texts may create subjects without directly describing them. What de Man's sequence omits, however, is the ear and hearing. In *The Prelude* hearing is figured as one of the vital senses. This has to do with the poem's sometimes apprehensive seeking out of a sympathetic auditor. But its scope extends beyond this, to a form of reading and knowledge which has the capacity to attend to what seeing cannot register; as, for example, in Wordsworth's account of climbing Snowdon where 'The soul, the imagination of the whole' (1805, XIII: 65) is discovered in a chasm:

> A deep and gloomy breathing-place through which
> Mounted the roar of waters, torrents, streams
> Innumerable, roaring with one voice.
>
> (1805, XIII: 57–9)

Hearing can detect a powerful intimation of the dialectic of the one and the many, where the mind can simultaneously register a multiplicity of sounds and their unity. Hearing makes present to consciousness what cannot be seen, or pictured. In Coleridge's terminology, quoted earlier in this essay, it unfixes the mind's attachment to a single image, by suffusing the visible scene with a sense of invisible depth. Again the poem registers a turn in awareness which is at the same time the opening up of a new reality. This effect in the Snowdon episode is the equivalent of Wordsworth's summoning of 'something evermore about to be' in his reflections on crossing the Alps in Book VI of the poem. In the sensory order of the poem, hearing is peculiarly attuned to what is 'about to be', and therefore to a structure in which absence is not exclusively allied to deprivation or loss but to a prophetic sense of something about to be announced or renewed.

This returns us to the question of autobiography, and the predominance within de Man's account of a metaphor of autobiography as a picturing of self and voice which is doomed to display the absence of those very features it wants to depict. But what if the metaphor of autobiography as picture is insufficient for the poem? What if it suggests a concept of what it means to make the self intelligible which turns out to be irrelevant? The specular function of memory in the poem, the way in which it offers scenes from Wordsworth's past, is one form of writing in the poem. But this runs in parallel with another, where autobiographical writing assumes a voice and a listener, Wordsworth *telling* the story of his own life. De Man's interpretation suggests that autobiography taunts us with the possibility of a completeness of representation that can never be realized. Hegel, in his *Aesthetics*, provides a different account which, although not directly about *The Prelude*, has an uncanny relevance to it:

> By displaying what is subjective, the work, in its whole mode of presentation, reveals its purpose as existing not independently on its own account but for subjective apprehension, for the spectator. The spectator is as it were in it from the beginning, is counted in with it, and the work exists only for this fixed point, i.e. for the individual apprehending it.
>
> (Hegel 1975, II: 806)

Applied to *The Prelude*, Hegel's account acknowledges the incompleteness of autobiography, but this is not a condition of the work's failure but its possible success. As the previous discussion of Coleridge's role in the poem has indicated, *The Prelude* consistently declares its purpose as existing for a subject who will realize what the poem is about through a sympathetic act of reading. In this sense the poem's vulnerability to rejection is simultaneously the source of its power. This may be a source of anxiety in the poem, but not of a kind described by de Man, where the writing of autobiography puts the poet in an unresolvable contradiction, rejecting the very terms which make autobiographical writing possible in the first place. Wordsworth persists in believing that his terms can be taken on trust. This is a possibility that, in the end, de Man cannot tolerate.

SUPPLEMENT

NIGEL WOOD: Your answer to de Man on *The Prelude* revolves around the fact that he is selective about his analogies, and so does not take into full account the more consolatory moments of the poem which counterbalance these moments of loss. How balanced (in this sense) do you regard the poem as being? Are there passages (not quoted by de Man) where the poetry expresses negative emotions without the unbidden return of identification?

JON COOK: I am not sure that my answer to de Man is quite as you define it. My reading of the significance of transitions in the poem differs from his. Where he sees the transitions recorded in the 'spots of time' passages as to do with the separation of consciousness from nature, an awareness of mortality, or a chastened understanding of imaginative excess, I find a more robust dialectic where moments of bafflement, loss or disappointment are followed by unanticipated satisfactions or new forms of relation between consciousness and nature. These new forms are not always strongly marked in the poem, and the restorations they stand for can come at some distance from moments of negative feeling. But my claim is that this is a consistent element in the poem, surviving even the strongest expressions of negative emotion.

NW: In your view, is there such an entity as a 'Romantic verse narrative' that can comprehend works as various as *Prometheus Unbound* or *The Eve of St. Agnes*? Similarly, is the term 'Romantic' still useful?

JC: Like other generic terms, Romantic verse narrative is useful as long as it is recognized as impure, entangled with epic, lyric, and, in the case of Byron and Wordsworth, novelistic forms. What I think distinguishes Romantic verse narrative from, say, the long eighteenth-century miscellaneous poem is its fascination with imagining change and transformation, the emergence of new shapes of the self and society which usually have to do with escape from or the overthrow of a version of tyranny. Another way of putting this is to say that Romantic verse narrative tests the implications of liberty, without the cards being so strongly stacked in favour of social determinism as they are in subsequent nineteenth-century fiction.

NW: On p. 47, you claim that 'As a whole *The Prelude* may be understood as a persistent testing of the validity of this structure [the succour offered by the same powers of imagination that had earlier been found wanting]'. Is this true of *all* forms of the poem: 1799, 1805, 1850, even the Dove Cottage MSS? Or more true of one version than others? Did this form of imaginative redress evolve as a trope?

JC: The brief answer is yes. The concern with the restorative force of 'spots of time' is there from the 1799 version of the poem, and continues through until 1850 despite Wordsworth's increasing political and religious conservatism.

NW: You commence your essay by making the point that we know more about *The Prelude* than Wordsworth's contemporaries ever could. The 1805 version was unknown outside a close-knit circle, for example. To a Derridean, though, the reading of a text is always a contemporary phenomenon, where, *of necessity*, the various points of origin of the lines are effaced. Could you say more about the consequences of this 'historical displacement'?

JC: I think it is helpful to sustain a tension between Wordsworth's early nineteenth-century and his late twentieth-century reputation. When Wordsworth completed the 1805 *Prelude* he was still a relatively obscure poet whose *Lyrical Ballads* had attracted some critical attention but not of a kind that would give him the public reputation of a writer like Crabbe. The critical question is whether late twentieth-century readers, with their access to the 1805 *Prelude*, understand Wordsworth better than his contemporaries did. Or is he an example of a writer whose greatness now depends on academic institutions and on the considerable investments made in him by the literary critical industry? I am suggesting that attention to such historical displacements can alert us to the processes which confer literary value on an author for different works at different times. Underlying this is a question about the function of criticism. In reading *The Prelude* do we shape the work to answer our own cultural and psychological needs, or does the poem have a meaning which subsists across different historical periods?

NW: Do you see Coleridge (as the figured ideal auditor) as anything other than a rhetorical 'presence' in the work, or is there something more apposite about the choice which a further glance at his life and friendship with Wordsworth would illuminate?

JC: Coleridge is more than the ideal auditor of the poem. He is its alter ego, the other poet whose growth concerns Wordsworth, a figure who provides both contrast and similarity. At a more immediately biographical level, the poem hints at the strains in the relationship between the two men. The poem is written in Coleridge's absence, as though to compensate for his loss. It comes to an end in the 1805 version with an anticipation of Coleridge's return and the hope of renewed work together. It is as though Coleridge's movements, and Wordsworth's surmises about his psychological condition, are a motor force in the poem. Once Wordsworth is confident of Coleridge's return, the work of the poem ceases. In fact the two writers did not recover the friendship that produced *Lyrical Ballads* in 1789.

CHAPTER 2

Romantic Space: Topo-analysis and Subjectivity in *The Prelude*

PHILIP SHAW

[Materialist criticism, usually associated with Marxist thought, stresses the determining social (including class) interests that are the true motivation of any art work. Individuals feel free to act as if they were individuals, and yet existence is always ultimately controlled, not by the biologically (individually) derived sense of the psychological subject, but the relationship one takes up as regards one's class and productive capacity ('the mode of production') in any given society. Our perspective is a partial one, and is capable of analysis by regarding it as an inflection of a more general set of preconceptions about society, and one's place in it, that is deemed *ideological*.

Marx provided a dialectical model for the interpretation of history, in that the economic 'base' and the influenced 'superstructure' of reactions to it (in legal, philosophical and political discourses among others) interact, achieving new syntheses, that in their turn provide changed economic conditions and, inevitably, altered perceptions. Principally, the model is a historical one and accounts for change through time more or less applicable in a variety of topographies. Philip Shaw illustrates the consequences for literary study of approaching these materialist propositions from a position that explores the variations in social life in space rather than through time. For those more used to tracing significant historical change in the bringing together of causes and ensuing effects, this is a significant change of gear. More commonly distrusted as a basis for materialist analysis, 'space' is not regarded by philosophers such as Henri Lefebvre, Gaston Bachelard and Maurice Blanchot as a term for merely convenient classification, such as 'the history of France' or 'the poetry of the English Lake District'. The emphasis is rather more on physical geographies: how social organization can be explained by a concentration on the way social space is organized. Land-scapes are never fixed and inert; the ways in which they are exploited to become productive, or even divided up to facilitate the leisure industry, all leave their mark. 'Space' always signifies something about communal intentions, and it is not just a question of decoding what is 'there', for space is, as Lefebvre realizes, *produced* before being read and produced, not just to be read in a form of aesthetic detachment, but rather to be *lived* – both as an arena for production (of all kinds) and consumption, and also for interaction, whereby our more direct ideas about what the country and the city, for example, 'are', is formed. It does not just involve a mapping of physical space (the 'street', the collective farm'), but goes further to discover hidden imperatives that are deduced from the reasons why space is constructed in the way it is and thus how a complex of social practices is performed in relation to it. As far as the consequences for literary study are concerned, we ought to be reminded that there are forms of aesthetic effect and other forms of superstructural discourse that count as production.

In a poem such as *The Prelude*, which aims to chart both the relationship between a particular perceiving subject and a series of locations and also illustrates the attempt to construct a personal 'space' or individual ego, spatial relations are not just those that involve physical areas. To risk a reductive description, it also implies a written relationship (detached? empathic? generic?) between the writer's perceptions and a chosen object. Blanchot regards the 'space' of literature as a process of 'seeing' which 'presupposes distance': a 'decisiveness which separates, the power to stay out of contact and in contact avoid confusion'. The 'I' must remain authorita-tive and resist the temptation to lose selfhood in a fascinated identification with the described object: 'what fascinates us robs us of our power to give sense' (Blanchot 1982: 32). Similarly, Bachelard, in his consideration of the way spatial metaphors order our thoughts, is unsparing in his determination to analyse them as propositions as opposed to observations, a cartography of the will rather than the Real (see Bachelard 1969: 211–31).

A priority is therefore given to the ordering of experience as well as how the poet's mind develops in time. Before this description gives an impression of this line of enquiry as interested in just psychological matters, we should be reminded that such lines of demarcation are also propositions about what is perceived as 'everyday life', in Lefebvre's terms. 'Social space' is always *produced* (and used), and is never the result of some natural process in an architect or town planner's mind. For Lefebvre, 'space' has very much more the force of the action of 'spacing' and so defining items one from the other. It is not to say that it promotes an ignorance of history, as all human activity has one, even that to do with perception. Instead of finding the outside of consciousness as immutable or *essentially* unchanging (Lakeland dells or Cambridge colleges), Lefebvre constantly returns us to the fact of its *production*, and so alerts us to the 'illusion of natural simplicity': a 'mistaken belief that "things" have more of an existence than the "subject", his thoughts and desires' (1991: 29).

I refer to New Historicism in my Introduction (pp. 23–6) and so do not need to detail its strategies. Shaw takes up one of its strands: that of the return to History taken by Marjorie Levinson and Alan Liu when they discover the *function* of landscape and the depiction of apparently personal perspectives on it. Nature, therefore, has a function in *The Prelude*, that of keeping the world in a manageable aesthetic frame. Once we follow Wordsworth into cities or even scenes of stirring historical change, then a crisis of perception occurs, where the powers of the subject to keep itself sacrosanct are challenged.]

NIGEL WOOD

Part 1

> *Geography is nothing but history in space*
> Elisée Reclus[1]

> *A traveller I am*
> The Prelude *(1805, III: 196)*

In this study of *The Prelude* I will be exploring the concept of space as a tool for critical analysis. The reason for this is simple: the grand narratives of history – both old and new – have tended to overcontextualize social life as the 'unfolding' of being over time; little, if any, attention has been paid to the 'emplacement' of being within space (Soja 1989: 4). This is due, in large part, to the reluctance of critical theorists to examine the presuppositions of historical analysis. For the majority of these critics, immersed in the categories of 'classical' Marxism, time simply is the accepted vehicle of mobility and change; space, on the other hand, has negative connotations of inertia and stability – useful, at best, as a 'neutral' support for geographical descriptions of 'place'. The resultant binary opposition has been aptly characterized by Michel Foucault: 'Space was treated as the dead, the fixed, the undialectical, the immobile. Time, on the contrary was richness, fecundity, life, dialectic' (1980: 70).

By linking space to reification and inertia, Foucault reminds us that the distrust of spatialism is, to some extent, a consequence of the general critique of commodity fetishism. According to Marx's definition, when things become commodities, they 'lie' in order to conceal their origins in material production. As a result, commodities set themselves up as absolutes, and so become, in the words of the French Marxist philosopher, Henri Lefebvre, 'more "real" than reality itself' (1991: 81).[2] Space, because it is figured as a floating 'abstraction' or 'pure form', works in much the same way. As an absolute it succeeds in disguising the practical reality of social relationships. To assert space as an analytical tool, therefore, within the framework of traditional Marxism, would be to risk the charge of reification. Dialectics would be supplanted by idealism.

There are, however, a number of countercurrents within the tradition. In a recent work entitled *Postmodern Geographies* (1989), the radical geographer, Edward Soja, has sought to modify Marx by arguing the case for a dialectics of time *and* place. To begin with, he claims, space is not a pure, empty abstraction or formal category, but a material *product* – a product that embodies and dissimulates social relationships and the form of these relationships. The environment, in other words, is both determining and determined, at once a product to be used and a means of production. As an example, think of a natural space, a horizontal plain. Before long the plain is overwritten with marks and inscriptions: signifiers of cultivation and other human activity. The 'furrows, the patterns of sowing, the boundaries, be they hedges or wire fences, designate relations of production and property' (1991: 83). Immediately, to quote again from Lefebvre, the environment is thrust into a dialectic: 'though a product to be used, to be consumed, [space] is also a means of production; networks of exchange and flows of raw materials and energy fashion space and are determined by it' (1991: 85).

In this view, space has become 'social': neither an autonomous category, in the Kantian sense, nor an inert landscape, in the standard geographical definition, but a lived space informed by the immaterial and material traces of human agency.

We can go on now to 'map' history as a series of spatial events: say, the transition in rural topologies from share cropping to intensive farming or the shift in urban environments from feudalism to late capitalism. An entire 'history' could be written on city space; for example, a spatial analysis of Paris from the 1789 Revolution to the *coup de tête* of 1848, from the Communard revolt of 1871 to the May day riots of 1968. In Britain during the nineteenth century, topo-analysis could be applied to the conflictual spaces of Peterloo and Spittlefields, the monumental significance of the Crystal Palace and the Albert Memorial, or turned on the colonial spaces of the Third World. The possibilities, as they used to say, are endless.[3]

But what relevance does this have to literary studies? As a literary critic interested in the writing and culture of the Romantic period – an area of research dominated, in recent years, by the influence of Jerome McGann and the school of New Historicism – it seems to me that we can no longer afford to ignore the subversive potentials of space, especially if we are to counter the formalist tendencies that continue to dog the academy. Take, for example, two recent collections of essays: Stephen Greenblatt's *Representing the English Renaissance* (1988a) and H. Aram Veeser's *The New Historicism* (1989). If these are anything to go by, it would seem that the new materialist critics have reneged on their commitment to politicizing the category of the aesthetic. Having collapsed the distinction between literary and non-literary texts – such 'boundaries are contested, endlessly renegotiated, permeable' (Greenblatt 1988a: vii) – the history of the New Historicists has become 'indistinguishable' from the 'floating cultural category' it was meant to replace (Klancher 1989). As Frank Lentricchia argues, while in theory 'nothing is outside politics', in practice the ceaseless 'circulation' of historical and artistic discourse indicates a 'desire' on the part of New Historicists 'to get outside politics' ('Foucault's Legacy – A New Historicism', in Veeser 1989: 237). The 'self-subversive tug in historicist discourse' thus ensures 'that there is always something left over' – something, in other words, that will 'escape' the determinism of the social (Veeser 1989: 241). In leaving a part that is 'purely' literary, something that is 'evermore about to be' (1805, VI: 542), the emergent textuality of New Historicism resembles Romantic transcendence. In both cases, we lose contact with the Real. History becomes 'text' and no longer figures as *lived* experience.

To deliver the text back into the realm of 'everyday life' – the phrase is Henri Lefebvre's[4] – we must adopt a number of strategies. The first will begin with a reconsideration of the privilege accorded to 'reading'. This may sound bizarre in the present context – I am, after all, engaged in the business of literary study – but I feel that it is time to address the effects of the current, almost obsessive concern with reading as the interpretation of forms, genres and linguistic codes. Although space embodies a discourse, or language, it is far more than a space of signification. In reality, as Lefebvre puts it, space is '*produced* before being read; nor was it produced in order to be read and grasped, but rather in order to be *lived*' (1991: 143). To read space, therefore, we must reapproach the very notion of interpretation. This will turn, as I will show in Part 2, on the possibility of 'recreating' lived experience.

A second strategy will be to undermine the traditional axes of critical thought. History, according to Soja (via Foucault), is not just a catalogue of diachronic or 'vertical' moments; in practice it opens out onto a network of horizontal elements, 'an ensemble of relations that makes them appear as juxtaposed, set off against one another, in short, as a sort of configuration' (1990: 18).[5] To interpret the synchronic 'configurations' of literary history, the points, that is, where aberrant, unexpected meanings break through the temporal discipline of narrative, we must level the 'verticality' of the linear text. Traditional historicism, in other words, must be toppled so as to 'allow other, more "lateral" connections to be made':

> The discipline imprinted in a sequentially unfolding narrative predisposes the reader to think historically, making it difficult to see the text as a map, a geography of simultaneous relations and meaning that are tied together by a spatial rather than a sequential logic.
>
> (Soja 1990:1)

In this essay, part of this process will involve the setting up of correspondences between structural and phenomenological being – which I will go on to define, via Lefebvre, as the relationship between dominant ideologies and the unstructured moments of everyday life. To begin with, however, I want to open up a theoretical space for explaining the difference between temporal and spatial selves. As we shall see, Soja is not alone in stressing the importance of space to an understanding of individual and collective modes of subjectivity. In the reading of Romantic space that follows from this section, I will be making reference to a variety of spatial thinkers, including Walter Benjamin, Gaston Bachelard, Frederic Jameson and, most importantly, Henri Lefebvre, whose major work *La Production de l'espace* (1974) has recently been translated into English.

I said I would disrupt the flow of the linear text. The time has come, then, for a detour.

The Cabinet of Sensations

Well before the invention of postmodern geographies, the Marxist critic, Walter Benjamin, completed a number of topographical 'experiments'. Benjamin's essays on city space, collected in English translation in a volume known as *Reflections* (1978), are crucial to an understanding of the relationship between geography, history and everyday life. Throughout these essays, spatial metaphors are used to collapse standard hierarchical divisions between story and history, self and collectivity, the aesthetic and the political. Above all, Benjamin uses space as a refusal of verticality and depth – traditional motifs for the constitution of history and subjectivity. Thus he writes in 'A Berlin Chronicle' (1978: 5): 'I have long, indeed for years, played with the idea of setting out the sphere of life . . . graphically on a map'. The map enables Benjamin to reject time, which has to do 'with sequence and what makes up the continuous flow of life', in favour of space with its 'moments and discontinuities', its insights and illuminations (1978: 28). In the course of the 'Chronicle', spatiality subverts the synchronic rhythm of historical subjectivity in order to give free run to the horizontal play of geographic being: a shaft of sunlight under a bedroom door, the smell of bodies in a classroom, the swarm of the covered market, the cafés and brothels of the poor quarter. Benjamin drifts through times as if he were picking pebbles from a beach. The image is an appropriate one, for the spatial subject collects topophilia in much the same way as an archaeologist or museum curator collects relics: 'He who seeks to approach his own buried past must conduct himself like a man digging . . . the images, severed from all earlier associations . . . stand – like precious fragments or torsos in a collector's gallery' (1978: 26). Unlike traditional modes of autobiographical narrative, Benjamin's fragments cannot be arranged in any kind of sequence or logical order. The product of the 'Chronicle' is a collocation of movements and memories; the recording of a 'buried life' that is always in the process of recovery, never given whole or complete.

If Wordsworth could have read Benjamin's text he would probably have dismissed it as an exercise in fancy, a mere 'cabinet of sensations' (1805, II: 228–9). The chance juxtaposition of mental *topoi* is a proce-dure that seems alien to the general chronological approach of *The Prelude*. Leaving aside the enigmatic qualities of the 'spots of time' (1805, XI: 257), *The Prelude* is a work almost wholly taken up with narrative description. There is, indeed, something threatening about the conception of the text as an exercise in intellectual 'town planning':

> But who shall parcel out
> His intellect, by geometric rules,
> Split like a province into round and square?
>
> (1805, II: 208–10)

More often than not, *The Prelude* favours 'images of interaction' – wind and water, caverns and mountains, and so forth – over images of con-structed space. The former are said to 'mediate' between the inner and outer world, the latter are depicted as splitting these worlds in two (Lindenberger, 1964: 69–83). Thus in Book II, constructed space seems part and parcel of 'that false secondary power by which/In weakness we create distinctions' (1805, II: 221–2). To give in to this tendency would be to substitute a space of metaphysical depth for the 'puny boundaries . . . of outward shows' (1805, II: 223–5): for a world of pure surfaces, in other words – and Wordsworth, we must recall, is one who believes in the reality of an 'under-presence' (1805, XIII: 71). Thus, in Book III he writes, as if teasing the superficial affectation of the modernist *bricoleur*:

> Carelessly
> I gazed, roving as through a cabinet
> Or wide museum, thronged with fishes, gems,
> Birds, crocodiles, shells, where little can be seen,
> Well understood, or naturally endeared,
> Yet still does every step bring something forth
> That quickens, pleases, stings — and here and there
> A casual rarity is singled out
> And has its brief perusal, then gives way
> To others, all supplanted in their turn.
>
> (1805, III: 651–60)

'Carelessly I gazed'. Instead of fixing on an image of permanence and universal sway, the Wordsworthian self is shifted through a set of metonymic relays: the 'gaudy congress' (1805, III: 661) of fishes, gems, birds, crocodiles and shells. It is as if, having temporarily foresaken the discipline of metaphor, the self were being convulsed in a giddy display of spatial sonorities, 'Of things by nature most unneighbourly' (1805, III: 662). As stratified space breaks up, individual subjectivity breaks down. The centred self drifts towards the dilettantism of the decentred or centrifugal subject, to pleasures that 'quicken', 'please' and 'sting'. With the gaze unable to find a surface on which to rest, the subject cannot be constructed as a self-reflective 'I'.

An obvious analogue to this, in eighteenth-century literature, is the contesting of gaze that occurs in Thomson's *Seasons* (1981). In the savannah grasslands section of 'Summer', for example, the dominance of the eye is temporarily disrupted:

> From these the Prospect varies. Plains immense
> Lie stretched below, interminable Meads,
> And vast Savannahs, where the wandering Eye,
> Unfixt, is in a verdant Ocean lost.
>
> (690–3)

Thomson usually structures space on neo-classical lines with the subject situated at the focal point of a long, conic field of vision. Here, however, the order of presentation, which normally proceeds from foreground to middleground and finally to background, is undone, 'lost' in a series of 'interminable' plains. It is as if the confused perspectives of Romantic space were feeding back into the topographical poem of the eighteenth century. In both cases, the subject is drawn away from the 'deep space' of the pastoral tradition and thrust into the 'layered space' of modernity.[6]

Let us return now to the cabinet section. With the eye 'Unfixt', to borrow Thomson's phrase, it seems that the temporal binding of the self has come unstuck. The viewer reels with 'a barren sense/Of gay confusion' (664–5). But the effects of intoxication are only temporary. Wordsworth must, after all, draw 'profit' from the experience (668). Hence memory intervenes to restructure the discontinuity of space in the regulative rhythm of linear narrative. Through the restorative gaze of the 'after-meditation' (648) a temporal economy is deployed at the same time as the self is reclaimed as its organizing centre. Having reaffirmed the self as a locus of vision, Wordsworth can go on to map space as a kind of existential journey or itinerary: turn wheresoever it may, the subject cannot miss its way (1805, I: 19).

The reduction of space to a picturesque form of seriality constantly threatens to overwhelm the self. Wordsworth provides two responses. The first is to deny his tendency to succumb:

> a strong infection of the age,
> Was never much my habit—giving way
> To a comparison of scene with scene,
> Bent overmuch on superficial things,
> Pampering myself with meagre novelties
> Of colour and proportion, to the moods
> Of Nature, and the spirit of the place,
> Less sensible.
>
> (1805, XI: 156–63)

The second is to claim 'a power like one of Nature's' (1805, XII: 312), holding up 'before the mind, intoxicate/With present objects . . ./ . . . a temperate shew/Of objects that endure' (1805, XII: 33–6). The point is, however, that Wordsworth does frequently 'pamper' himself; a 'craving' for new combinations and new forms exists alongside the sober, centred self, as is made clear from the long, descriptive section devoted to life at Cambridge.

Throughout this description, Wordsworth presents his reflections in terms drawn from the discourse of cartography. Thus, in Book VI, he looks back on the 'Good-natured lounging' of his student days to 'behold a map/Of my Collegiate life' (1805, VI: 202–3). But Wordsworth, unlike Benjamin, uses cartographic imagery to devalue his experience. In Book III, for example, Cambridge presents the Romantic subject with a world of flat 'surfaces' and abstract 'spectacles'. In contrast to the sublime verticality of the Lake District, we see Wordsworth at large on a 'populous plain' (1805, III: 195), his sight 'dazzled by the novel show' (203). Collegiate life is characterized, by turns, as 'empty' and 'superficial' (211–12), theatrical (259) and playful, 'unprofitable' and riotous (251–2), 'trivial' and 'gaudy' (457–8). In the absence of 'majestic thoughts' (210), the subject 'Drift[s] about along the streets and walks' (253), losing the deep self in a way that is similar to the discontinuous progress of the 'Chronicle'.

As Wordsworth wanders, the 'Imagination sle[eps]'. 'And yet not utterly' (260–1) for, a few lines later, we are told that he sleeps where 'generations of illustrious men' have 'slept' (263–5). The imagination, in other words, is lodged in a cultural tradition that corrects the negative connotations of line 260. To counter the laziness that makes of life a 'floating island' (340) – aimless and unanchored – Wordsworth peels open the surfaces to reveal 'Caverns' (246) and 'catacombs' – places of depth where 'Perennial minds lie visibly entombed' (346). Thus, while the subject displaces itself in idle pursuits, meaning is preserved in the eternal space of death.

The reinsertion of an 'under-soul' (540) affords Wordsworth the opportunity to indulge in some mental constructions. Against the drift of social space in Cambridge he refashions the university on an idealist plane. If the former is given over to the intoxicating, artificial world of surfaces and present things (1805, III: 301–9; XII: 33–6), the latter is devoted to solitary, sobering activity. Wordsworth's mental Cambridge is marked then by its 'purity and depth' (1805, III: 443); it is a place bearing the stamp of 'awe' (447): it is a place, in other words, of recentring. Later on, memory will refashion the real Cambridge as a 'republic', where brothers stood 'Upon equal ground' in 'subservience . . . /To God and Nature's single sovereignty' (IX: 228–42). The spectacle and surface will have been forgotten, 'sovereignty' will have precedence over the 'inferior exhibition' (III: 606).

We return now to the 'Chronicle'. Benjamin's interest in self-mapping leads him away from mental space and towards an affirmation of the loss of centre that occurs in the social. It is as if, to prefigure the

Situationists, Benjamin were celebrating the experience not of a return but of a continuous, drunken *dérive*:

> Now . . . in reconstructing [the map's] outline in thought without directly reproducing it, I should, rather, speak of a labyrinth. I am not concerned here with what is installed in the chamber at its enigmatic center, ego or fate, but all the more with the many entrances leading into the interior.
>
> (Benjamin 1978: 31)

Less concerned with the need to order experience, to locate the self within the restricted economy of reflection, Benjamin casts himself as a nomadic *flâneur*. Although Benjamin acknowledges the 'interior', space, for the wanderer, is not that which shelters the self but that which sends it into exile. To put this in philosophical terms, Benjamin describes a space that has more in common with the dispersal of Jewish space-time than with the 'sheltering' space of Heidegger – the existentialist philosopher with whom Wordsworth is often associated. As Françoise Collin puts it in her study of Blanchot: 'Jewish space-time is not history but wandering [errance]'. And wandering is an error that leads the self away from the interior, it is 'the fact of being on the way without ever being able to stop' (Collin 1971: 75). Benjamin's space is productive, therefore, to the precise extent that it resists the predilection for space as dwelling and presence.[7]

To set up an opposition: Benjamin is the cartographer of wandering and outer space; Wordsworth the historian of being and inner space. As I write, however, the opposition seems too easy. I am simplifying Wordsworth in order to emphasize modernist 'play' and to ignore the possibility of Romantic 'excess'. I am, moreover, neglecting an important aspect of the spatial: the link between concepts of space and social reification. For the purposes of this essay, then, the Romantic space that I describe will not be the space of 'literature', of 'ideology', or of 'psychoanalytic topographies' (Lefebvre 1991: 3). Although these spaces will be investigated, in so far as they contribute to a significant qualification of the spatial, I am much more concerned with Lefebvre's concept of social space (or its synonym 'everday life'). To put this concept into practice we must first of all represent Wordsworth in the space in which he seems most comfortable. If we are going to tamper with Romantic space we had better be certain that we can identify how it has been constructed.

Wordsworth: Geometry and History

In the cabinet of sensations section the subject is rescued from spatial discontinuity and delivered to the linear flow of personal history. We will return to this phenomenon in Part 2. I want now to investigate the connection between phenomenological or 'mental' space and material or 'social' space. I take my example from Book VI of *The Prelude*. Wordsworth begins this section by describing his return to Cambridge:

> I turned my face
> Without repining from the mountain pomp
> Of Autumn, and its beauty (entered in
> With calmer lakes, and louder streams) . . .
> You and your not unwelcome days of mirth
> I quitted, and your nights of revelry,
> And in my own unlovely cell sate down
>
> (1805, VI: 9–16)

Sequestered in the interior space of the undergraduate's little 'cell', Wordsworth's mind drifts away from the realm of the social and towards 'The hemisphere/Of magic fiction' (102–3): the literary space of Spenser and the poets. In this space imagination transcends the material world in order to refashion the subject as a work of literature. Thus we see Wordsworth engaged in a Bloomian 'struggle' with 'the dread awe/Of mighty names' (72–3). Here, the reference to Spenser is of course not without significance; as Bloom *et al.* put it: 'Coleridge credited Spenser with being the great inventor in English poetry of the "land of Faery, that is, of mental space"' (1979: 34). It seems to me, however, that we can detect a further and perhaps more dominant influence in the philosophy of Immanuel Kant.

For Coleridge and for Wordsworth, mental space has far more to do with the philosophy of transcendence than with the Faery land of medieval romance. This is born out in Book VI of *The Prelude* during the course of a long speculation on 'geometric science':

> With Indian awe and wonder, ignorance
> Which even was cherished, did I meditate
> Upon the alliance of those simple, pure
> Proportions and relations with the frame
> And laws of Nature . . .
> Yet from this source more frequently I drew
> A pleasure calm and deeper, a still sense

Of permanent and universal sway
And paramount endowment in the mind

(1805, VI: 142–53)

In contrast to the rhetorical agonistics of the Bloomian landscape,
geometry proposes a universe that is happy and calm, regular and
knowable – an a priori realm 'fitted' to the individual mind. At this
point, therefore, it appears that mental space has triumphed over both
literary and social space. Then a strange thing happens:

And as I have read of one by shipwreck thrown
With fellow sufferers whom the waves have spared
Upon a region uninhabited,
An island of the Deep, who having brought
To land a single volume and no more—
A treatise of geometry—was used,
Although of food and clothing destitute,
And beyond common wretchedness depressed,
To part from company and take this book,
Then first a self-taught pupil in those truths,
To spots remote and corners of the isle
By the seaside, and draw his diagrams
With a long stick upon the sand, and thus
Did oft beguile his sorrow, and almost
Forget his feeling: even so—if things
Producing like effect, from outward cause
So different may rightly be compared—
So it was with me then, and so will be
With poets ever.

(160–78)

The passage can be read in a number of ways, the most obvious of
which is the reading that replicates a 'Romantic ideology'. Herbert
Lindenberger, for example, writes 'of a tendency throughout *The
Prelude* to isolate objects in order to connect them at a deeper level:
islands, whether real or figurative, are places which cut you off so that
these connections may be made' (1964: 83). Using isolation as the means
towards 'interaction', the passage then becomes an extended metaphor
for the workings of the transcendental imagination. But there is a real
issue at stake here, one that involves the materiality of a social landscape.
In recovering this landscape, what 'happens' is the return of the
repressed: social space breaks through the covering of pure 'relations'

and 'Proportions' to restore a sense of history; for although the land-scape of the island is apparently removed from the conditions of everyday life, in ideological terms the process of isolation is far from innocent.

To read this space we must place the poetry alongside a passage from John Newton's *An Authentic Narrative* (1782). The section with which Wordsworth would have been most familiar reads thus:

> Though destitute of food and clothing, depressed to a degree beyond common wretchedness, I could sometimes collect my mind to mathematical studies . . . I used to take [Euclid] to remote corners of the island by the sea-side, and draw my *diagrams* with a long stick upon the sand. Thus I often beguiled my sorrows and almost forgot my feeling – and thus, without any other assistance, I made myself in good measure, master of the first six books of *Euclid*.[8]

In truth, John Newton had never been shipwrecked. Although best known for his work as an evangelical preacher, he was, at that time, the captain of a slaving ship: the slave trader read Euclid to relieve himself of guilt and depression. In the section from *The Prelude* Wordsworth uses Newton to focus his thoughts on the relationship between subjectivity and space – more specifically on the idea that abstract concepts can only be apprehended through the exercise of individual reason. The emphasis on mental space is used, however, to hide an ideological point. For both writers the transition from social reality – Africa and the slave trade in Newton's case, the 'artificial life' of Cambridge in Wordsworth's (1805, III: 591) – to mental category can only be achieved by reducing space to the isolated, empty and essentially ungraspable structure of the Kantian subject, the formal structure of historical transcendence. This results in the creation of a rift between the mental sphere on the one hand and the material or social sphere on the other. In the terms given us by Lindenberger, Wordsworth's shipwrecked mariner, although accompanied by 'fellow sufferers' is the perfect image of this isolated Romantic subject:

> Mighty is the charm
> Of those abstractions to a mind beset
> With images, and haunted by itself
>
> (178–80)

Through abstraction, then, social space is able to take on the 'higher' form of 'an independent world/Created out of pure intelligence'

(186–7). In real terms, however, a material landscape has been placed on the side of the dead, the fixed and the undialectical. With space contained in this way, the message for poets and slavers alike is clear: social reality can be transcended – or (less charitably) ignored – through an exercise of pure reason.

Space and Subjectivity

Social space is threatening. It threatens to undermine the privileged role of the transcendental subject within post-Kantian philosophy, the most striking feature of which is its continuing reliance on categories drawn from the realm of the aesthetic. For Kant, the subject is held together by its ability to produce itself within the limits of the a priori. But with the subject unable to provide an adequate presentation of itself to itself – because understanding must 'reduce' an idea of pure reason to make it into an intuitable formation – there is only the alienation of 'empty form'. As a result of this reliance on the aesthetic a breach occurs between the *bildende Kraft* (formative skill) of the artist and its correlate in natural organic production: in the former the subject is produced; in the latter it simply *is*.

Phenomenology can be summed up as the attempt to paper over this breach. In Romanticism it manifests itself in the frequent allusions to the unity of organic and artistic modes of productivity. If art provides the subject with a framework for self-constitution it does so on the assumption that it can combine creativity and critical reflection in a single, unmediated and immediate fashion. Here, 'art' is a synonym for mental space. In post-Kantian philosophy the 'work' of the subject is a strictly aesthetic labour; it is unrelated to the instability of socio-political contexts. This has obvious appeal for certain 'literary' philosophies. The French philosopher, Gaston Bachelard, for example, writes of space in terms of the 'isolated [poetic] image' (1969: xi): independent of historical causality, able to speak with a language 'so new that correlations between past and present can no longer be usefully considered' (xxv), poetic space 'separates us from the past as well as from reality' (xxx). Having purged the image of material associations, Bachelard's poetic space can be 'considered as an origin of consciousness' (xxiv). As with Kant, therefore, the establishment of mental space is used to form the basis of a 'pure' phenomenology. But in order to do so the subject must first be 'desocialized'. The reason for this is simple. For Bachelard the self is transhistorical, its authentic condition is a state of 'intimacy'. Phenomenology can only recover this condition

'by ridding history of its conjunctive temporal tissue' (9). Space therefore resists history in order to restore the imagining consciousness to
a mythic state of indivisibility.

Topo-analysis, in Bachelard's work, is piquant and attractive; it is
also reductive. In spite of assertions to the contrary, the spatial imagination is not on the side of 'freedom' but of reification. By negating social
space for the sake of 'solitude' the subject is divorced from the sphere
of everyday life.[9]

A more sophisticated version of the spatial subject has been investigated by Frederic Jameson. In a justly celebrated essay, *Postmodernism,
or, The Cultural Logic of Late Capitalism* (1991), Jameson supplies us
with a model for understanding contemporary culture. According to
Jameson, we now grasp social reality 'synchronically' – in other words,
in space rather than in time. Consequently 'a model of political culture
appropriate to our own situation will necessarily have to raise spatial
issues as its fundamental organizing concern' (1991: 51). Like Soja,
Jameson insists that space cannot be reduced to the conventional
Kantian conception of an 'empty formal container': a 'categor[y] of
experience so all-encompassing' that it cannot itself 'enter into the
experience for which it stands' (364). Following Lefebvre, Jameson
stresses that space is at once abstract *and* material; there is, he writes,
a *'correlation* between these hitherto universal and formal organizational
categories . . . and the historical specificity and originality of the
various modes of production' (364; emphasis added). Thus, far from
being a purely abstract concept, an idea that would reciprocate the
Romantic ideology of post-Kantians such as Coleridge and Bachelard,
space for Jameson is always already social space and as such cannot
be separated from the socio-economic relations in which it is really
lived.

Having witnessed the politicization of Kant, we are led, via Lefebvre,
to the following conclusion: *'all* modes of production are not merely
organized spatially but also constitute distinctive modes of the production of space'. This raises some obvious problems for the concept of
the subject, for if space is at once a product and a means of production,
then, as we have seen, the notion of mental space must be revised.
As Lefebvre argues, philosophers from Kant onwards have focused on
'mental space' as something set apart from the conditions of daily life,
as if the production of the subject could be abstracted from the production of the social. The 'net result' of such thought, borne out in the
dazzling *topoi* of Bachelard's 'poetic space', is the belief in mental space
as something 'extra-ideological' – separable, that is, from social space.

When Jameson gives us his theory of subjectivity, then, the aim is to resist the spatial fetishism of post-Kantian thought. To do so, he invokes the idea of 'cognitive mapping', a concept with echoes of Benjamin but which is in fact borrowed from Kevin Lynch's classic study, *The Image of the City*. Taking his cue from Althusser's redefinition of ideology as 'the "Representation" of the imaginary relationship of individuals to their real conditions of existence', which 'interpellates individuals as Subjects' (Althusser 1971: 162, 170) and connecting this to Lynch's work, Jameson comes up with the following thesis: the cognitive map 'enable[s] a situational representation on the part of the individual subject to that vaster and properly unrepresentable totality which is the ensemble of society's structures as a whole' (1991: 51).

For Jameson, this concept of 'positive ideology' has the advantage of stressing the gap between individual and social being; between 'phenomenological perception' on the one hand 'and a reality that transcends all individual thinking or experience on the other; but which ideology, as such, attempts to span or coordinate, to map, by means of conscious and unconscious representations' (415–16). Now, while the concept of cognitive mapping has obvious attractions – it does, after all, explain how subjects locate themselves in social space – there is, it seems to me, a fundamental problem with Jameson's reading of Althusser. Like Althusser, Jameson reduces individuals to functional supports of the system. Because subjectivity and ideology have been identified with the Lacanian Imaginary – and the Imaginary coordinates an *illusory* relationship with the Real – we get no sense of the subject as something that is able to *resist* the imposition of social structures. In a sense, therefore, Jameson has opened up a gap between phenomenological and structural being that he cannot, in fact, close:

> cognitive mapping, which was meant to have a kind of oxymoronic value and to transcend the limits of mapping altogether, is, as a concept, drawn back by the force of gravity of the black hole of the map itself (one of the most powerful of all human conceptual instruments) and therein cancels out its own impossible originality. A secondary premise must, however, also be argued – namely, that the incapacity to map spatially is as crippling to political experience as the analogous incapacity to map spatially is for urban experience.
>
> Jameson (1991: 416)

If the concept is so disabling why bother with it?

When Lefebvre considers the relationship between subjects and ideology he begins with an attack on the idea that our relationship with the Real is a 'product' of the symbolic. To assume, along with Lacan, Althusser and Jameson, that signs are primordial, and that reification is a natural or universal condition, is to make the mistake of confusing the reality with the abstraction, social space with mental space. Seeking to resist this formation, Lefebvre follows Nietzsche in claiming that 'language in action' (*parole*), is more important than 'language as a system' (*la langue*) (1991: 138). Words are simply metaphors for 'things' – they do not pre-exist 'the reality of the senses, of bodies, of wishes and desires' (1991: 139). The body, therefore, is primary. Against the reflective surface of language, it offers itself as a kind of 'anti-mirroring' effect; one that holds representation, and hence reification, in reserve. Thus, far from being a purely linguistic form, the subject is first of all felt and experienced through physical gestures and movements; a spatialization of subjectivity that 'does not consist in the projection of an intellectual representation, does not arise from the visible-readable realm' (1991: 200) – does not, in other words, cohere in either the spatial idealism of traditional phenomenology or the spatial structuralism of Althusser and Lacan.

To sum up: the space of the body is texture reasserting itself against text. In its depth, opacity and warmth, the body 'returns' as an irreducible force to counter the abstract translucency of pure form. This means that the subject occurs as a productive 'interplay' between semiotic disembodiment and material re-embodiment, 'between', as Lefebvre puts it, 'uprooting and reimplantation . . . spatialization in an abstract expanse and localization in a determinate expanse' (1991: 203). Having thus reintroduced a concept of agency to the Althusserian thesis, there are no limits to the spaces that the subject may claim or be claimed by in its progress through everyday life.[10]

The task now is to map this 'interplay' as it occurs in *The Prelude*.

Part 2

Space in (New) History

The New Historicism has had a tremendous impact on Wordsworthian studies. Recent critical works by Marjorie Levinson, Clifford Siskin, David Simpson and Alan Liu have all been marked by a willingness to 'return' the text to history. The reason for this is twofold: first, to resist the institutional hegemony of the Yale school – the so-called 'critics of consciousness' (variations on a New Critical theme and all post-Kantians to a (de) man); second, to shift the emphasis away from discussions of unitary or integrated 'selfhood' and towards an examination of the socio-discursive conditions in which 'subjects' are produced. For many of these critics, the latter project entails the adoption of Althusserian concepts of subjectivity where the self is conceived as a provisional conglomeration of 'subject-positions': an illusory product of the relationship between linguistic and social codes. We have already seen the shortcomings of this theory. By locating the self exclusively in the mental space of discourse, the material space of everyday life is denied. Consequently, the subject falls into an abyss of aesthetic enervation. The New Historicist subject is therefore as empty and inadequate as the Romantic archetype it was meant to replace.

But if the latter can be forgiven for its epistemological naivety must we continue to make excuses for the former? I tend to agree with the notional conclusions of Jon Klancher in his essay 'English Romanticism and Cultural Production' (1989). Theories of Romantic subjectivity remain useless unless they resolve the question of 'grounding' that New Historicist theories have yet to deal with; it is not enough to shuttle texts between deconstructive and reconstructive 'move and countermove', as if aesthetic forms and historical practices could be circulated endlessly (Veeser 1989: 81). If our criticism is to rejoin the world of social praxis, somewhere, somehow, a ground must be applied – what better ground, then, than the practical reality of social space?

Strangely enough, in both Levinson and Liu, the material for a resurgence of social space is already there. In Levinson's *Wordsworth's Great Period Poems* (1986), this involves a recreation of the spatial politics of Tintern Abbey and the Lake District; in Liu's *Wordsworth: the Sense of History* (1989b), an analysis of the historical space of the Simplon Pass. The problem is, however, that neither critic has solved the problem of how we are to *read* these spaces. Social space, as we have seen, cannot be reduced to a system of signs; it cannot be approached by way of the abstract realm of textuality. The reading of social space that I therefore propose will require a kind of phenomenological perception; not the closed, idealist form of Kant and Bachelard (the sort that ends up 'reading' the subject in terms of its identification with aesthetic categories), but the imaginative reconstruction of real spaces and real times. To quote from Kristin Ross: 'By imagining the lived experience of actors in particular oppositional moments . . . one can avoid an analytic structure that insists on starting from the (predetermined) result' (1988: 11).

Through the recreation of everyday life, therefore, we move from mental space to social space; we shift, in other words, from theory into practice. And in doing so we question not only the past but also ourselves.

Maps and Pictures

To open Romantic history to the reassertion of social space we must draw on the 'semiotic disembodiment' of the mental map. The common assumption about Romantic mapping is that it did not exist. More often than not, Romantic subjects are shown to be involved in what Jameson refers to as 'pre-cartographic operations' – existential journeys that are plotted by itineraries rather than maps. Thus, in a poem such as Byron's *Childe Harold's Pilgrimage* (1812–18), the hero's wanderlust is organized around the 'still-subject-centred progress' of the tourist, along which various 'significant key features' are marked – cities, mountains, rivers, lakes and so on (Jameson 1991: 52). Similarly with Wordsworth's *Prelude*, the confident assertion of Book I – 'and should the guide I chuse/Be nothing more better than a wandering cloud/I cannot miss my way' (1805, I: 17–19) – is usually taken as a signal that Romantic subjectivity is at home in the world. With the whole universe as a *topos* for being, the stages of the journey from youthful naivety to mature self-knowledge can be traced without maps and consequently without any anxiety over representational collapse. Such is Wordsworth's faith in the itinerary – 'theme/Single and of determined bounds' (1805, I: 669–70) – that any aspects of nature, even the most fragmented parts, 'a twig or any floating thing' (1805, I: 31), can serve as a 'guide' to coordinate the relationship between individual being and universal totality.

Problems occur, however, when Romantic writing calls this relationship into question. It is one thing to trust your course to one of nature's fragments, as if subjectivity were always already given or 'complete', quite another to lose the sense of its necessary connection with the 'material re-embodiment' of social space. The point is that Wordsworth's journey has more practical concerns than traditional readings of *The Prelude* would care to admit. If we take the model of the tour as the basic motivation behind the poem, as Alan Liu suggests, then the conventional ascription of 'mystical pilgrimage' begins to look rather shaky. For *The Prelude*, unlike the *Morte D'Arthur* or *The Pilgrim's Progress*, is best understood as a journey without a goal; it is less concerned with finding something than it is with making sense of the passage; and this, as Liu reminds us, can only be achieved from a retrospective point of view: an account of things that seeks to bridge 'gaps' or 'breaks' in the itinerary through the 'thought [of] continuity' (1989b: 6). Cognitive mapping, therefore, in Jameson's sense, is present at every level of the poem.

Given that a form of mapping exists in *The Prelude*, the question arises of how Wordsworth forges continuity. In a territory without structural coordinates, the self can only be written, as it were, after the fact. Continuity can only be established in the temporality of writing. But looking back into the past Wordsworth must first insert a compass; a spatial element to ensure that the tour *could* always have been comprehended as a totality. From point to point, nature leads the way. But if Wordsworth can trust to nature for a guide, it is because nature is being used as a screen memory to disguise a more troubling thought: the idea that subjectivity is dependent not on a map, but on a body and its physical location in space. So what, then, is nature?

Since the work of T.J. Clark and John Barrell, critics of Romantic representation have argued that the appeal of Romantic nature is built on its status as a pictorial 'landscape'; on its reception as a visual 'commodity' rather than as a natural or self-engendered 'work'.[11] Outside the landscape, the manifestation of an aesthetic 'frame' enables the subject to be constituted as a viewer – aloof and detached, located in a continuous mental space beyond nature and the contingency of social production. Above all, it helps to assert the independent power of the creative imagination. Thus, as Lefebvre writes:

> The power of a landscape does not derive from the fact that it offers itself as spectacle, but rather from the fact that, as mirror and mirage, it presents any susceptible viewer with an image at once true and false of a creative capacity which the subject (or Ego) is able, during a moment of marvelous self-deception to claim as his own.
>
> (1991: 189)

In *The Prelude*, therefore, whenever social space threatens to overwhelm the self, to return it to the body, as in Revolutionary France, the 'power of landscape' intervenes as a kind of supplement or mark to relegate social space to the background and to reaffirm the mental space of imagination. As Liu indicates, the picturesque framework of Wordsworth's thought is no accident. Within *The Prelude*, nature is never self present, it always appears as landscape, as something framed by the visionary structure of aesthetic 'keeping'. For it is only by establishing a perspectival system, one that uses the middle ground of nature to relegate social space to the role of a backdrop, that the tourist 'I' can 'appear in the foreground' as something 'strong in itself' (1805, VI: 547); 'a self-generated "original" denying history . . . conventionality' (Liu 1989b: 12) – and, we should add, the space of the body.

The progress of *The Prelude* is based, then, on the denial of physical space: that which would overlay the pathos of phenomenological being, either with too much 'reality' (the incommensurability of the revolutionary 'event') or with too much 'representation' (the alienation of objective structures).

In the following, I will recreate the pattern of this denial by examining the function of nature in Wordsworth's treatment of the French Revolution. Here, as we shall see, the perspectival system, or map, is under constant threat of attack, not from imagination or history, but from the return of the social body.

Swarms and Dances

The passage I am most interested in is located in Book VI, and is concerned with the relationship between observers and revellers, and also between the individual and the collective that Wordsworth refers to as the 'swarm'. My insight into the significance of the latter term has been developed through a reading of Kristin Ross's superb study of Rimbaud, *The Emergence of Social Space*. To take us into the world of the swarm, I will begin with a little scene-setting.

When Wordsworth and Jones arrived in France on 13 July 1790, it was to find

> blessedness
> Spread like a fragrance everywhere, like spring
> That leaves no corner of the land untouched
>
> (1805, VI: 368–70)

It is one year after the fall of the Bastille – an act of levelling marked in line 357. In the passage that follows, our attention shifts from the vertical axis of history to the horizontal axis of social space. Here, the focus would appear to have moved also from the isolated gaze of the individual to the communal body of the populace:

> Unhoused beneath the evening star we saw
> Dances of liberty, and, in late hours
> Of darkness, dances in the open air.
>
> (1805, VI: 380–2)

The travellers are witness to the free action of the liberty dance: a corporeal space denoting the transition from the individual being of 'housed' space – the comforts of the Heideggerian 'dwelling' – to the social being of nomadic space.

It is not long, however, before we are returned to the sheltered realm of the after-meditation: the mental space where Wordsworth and Jones are cast as tourists. Thus, as the journey proceeds, the social space of Revolutionary France takes on the form of a landscape painting in the mind, with each scene composed as if the subject were looking out from the vertex of a perspectival cone. As the travellers glide on the surface of the Saône, they construct a world that is entirely transparent – a pictorial world that has been drained of matter and extension. With each turn of 'the flowing stream' space is transformed into a sequence of spectacles to be grasped in the pleasure of a gaze. It is as if the eye were roving over a canvas or a set of *articles de luxe*:

> Enchanting show
> Those woods and farms and orchards did present,
> And single cottages and lurking towns –
> Reach after reach, procession without end
> Of deep and stately vales.
>
> (1805, VI: 387–91)

In the next passage, however, the discourse of the Romantic nature trail collapses. At this point the observers suddenly become participants, leaving the protection of the framework to step into the middle ground; at once destroying the rules on which the picture had been formed and restoring the lived experience of the Revolution:

> We rose at signal given, and formed a ring,
> And hand in hand danced round and round the board;
> All hearts were open, every tongue was loud
> With amity and glee . . .
> And round and round the board they danced again.
>
> (1805, VI: 406–13)

The religious echoes of these lines, all 'hearts were open' and all desires known, from the collect, corresponds with the messianic phase of the French Revolution. But rather than history, reason and sense, what has most place here is the intermingling of political and libidinal desires: the levelling of the transcendent signifier and the opening of sensational virtuality. In the lateral space of the dance, the language of the eucharist and the rhetoric of social transformation are accelerated to the point where signification becomes denotation, leaving subjectivity convulsed in an incantatory rhythm of gestures, motions and directions: 'round and round . . . round and round'.

As the body escapes from the 'gravitational pull' of stratified space the perspectival system is broken up; thus the importance of intransitive verb forms and impersonal pronouns. For an instant, 'we' are close to the surging 'erotico-politics' of Rimbaud, the poet of the 1871 revolution. In this moment of spatial hypersensation *The Prelude* veers towards 'a devaluation of individual subjectivity in favor of the construction of a (virtual) group subject' (Ross 1988: 113). But the moment is brief, the dance ends, we are back in the world of Romantic 'solitude' (1805, VI: 424); the 'temperate [and temporal] shew/Of objects that endure' and not 'the busy dance/Of things that pass away' (1805, XII: 33–6).

Looking back now to lines 398–9 of Book VI we can see the potential danger of the dance. For here, Wordsworth installs a pre-emptive warning within his text: 'Like bees they swarmed, gaudy and gay as bees;/Some vapoured in the unruliness of joy'. As the soberness of the transcendent subject succumbs to a form of drunken collectivity, insect imagery becomes increasingly prevalent. The political implications of this theme can be extracted by placing the lines quoted above alongside a verse from Shelley's 'Song to the Men of England' (1819):

> Wherefore, Bees of England, forge
> Many a weapon, chain and scourge,
> That these stingless drones may spoil
> The forced produce of your toil?

In Shelley's poem, the weapons which the 'Bees' 'forge' become instruments of their own subjection. The seeds of revolt are sown, however, at the level of the metaphor. By depicting the workers as bees and the ruling classes as 'stingless drones', power relations are reversed. The task of the working classes is to realize this reversal, making it literal in the realm of social praxis. Wordsworth, of course, is distrustful of this metaphor. Whenever insect imagery occurs in *The Prelude*, it is usually placed in opposition with sobering images of humanity. Here, the 'unruliness' of the French bees directs us towards a number of episodes where collective 'joy' has given way to the riotous pleasures of the many; where, to put it another way, the 'swarm' transforms the static landscape into a vibrant, molecular space of libidinal desires.

The beginning of Book IX, for example, sees Wordsworth back

in France, having adopted, once more, the attitude of 'the sauntering traveller' (1805, IX: 34). In contrast to the festive scenes of June 1790, the subject enters into a world 'rocked by storms' and 'hubbub wild' (49–56). It is as if social space had suddenly entered the city to overturn the representation of nature as pictorial commodity. Once again, however, social space is evoked in terms drawn from the discourse of tourism: 'The Arcades I traversed in the Palace huge/Of Orleans, coasted round and round the line/Of tavern, brothel, gaming-house, and shop' (50–2). By 'reading' Paris through the template of the leisurely stroll, the subject distances himself from the violence around him. The detachment cannot be sustained for long, however. As Wordsworth pauses at the ruins of the Bastille to gather up a stone, he pockets the souvenir 'in the *guise*/Of an enthusiast' (66–7; emphasis added). The gap between fiction and reality begins to close. Whenever the mask drops, the gaze of the tourist is assaulted by a collocation of 'Loose and disjointed' things (107): the 'hissing' of Factionists, the 'ant-like swarms/Of builders and subverters' (58–9). The resurgence of the swarm leads Wordsworth to a moment of existential crisis:

> Oh, laughter for the page that would reflect
> To future times the face of what now is! . . .
> The land all swarmed with passion, like a plain
> Devoured by locusts — Carra, Gorsas — add
> A hundred other names, forgotten now,
> Nor to be heard of more; yet were they powers,
> Like earthquakes, shocks repeated day by day,
> And felt through every nook of town and field.
>
> (176–83)

The description of the land 'all swarmed with passion' is a harsh indictment of the festive collectivity depicted in Book VI. There, to paraphrase a remark of Walter Benjamin's, the loosening of the self by intoxication allows the people to step outside the realm of ideological intoxication.[12] Here, by contrast, it leads to an alarmist evocation of the bio-power of the crowd, a form of mass desubjectification in opposition to the integrative power of the individual mind. Nature explodes in a kind of rural violence: an upsurge of materialism against organicity, against the 'real solid world/Of images' (1805, VIII: 604–5; strange Kantian paradox!) and against the restorative powers of imagination. Its effect, to paraphrase Ross, is to make the Words-worthian self tremble at the threat of a return to the multiple, repetitive motions of the 'names of history' (Ross 1988: 67). In the realm of material space, a multiplicity of diverse voices act on the subject, driving it towards a hyperbolic sublime. The outcome is an exacerbation of mind beyond the 'counterpoise' of nature (1805, XI: 31–2).

Cities of the Plain

The French Revolution sections lead, obviously enough, into a closer examination of Wordsworth's treatment of the city. To begin with I will cite a passage from Geoffrey Hartman's signal work, *Wordsworth's Poetry, 1787–1814* (1964):

> A further sign of the imagination threatening its ties is revery, that abstracted, dream-like void which enables Wordsworth to pass unscathed through London. The poet thinks it a gift of nature, yet it removes him as much from nature as from man. 'Of that external scene which round me lay,/Little, in this abstraction, did I see,' he remarks of a previous strong moment of revery [1850, IV: 160–1].
>
> (1987b: 238)

Reading with Hartman (and thus 'with' Wordsworth) we may interpret the city sections as reaction formations to the 'superficiality' of the social world, all the 'surfaces of artificial life' (1805, III: 590) that threaten the deconstruction of the self. The entry of the poet into the urban environment, therefore, functions as a kind of *via negativa*, a staged denial of solitary *and* social authenticity prior to their (temporary) restitution in the mental space of imagination. In isolation, however, imagination is dangerous; as 'an abstracted, dream-like void' it threatens to negate not only the city but also the 'relationship' that connects the poet with the world. Yet the risk must be taken, for in *Wordsworth's Poetry* imagination is used to protect *The Prelude* and a certain theory of reading from a far greater threat: the material apocalypse of the social, that which would negate hermeneutic depth in a surface flow of 'men and moving things' (1805, VIII: 158).

Throughout *The Prelude* we are reminded that city space is alienating: if rural life 'shapes . . . the soul' and 'Gives movement to the thoughts . . . /With order and relation' (1805, VII: 726–30), urban life is 'an unmanageable sight' (709), at once uniform and extraordinary, rapid and languorous. It works to dull the imagination. This is why, according to Hartman, 'so much space is given . . . to fairs and festivals, to primitive and sophisticated amusement, in a word, to distractions' (1987b: 239). The 'space' that Wordsworth donates to the 'immediate, external stimuli' of the masses is a primitive substitute for the lasting, internal pleasures of imagination. Hence, in Book III city life in Cambridge is described, variously, as a 'motley spectacle' (1805, III: 29) or 'novel show' (203); an 'inferior exhibition, played/By wooden images, a theatre/For wake or fair' (605–7). In Book VII, London is made up of 'shifting pantomimic scenes' (1805, VI: 283). The terror of the simulacra climaxes with the 'monstrous' spectacle of Bartholomew Fair: a work to lay the 'whole creative powers of man asleep' (653–5). The negative way of the Wordsworthian imagination is therefore linked to the resistance, noted earlier, of the individual subject to the social body of the crowd. Imagination opposes the 'swarm' (699), stasis transcends the 'illimitable walk' (159), articulation resists 'anarchy and din' (660).

The tension here, between the imagination of the autogenerative individual and the will of the desubjectivized crowd is crucial to our understanding of *The Prelude*. It is based, first of all, on the assumption that material space can be subdued, reduced to something static and unchanging, ideal and transcendent. In practice, however, what Wordsworth discovers in the city sections is a space of shifting multiplicity, a physical texture that refuses to be overwritten by the abstract textuality of imagination. In a very real sense, therefore, city space is the true Wordsworthian 'other', one that refuses sublimation in the *via negativa*. For the purposes of this essay we must recreate those moments where the city breaks through the strategies of mental resistance.

Book VII 'fixes' the subject in a society contrasting to some degree with the academic bowers of Cambridge and the 'unfenced regions' of the Lakes. Since childhood he has been haunted by the 'sights and shows' of fancy: the 'green groves' of pleasure parks and 'fairy cataracts' (123–5), 'Streets without end and churches numberless' (133). It is not long, however, before the 'wondrous power of words' is displaced by hard reality. The London that Wordsworth looks upon from line 139 oscillates between mental and physical perspectives: the steady self-confirmation of the classical vista and the 'quick dance' of modernist fragmentation (156). One aspect of city space that Wordsworth must resist is its tendency to level the imagination. Hence the rhetoric of the conducted tour. To establish distance, Wordsworth views London from the mediatory standpoint of the guide book or panorama. Thus, as the tour proceeds, the pronouns shift from 'I' to 'we', and from 'me' to 'us'. Spatial, temporal, reading and class relations have been synthesized into the empty, translucent and transcendent form of the 'tourist' subject. To read against the grain of this subject 'we' must therefore look more closely at the texture of our guide.

Lines 154–70 are marked by an anaphoric structure of nouns or headwords in combination with modifiers and qualifiers: 'the Babel din', 'The endless stream of men', 'the illimitable walk' (157–60):

> The wealth, the bustle and the eagerness,
> The glittering chariots . . .
> The scavenger who begs with hat in hand,
> The labouring hackney-coaches, the rash speed
> Of coaches travelling far, whirled on with horn
> Loud blowing, and the sturdy drayman's team,
> Ascending from some alley of the Thames
> And striking right across the crowded Strand
> Till the fore-horse veer with punctual skill . . .
>
> (161–70)

The accumulation of definite articles – 'the' rather than 'there is' – forces London out of memory and into the experiential present of deixis. It is as if the temporal depth of the verb 'to be' had been flattened out. In the absence of this depth it becomes very difficult to establish relationships between things: the poetry is demonstrative rather than descriptive. As the series accelerates we are unable to assemble the nouns in hierarchical categories: the city 'strikes' the eye (155), coaches are 'whirled on' (166). Throughout, active verbs seize on the object in order to subvert classification. The verticality of vision is toppled to emphasize horizontal configurations of movement and rapidity: 'the quick dance/Of colours, lights and forms' (156–7), of 'moving things/From hour to hour' (158–9), the 'rash speed' of the coaches (165). What emerges from this is close to the intoxicatory effects of the dance sections, a notion reinforced by the fact that the horses in lines 167–70 are part of a 'drayman's team'. Here, the 'fore-horse' veering with 'punctual skill' plays on an unfortunate ambiguity of metaphor: the tenor, as it were, runs away with the vehicle.

We can proceed now to examine a number of emblematized themes. The first involves what I will refer to as the 'drunkenness of words', their capacity to drift in and out of the mental space of dominant ideologies. The politicization of language is a prevalent theme of the London book. Between lines 171–83, for example, advertising slogans conjoin with repetition – 'face to face—/Face after face . . . /Shop after shop' (172–4) – to dazzle the consumer with 'symbols' and 'blazoned names' (174). The shopfronts are 'inscribed from top to toe' with huge letters, 'like a title-page' (176–7): words that are, in every sense excessive, larger than life, irresistible. Here, the hyperbole of verbal signification opens on to a generalized gap between sign and referent. Alongside the advertising texts, significant historical presences such as 'Boyle, Shakspear, Newton' (182), foundations of the Enlightenment, are transformed into absurd figureheads. This theme of cultural debasement is continued in a later passage where literary language itself succumbs to the denotative language of the market. Here, 'files of ballads dangle from dead walls' alongside 'Advertisements of giant size'. As the space of mercantile capital presses 'forward in all colours on the sight' (209–11), dominating our field of vision, the belief in inner meaning is undermined. The result is, of course, horrifying to anyone with a stake in poetic truth. In the city, the still, small voice of literary language loses its capacity to signify. Put another way, under the conditions set by capital, the exchange value of the sign encroaches on its use value; the music of humanity is usurped by the silent roar of the slogan.

The second theme is related to the intrusiveness of representational or pantomimic space. Shortly after this section Wordsworth reinscribes himself in the role of the *bricoleur*. This time, however, the subject is cataloguing people not things:

> Now homeward through the thickening hubbub, where
> See—among less distinguishable shapes—
> The Italian, with his frame of images
> Upon his head; with basket at his waist
> The Jew; the stately and slow-moving Turk,
> With freight of slippers piled beneath his arm.
> Briefly, we find, if tired of random sights . . .
> . . . all specimens of man . . .
>
> (1805, VII: 227–36)

The key word in this cabinet of sensations is 'specimens'. It allows Wordsworth to distance himself from the chaos of the crowd, substituting the singularity of the collector for the multiplicity of the collective. Abstracted from the contradictions of urban space, we can proceed at 'leisure', moving from outward scenes to descriptions of 'the spectacles/Within doors' (245–6). Here, we are presented with the miniature world of the panorama exhibition: 'mimic sights that ape/The absolute presence of reality' (248–9). Strangely, Wordsworth seems to value this encounter with imitation. The reasons for this are complex and are linked to the problems of Kantian self-production.

We can explain it, however, by way of an excursus into the theory of the panorama. To paraphrase Nicholas Green's comments on mid-to late nineteenth-century French exhibits, in the panorama, the 'play on illusionism' sets 'the experience of reality . . . off against the recognition of a clever counterfeit'; the artistic model, in other words, transforms reality into a pictorial commodity, a 'treat, to be consumed by the eyes' (Pugh 1990: 170–3). In Wordsworth's London this forms the basis of a model of self-fashioning. As we gaze at the exhibit our attention shifts between the well-crafted artistry of the display and its 'realist' evocation of the external world. This constant oscillation enables the imitation to sustain the idea of landscape as a model of 'luxury consumption' (Pugh 1990: 173). In doing so, however, it also presents the subject with a 'mirror' (1805, VII: 250) in which to produce the illusion of integrated subjectivity. From a point just beyond the frame we gaze at a '*whole* horizon on all sides', we are 'Plant[ed] upon some lofty pinnacle' (259–61; emphasis added). Having elevated ourselves from the broken perspectives of the horizontal plane a subjective ideal is reconfirmed. In the realm of spatial imitation the newly integrated 'Traveller' sees all (279–80).

From the point of view of spatial critique, however, the tension between self-fashioning and artistic production is exacerbated to the point of implosion. The reproduction of the classical vista is dialogized from within by its setting in the fragmented framework of urban space. Thus, when we turn away from the 'order of things' in the panoramic exhibition it is to enter into the 'shifting, pantomimic scenes' of Sadler's Wells: a world of 'Saw singers, rope-dancers, giants and dwarfs' – entertainment, as Wordsworth notes, for 'the rabblement' (283–96). The disorderly conduct of this particular show contrasts markedly with the frozen perfection of the panorama. While the former is enjoyed as a collective experience, the latter is endemic of solitariness and deprivation; it is a veritable figure of the sovereign imagination.[13]

We return to the trope of signification in lines 418–550. With the imagination asleep once more (499–516), words drift away from the centre. No longer anchored to the pure transparency of sense, they revert to the noisy opacity of non-sense – as if language had become a counter-spirit. The effects are felt at every level of society. In the 'never-ending' discourse of the lawyer: 'Words follow words, sense seems to follow sense' (540). In the holy church, the priest leads his voice 'through many a maze' (551), obfuscating symbolic truth for the sake of theatricality. If here, the discourse of the professional classes represents an extreme of linguistic disembodiment, that of the lower classes demonstrates the limit point of linguistic re-embodiment. The body of the rabblement is in 'uproar' (296). A cripple '*lies* at length beside a range/Of written characters' (221-2; emphasis added). A female vendor 'scream[s]' (198). Even at the level of gender the body forces language to veer away from its sanctioned purpose. Wordsworth is shocked, for instance, when he hears, for the 'first time . . . /The voice of woman utter blasphemy'. The disparity between the oath and the 'outward shape' of the prostitute divorces 'humanity' from the 'human form, splitting the race of man [and the signifier]/In twain' (418-27). In the city, therefore, the gap between sign and reality, imagination and nature is intolerable; everywhere, the 'outward shape' fails to harmonize with the inner meaning. Only at night, when the streets are emptied and the 'spectacle' is 'still', can the imagination find peace to match the 'solemnity' of nature. Life, for the most part, is noisy and frivolous, unmanageable and confused; the peace, as Wordsworth eventually admits, is 'falsely *catalogued*' (624-43; emphasis added).

The second instance of a spectacle laying the 'creative powers of man asleep' (655), occurs towards the end of Book VII:

> What say you then,
> To times, when half the city shall break out
> Full of one passion—vengeance, rage, or fear—
> To executions, to a street on fire,
> Mobs, riots, or rejoicings?
>
> (645-9)

Wordsworth goes on to depict St Bartholomew's Fair, invoking the aid of the Muse to lift us 'Above the press and danger of the crowd' (658). In a gesture towards the Augustan space of John Gay's London poem, *Trivia* (1716), the Muse allows the poet to be transported in security.[14] The passage that follows from this is important and deserves to be quoted in full:

> what a hell
> For eyes and ears, what anarchy and din
> Barbarian and infernal—'tis a dream
> Monstrous in colour, motion, shape, sight, sound.
> Below, the open space, through every nook
> Of the wide area, twinkles, is alive
> With heads; the midway region and above
> Is thronged with staring pictures, and huge scrolls,
> Dumb proclamations of the prodigies;

And chattering monkeys dangling from their poles,
And children whirling in their roundabouts;
With those that stretch the neck, and strain the eyes,
And crack the voice in rivalship, the crowd
Inviting; with buffoons against buffoons
Grimacing, writhing, screaming; him who grinds
The hurdy-gurdy, at the fiddle weaves;
Rattles the salt-box, thumps the kettle-drum,
And him who at the trumpet puffs his cheeks,
The silver-collared negro with his timbrel,
Equestrians, tumblers, women, girls, and boys,
Blue-breeched, pink-vested, and with towering plumes.
All moveables of wonder from all parts,
Are here, Albinos, painted Indians, dwarfs,
The horse of knowledge, and the learned pig,
The stone-eater, the man that swallows fire,
Giants, ventriloquists, the invisible girl,
The bust that speaks, and moves its goggling eyes,
The waxwork, clockwork, all the marvellous craft
Of modern Merlins, wild beasts, puppet-shows,
All out-o'-th'-way, far-fetched, perverted things,
All freaks of Nature, all Promethean thoughts
Of man—his dulness, madness, and their feats,
All jumbled together to make up
This parliament of monsters. Tents and booths
Meanwhile—as if the whole were one vast mill—
Are vomiting, receiving, on all sides,
Men, women, three-year's children, babes in arms.

(659–95)

Beneath us, what has precedence are the gerundial forms: 'chattering',
'whirling', 'writhing, screaming', 'goggling', 'vomiting, receiving'.
Language is in a constant state of process, producing a 'space' that
'is alive'. To Wordsworth, however, the fair has nothing to do with
celebration. From our perspective above the crowd it would appear
to have more in common with the blank chaos of industrialization:
'as if the whole were one vast mill'. The gerund forms stress the
insectivorous nature of the scene: a series of mindless productive and
reproductive moves. As riot and industry go hand in hand, then, it
seems that only imagination can maintain an effective resistance against
dehumanization. This view is confirmed in lines 696–713. The failure

of the 'swarm' (699) to overcome the unsavoury aspects of modernity is due to the fact that it produces and is produced by

> the same perpetual flow
> Of trivial objects, melted and reduced
> To one identity by differences
> That have no law, no meaning, and no end . . .
>
> (702–5)

City space and the social body it embraces are characterized in the form of a counter sublime: – 'By nature an unmanageable sight' (709) which works to undermine reason. Thus we are prepared for the reassertion of mental space.

The conclusion to this book is usually read as a triumphant affirmation of imaginative power. Critics such as Hartman and Lindenberger, for example, would point to the accumulation of pastoral images for evidence of completion or harmony. Thus, the 'unmanageable' fair is juxtaposed with the 'steady form' of the mountain; the babble of the city with the 'changeful language' of the ancient hills. Nature is reinserted to counter the confusion of urban space. In contrast with the fragmented temporality of the panorama exhibitions, the pantomimes and fairs, the time of nature is 'Perennial'. It is measured by seasons and cycles. Thus, while moving away from the inert landscapes of the Augustan topographical poem, Romantic nature imagery includes its privileging of rhythm and harmony, of 'multitude,/*With* order and relation' (720–30; emphasis added). But to perceive rural space in this way requires an exercise of artistic control. If city space 'wear[ies] out the eye' (708), the subject must counter this by looking on nature with 'steadiness' (711). Only he who preserves an 'under-sense of greatest' can look on 'the parts/as parts, 'but with a feeling for the whole' (712–13). To restore the sense of landscape to metaphorical perfection, the subject must gather the flow of trivial objects under the rubric of imagination. But at the end of the text, what has been restored is not the real landscape – not the space of daily life and practical relations – but the false, aesthetic landscape of pastoralism. Nature is placed by Wordsworth within the text as an artistic mark to distinguish the subject from the social body. From the space of imagination, 'the press/Of self-destroying, transitory things' is composed as an 'enobling harmony' (739–41). Wordsworth resists historical space, therefore, to fashion himself in the artifice of eternity. It is this 'reality' that will overshadow the self-presence of the recuperative landscape in Book VIII.

Exit

The Veiling of Fleet Street

This will not be a conclusion in the ordinary sense. Rather I will attempt to 'perform' one final act of spatial subversion. I hope that the following will suggest to the reader spaces for dialogue rather than for completion.

In April 1808, a few years after completing the thirteen-book *Prelude*, Wordsworth spent some time in London in the company of Coleridge, who was suffering from ill-health. In a letter to Sir George Beaumont, Wordsworth recounts that he left Coleridge in 'a very thoughtful and melancholy state of mind':

> I had passed through Temple Bar and St Dunstan's, noticing nothing, and entirely occupied with my own thoughts, when looking up, I saw before me the avenue of Fleet Street, silent, empty, and pure white, with a sprinkling of new-fallen snow, not a cart or Carriage to obstruct the view, no noise, only a few soundless and dusky foot-passengers here and there; you remember the elegant curve of Ludgate Hill in which this avenue would terminate, and beyond and towering above it was the huge and majestic form of St. Pauls, solemnised by a thin veil of falling snow. I cannot say how much I was affected at this unthought-of sight, in such a place and what a blessing I felt there is in habits of exalted Imagination. My sorrow was controlled, and my uneasiness of mind not quieted and releived altogether, seemed at once to receive the gift and anchor of security.
>
> (de Selincourt 1967– , II.i: 209)

Such moments are not uncommon in Wordsworth; they appear as if from nowhere: a testimony to the power of 'unthought-of sights' in combination with the 'habits of exalted Imagination'. In such moments it seems as if the scission between the *bildende Kraft* of the subject and the idealized form of natural organic production has been resolved. Nature and culture, interiority and exteriority, become 'genuine counterpart[s]', 'brothers' to each other (1805, XIII: 88–90). Something, however, does not hold quite true. The reciprocal relationship between nature and art is marked by a *frisson* of undecidability.

Shortly before this incident, Wordsworth and Coleridge had visited the Thomas Angerstein collection (later to form the core of the National Gallery). The day, Wordsworth notes, 'was very unfavourable, not a gleam of sun, and the Clouds were quite in disgrace'. The scene is looked upon as an *objet d'art*, one that is sadly out of keeping: blank and uninspiring. In contrast, the pictures in the exhibition – Michelangelo's Sebastian', 'the new Rembrandt' – present the viewer with images of *'wonder', 'depth'* and *'high* pleasure' (italics in original) (II(i): 208). Art, in other words, restores the sublimity so lacking in reality. Thus, when we reach the St Paul's description, this 'unthought-of sight', which appears to break away from an intentional structure, fails to be anything but intentional. The entire scene, as Richard Noyes writes, 'is composed as an artist might arrange and harmonise it' (1968: 239). In the foreground, Fleet Street is 'silent, empty, and white with snow'. From the middleground the 'sweeping curve' of Ludgate Hill gestures towards the 'huge and majestic form' of the cathedral, 'solemnised by a thin veil of falling snow'. We could say, therefore, that Wordsworth's 'uneasiness' ('not quieted and relieved altogether') is pre-emptive of the fact that the category of the aesthetic has come to dominate his relation with the external world. The 'blessing' and 'security' that it provides is therefore double-edged. For while the act of veiling succeeds in disguising the material reality of city space – Fleet Street at that time was one of London's dirtiest and most crowded streets – it places the subject in a solipsistic universe of pure form.

There is, however, time for one final space – a space that veers away from our sight, a space of danger and chance, of distorting noise and opaque folds. From the quiet limit of imagination, the Romantic subject gazes on a world riven with violence – a world proclaiming itself in the excessive, passionate and terrifying form of the social: 'Grimacing, writhing, screaming . . . the whole swarm of its inhabitants' (1805, VII: 673, 699). It is a world that *The Prelude* cannot resist.

SUPPLEMENT

NIGEL WOOD: You seem to argue against the figural use of landscape or indeed social space in Romantic literature, or rather you claim that it has been *too* encoded by critics who share the Romantic Ideology. How can we reassess literary space as a material formation?

PHILIP SHAW: Obviously, in the wake of McGann, Barrell and others, critics today are a little more suspicious of the Romantic treatment of landscape. David Simpson's *Wordsworth's Historical Imagination* (1987), for example, does a fine job in recovering details of the political economy of the Lake District – details that Wordsworth in *The Prelude*, chose either to repress or to ignore. In writing of social space, via Lefebvre, however,

I have decided to sound a further note of caution. While the New Historicism would make the claim that it has liberated itself from the so-called Romantic ideology, it seems to me that it has not yet escaped the influence of its philosophical idealism. Critics, as far afield as Jean-Luc Nancy, Philippe Lacoue-Labarthe and Marjorie Levinson, have attested to a certain 'persistence' of Romanticism: the way in which Romantic poems seduce us into acts of critical completion while at the same time ensuring that a part is always 'left over'. Now, if we are to counter the refiguring of landscape that inevitably occurs in (some) New Historicist works, it seems to me that we must go right to the heart of this persistence. For, as Lefebvre writes, the 'Kantian legacy of transcendental spatial idealism pervades every wing of the modern hermeneutic tradition' (1991: 25), the net result of which

> is that a particular 'theoretical practice' produces a *mental* space which is apparently, but only apparently extra-ideological. In an inevitably circular manner, this mental space then becomes the locus of a 'theoretical practice' which is separated from social practice and which sets itself up as the axis, pivot or central reference point of Knowledge.
>
> (1991: 6)

In my opinion, the pivotal point of New Historicism, the part that escapes ideology, remains the category of the aesthetic. We see this especially in Greenblatt, where the return of literary, or Romantic space saves the day for an overly historicized subject. Only Liu, it seems to me, has come close to 'getting' at this point. To read literary landscapes, therefore, we must attend to those moments where the 'spatial idealism' of theory supersedes its origins in material practice.

NW: Louis Althusser claimed that Grand History did not exist and that it was composed of several Histories, all with their relative autonomy. How formative was Wordsworth's historical and/or geographical location?

PS: The importance of the Lake District in fostering Wordsworth's sense of self needs to be reassesed. Literary critics have approached *The Prelude* as a linear narrative. They have, in other words, read the text as a series of educative progressions: Wordsworth is formed in the Lake District; he is altered by Cambridge; challenged by the Alps; threatened by London; almost destroyed by France; restoration comes from the marriage of Nature and Imagination in the Snowdon episode. A recent environmental work, Jonathan Bate's *Romantic Ecology*, does nothing to challenge this view. We are still talking about the Lakes, on Wordsworth's own terms, as the 'origin' of mature sensibility. To counter this tendency I have sought to reverse the standard temporal flow. In so far as any location is 'formative', I have attempted to read Wordsworth as a poet of urban rather than natural or imaginative space. The Lake District is an important founding myth because it resists the pressure of the social: witness the restorative commentaries on London in Book VIII and Cambridge in Book IX. Wordsworth's 'home' is, it seems to me, an 'after-meditation' brought on by his terror of urban and industrial environments.

NW: Do you feel that Wordsworth's depiction of the coherent and cohering subject was an individual response, or one shared by several writers in the age?

PS: The notion of the 'cohering subject' was an idea that Keats certainly did not share. But Keats' own assertion of 'negative capability' must be scrutinized with some care. The dispersed self, beloved of mental topographers from Maurice Blanchot to Jacques Lacan, is no more 'radical' in its formation than the integrative self of the egotistical sublime. For Keats, the ability to die into the space of literature is predicated on the escape from a more worldly locus: the space of practical reality. Thus, in 'To Autumn', a pictorial landscape is used to cloak a social landscape (see McGann 1988: 15–66). Keatsian loss is a negative response to a world that Romanticism can no longer assimilate. Wordsworth comes close to this idea in the city sections except that here it is the performative discourse of the swarm, rather than the literary space of imagination, that leads the writer to a possibility of loss.

NW: You do not mention the usual anthology sections of The Prelude, that is, the childhood books (I and II) or the ascent of Snowdon/the Alps. Surely, 'Topo-analysis' of these episodes would be essential to give a full account of the poem. Are they different in kind or only in degree from the sections you have mentioned?

PS: I quite agree. A full account of space in The Prelude would require some consideration of the childhood books and the Alps/Snowdon sections. In this essay I have concentrated on Wordsworth's depiction of the city. This is partly for reasons of strategy – to redress a little balance – and partly to prepare the way for a more deconstructive reading. It is strange that the natural spaces of Books I and II, for instance, are scored with architectural metaphors – references to building, foundations and so on. Indeed, throughout the text, Wordsworth bases his model of permanence less on the archetypal endurance of nature, and more on the cultivated authority of the monument (see, for example, 1805, Book I: 127–31; 226–8; Book II: 292–5; Book XIII: 278, 430). This must be related to Kant's interest in architectural metaphors. See Derrida, 1987: 40–1, and also the interview and essays on deconstruction and architecture in Architectural Design (1989).

NW: How would you respond to Raymond Williams's thesis in his The Country and the City that place gives rise to literary structures of feeling, that is, genres, which take over from geographical considerations, even if we know, say, the Lake District intimately. Isn't The Prelude more a testimony to the topographical poem of the eighteenth century, such as Thomson's

The Seasons, than some personal or even contemporary preoccupation?
PS: I'm glad you brought this up, for in many ways Williams's thought is very close to that of Lefebvre. In *Marxism and Literature* (1977b), for example, Williams makes a distinction between 'structures of feeling', or 'experience', and the more formal concepts of 'ideology' or 'world-view'. Feelings, he argues, are social and material before they are articulated and defined by the processes of cultural exchange. Like Lefebvre, therefore, he is concerned with 'meanings and values as they are actively lived and felt' (Williams 1977b: 132) – with, in other words, concrete reality prior to representation. Now, while structures of feeling can be 'related' to formal systems, such as literary genre (1977b: 133), to suggest that the latter may 'take over' from social considerations, such as geography (defined by Lefebvre as a set of 'social relations', rather than as static 'place' or 'location'), seems rather mistaken. Take the example of the pastoral tradition. In *The Country and the City* (1977a), Williams argues correctly, it seems to me, that rural communities have been 'alienated' by the metropolitan bourgeois ideology of pastoralism. A literary genre, in other words, has disguised the reality of the productive forces and relations that permeate the countryside. To imply, however, that the relationship between poems and places can be *reduced* to a kind of intertextual dialogue has dangerous connotations of academic formalism, for which there is no need. To modify Williams a little, 'structures of feeling' or, as I would prefer, the unstructured moments of 'everyday life', break through genre (for instance, in Wordsworth's London) to return textuality to the base conditions of material production.

CHAPTER 3

Working *The Prelude*: Foucault and the New History

CLIFFORD SISKIN

[Clifford Siskin's essay poses two associated questions in particular: first, what is distinctive about the *academic* requirements for writing about Wordsworth's poetry; and second, how are we affected by the (usually tacit) discursive rules that govern what is 'knowledge', in itself and also about a literary work? Without answers to these preliminary enquiries, we may be restrained by irrelevant assumptions (not derived from the declared object for investigation) about just what is aesthetic as opposed to what is functional and what is 'relevant' critical comment. This can seem alien to 'proper' (but actually just traditional) critical concerns, based securely on the priorities given 'close reading', where a detailed focus on an individual text's 'words on the page' leads directly to either its evaluation or accurate interpretation. This approach is distrusted in several recent critical procedures for at least two reasons: first, it presupposes that such resulting information has been derived from some completely objective ground-rules that do not change in relation to the investigator (that is, her/his cultural/historical context); and second, in similar fashion, it places great reliance on our own context's canonical features in 'criticism', 'literature' and even 'subjectivity'. Unless we own up to the problem of the relativity of frames of reference, our criticism will be in bad faith: it will derive its authority from premises that pose as universals yet which are always historically *situated*.

Siskin mentions the influence of the sociologist/historian, Michel Foucault, on various forms of New History. During the vogue for formalist analyses of writing, using deconstructive strategies, in the 1970s and mid-1980s, there was always Foucault's dissenting voice, directing enquiry back to 'history'. Before we assume that this involves the return of traditional contextual studies of writing, where the writer is related to her/his historical background by a tracing of correspondences true of some 'spirit of the age', we need to assess Foucault's emphasis on investigations into discourse formation. For example, he set little store by analyses of the individual biography of the author, as such an entity only really emerges out of critical interpretation as an 'author-function'. The one heading, 'Wordsworth', does not refer to some unitary item and does not quite tally with the effective rhetorical and economic (or organizational) function it performs in critical discourse. An 'author' is always 'linked to the juridical and institutional system that encompasses, determines, and articulates the universe of discourses' (that is, writing described in terms of the constituting and usually tacit rules that allow certain references and even topics to be comprehensible to a certain set of addressees not just by what is denoted but what is suggested by the mode of address). These discourses are not affected identically 'at all times and in all types of civilization'. Historical difference between varied organizing principles behind the ordering of perception needs to be traced, but is not determined by the usual periodization by chronology, still less either by the reigns of certain monarchs or administrations under certain presidents or by apparently significant single events, such as a salient battle or economic change. An 'author-function' cannot be defined 'by the spontaneous attribution of a discourse to its producer', because that does not involve an explanation of how the larger structures of perception that contain the individual operate through the apparently individual case. Consequently, the 'author' does 'not refer purely and simply to a real individual, since it can give rise simultaneously to several selves, to several subjects – positions that can be occupied by different classes of individuals' (Foucault 1979b: 153).

The renewed interest in history is not necessarily a return to the familiar study of lines of influence or the unfolding of some national or even global destiny. In his *The Archaeology of Knowledge* (1969; trans. 1972) he stresses that, on the contrary, history is marked by discontinuity and ruptures between residual and emergent forces, breaks which traditional historical accounts efface 'in order to reveal the continuity of events'. The present task, Foucault saw, was to displace these perceived discontinuities and place them in the 'work itself' (1972: 13–14). This means not reading off the chosen object of study against a general master-explanation supposed to be more or less characteristic of some passage of time (a 'world-picture' or 'eras' of, say, expansion or capitalism), but, resisting that temptation, identifying several 'histories' embedded in, for example, a literary text: histories of book production, growth of a market, but, more radically, the unequal distributions of power in any culture. Foucault still finds mileage, therefore, in a focus on specific periods; his emphasis is less on the succession of recorded facts and more on what these phenomena can reveal of the chosen age's *episteme*, that is, the result of the configuration of contemporary discrete discourses that sets limits and also defines reality for people.

To move from one *episteme* to a succeeding one is never achieved by smooth transition as it alters one's grasp on reality.

It is a debatable point, however, whether Foucault ever encourages us to discover some 'reality' behind these archival traces, as the official explanations a society offers of its own activities cannot, by definition, indicate the deep changes that are actually occurring. 'Truth' is always bound to, and defined by, a particular *episteme* and is always, thus, a 'truth-effect', governed by a 'regime of truth' that validates its power. 'Power' is not primarily a result of temporal forces (military or political might, for example), but is nearer to the French *pouvoir*, the conceptual power to accomplish something, a possession not exclusively wedded to position within a power structure.

Foucauldian analysis of individual texts must work outwards from one piece of writing to embrace all the evidence that makes more and more secure one's identification of the competing discursive practices that are implicated. Indeed, Foucault rarely, if at all, interests himself in the interpretation of single texts mainly because the opportunity for dwelling on individual variations in his analysis is limited. Increasingly, the all-embracing category of 'power' implies that literature is rarely distinct from prevailing manifestations of its discourses. It may mask its assumptions, but, in the final analysis, it ceases to be a totally autonomous set of texts: 'Power is tolerable only on condition that it mask a substantial part of itself' (1981–7, 86). If all is power, then one merely swaps one form of it for another (see Culler 1988: 62–8).

Foucault does address certain clear priorities in his essay on 'Nietzsche, Genealogy, History', when he would aim to replace more traditional linear history with genealogy, a tracing of antecedents that are examined for their hold on us, the ways in which they have formed the present, at the same time as a renewed awareness less of our inheritance than of why we have broken away from it. Discourses exist only in an active way and do not demand ever more refined definitions of their 'being'. By laying hold on perhaps just single traits at a time one can trace myriad influences in the work as a whole. The genealogist will interrogate the integrity of the 'self, its recognition and displacement as an empty synthesis, in liberating a profusion of lost events' (1977: 145–6). For a recent example of this, see Jonathan Arac's *Critical Genealogies*, especially his precise account of '*The Prelude* and Critical Revision: Bounding Lines' (1987: 57–80), and also Siskin's own *The Historicity of Romantic Discourse* (see 1988: 114–24, 143–7).]

NIGEL WOOD

'*All gratulant, if rightly understood.*'
Wordsworth

'*Everything is dangerous.*'
Foucault

Theory

Past and Present

Forgive me for beginning with a little trick – after all, the whole purpose of this book is to effect the tricky (some would say 'magical') transformation of theory into practice. My trick is to make (prove?) my point in the *very act of making it*. I will assert the ongoing power of Wordsworth's *Prelude* – the way it continues to configure our professional and personal behaviours – by engaging in two quintessentially Wordsworthian habits: using my own personal experience as evidence; and framing that experience within a tale that contrasts the present with the past. So compelling were these behaviours to Wordsworth, that, when he tried to put his theories 'On Man, on Nature, and on Human Life' into practice, the initial result was not the intended 'philosophical poem' (Preface to *The Excursion* (1814), Owen and Smyser 1974, III: 5) called *The Recluse*, but an introduction composed of 'more lowly matter': the autobiographical descriptions of the 'Man/ Contemplating' that are *The Prelude* ('Prospectus', 94–6; Owen and Smyser 1974, III: 7).

I am going to take you back in my life not as far as the 'infant softness' (1850, I: 278) of *The Prelude*, but further than the 'five long winters' of 'Tintern Abbey' (2). In 1972 I wrote my undergraduate honours thesis on the 1805 and 1850 versions of *The Prelude*. More specifically, I patched together a new 'Prelude' that supposedly combined the best lines from each version into the poem that Wordsworth 'should' have published. I accompanied this new hybrid text with extended explanations of my editorial criteria and decisions. The result, I hoped, would not only earn me an 'A' (which it did), but would also, I fantasized, get picked up by a publisher for a paperback reading text aimed at undergraduates (which it did not). Like Wordsworth, whose plans in his early twenties for a 'monthly miscellany' on moral issues 'from which some emolument might be drawn' (de Selincourt 1967– , I: 118–20) also fell through, my subsequent journey into print has led me far from these early ambitions. Just as the poet turned from essays in monthlies to poems in books as he 'Yielded up moral questions in despair' (1850, XI: 305), so I find myself formally and conceptually estranged from my previous project.

Traditional literary histories have explained the Wordsworthian changes the way Wordsworth taught us to understand them: we have psychologized them. External events are assumed to cause internal effects in the psychic depths of the individual. The French Revolution, the Terror, and the death of Wordsworth's brother have all been used to 'explain' the shifting attitudes toward moral questions and the changes in literary output. Their accuracy as 'explanations', however, is secondary to their shared effect: finally, they all serve to shape Wordsworth's output into an *oeuvre* and the *oeuvre* into a celebration of the poet's personality. These histories become 'gratulant' Preludes, echoing the very past they are supposed to analyse.[1]

Permit me to break the habit. Although I could reveal some fairly compelling events, I would rather describe my estrangement from my earlier work by staying out of the Romantic depths and on the surface. There, I can tell a tale of discursive change within a discipline rather than a psychological tale of individual growth. What happened between that thesis and this paper, between then and now, was theory. Literary studies – the kind of knowledge production in which I participate – have been transformed by the form of writing we call 'theoretical'. What it has done, in the simplest and most important sense, is make us extraordinarily uncomfortable with our previous work. It does so by calling into question our assumptions about what we study, how, and why, but it does this not by deflating those assumptions with pinpricks of 'truth', and then inflating a new set of truisms, but by locating all assumptions within a *political* space by articulating how, since the eighteenth century, acts of knowledge production are exercises of power. 'My point', insisted the theorist Michel Foucault, 'is not that everything is bad, but that everything is dangerous' ('On the Genealogy of Ethics', in Dreyfus and Rabinow 1983: 231). The theoretical turn from absolute truths produces a pluralism in which, to borrow Vicky Spelman's phrase, 'nothing goes' (Sawicki 1988: 189).

The danger that I now recognize in my earlier work is how easily it went. I made a 'new' 'Prelude' without posing some fundamental questions about all the old ones – two-part, five-book, 1805, 1850 (*P*, 510–26). What kinds of writing are they? What literary and social functions do those kinds perform? Do classifications such as 'autobiography', 'confession', and 'epic' help us to understand why we have different 'Preludes' and why Wordsworth refused to publish any of them? Now that we have published them, what should we *do* with them?[2] Is it our job as literary critics to pick out – or construct – what is 'best'? If so, what criteria do we employ and what cultural ends do they serve? If not, what other kinds of knowledge can we, or should we, want to produce?

Theory confronts us with a political economy of knowledge: when something goes, something else does not; everything is dangerous when the production of any one kind means *not* to be producing another. When, for example, we classify *The Prelude* in the traditional manner, as a strictly literary tale of imagination, creativity, and love of nature, we cannot address it, as I will in the next section, as a text prescribing particular kinds of work – the division of labour that authorizes modern professionalism. To think theoretically, in other words, is to address the *historical* problem of what not to go for anymore.

I emphasize 'historical' because the issue is not what is 'bad' in any absolute sense; criticism, like any other form of writing, has functions that change. To question the present value of a past function, such as the provision of psychological explanations of change within the traditional literary tales described above, is not to assert an 'evolutionary' superiority over inherently useless or wrongheaded criticism. It is, rather, to denaturalize the conceptual limits of what may have worked in the past and thus establish, in the present, the possibility of different kinds of knowledge – knowledge that will, of course, be subject to other limits (Siskin 1988: 17). The turn toward theory that has transformed literary studies has thus also necessarily been a turn towards history. In fact, the rubric I use to classify how I would *now* write up *The Prelude* is 'new history' – a label that, as I will show shortly, can embrace a wide range of current scholarship, including the work popularly called the 'New Historicism'. To clarify my intentions and procedures, then, I will first trace the interrelations of theory and history within this kind of writing.

New History

When describing any genre, the temptation to define it often becomes irresistible, for the result is an object that can then be narrativized: a novel that rises, a lyric that blossoms, a kind of criticism that catches on. The first step in such definitions is to locate the object discursively by identifying the features that appear to be shared by the texts one wishes to label. The beginnings of a list of what John Bender calls New Historicism's 'vital signs' might include: an interdisciplinary turn; a predilection for thick description of tiny particulars – finding within an event or anecdote, as H. Aram Veeser puts it, 'the behavioral codes, logics, and motive forces controlling a whole society' (Veeser 1989: xi); 'the dissolution of boundaries between venerated aesthetic objects like novels or paintings and tracts, pamphlets, or legislation; the reading of institutions as "texts"; the treatment of subjectivity as a socially constructed . . . phenomenon' (Bender 1989).

The problem with such a list is figuring out what to do with it; what kind of knowledge does the list allow us to produce? Is it, on the one hand, only definitional, a means of deciding what works deserve the label? Or, on the other hand, is this also prescriptive knowledge: does it tell us how to write this particular kind of writing? Does the list, that is, simply present New Historicism as a specific kind of writing or offer it as a methodology? Opting for the latter possibility, with its promise of practical results, has become, I would argue, the single most problematic turn in the production of new historical criticism. Even if we were to assume that any one or combination of those definitional features could prescribe a methodology, any such methodology would not necessarily be appropriate for different problems and different historical moments. In the social sciences, for example, one looks for a methodology appropriate to a problem rather than assuming a 'good' methodology can and should be applied to problems as they arise.

To see what results from that latter assumption, we need only select from our list a feature such as the dissolution of boundaries between the aesthetic and the everyday. When it is applied as a critical imperative to the study of historical moments *before* the late eighteenth-century invention of the aesthetic as an autonomous discursive realm (Kristeller 1965), the boundaries are just assumed to be there – functioning in familiar ways – and historical criticism becomes ahistorical. To take the first step, breaking our sense of canonical limits, may be valuable; but to be swept along methodologically into the next, thinking that we have also found and broken the same limits *in the past*, is to miss the historical point. That has been the ironic fate of those 'radical' Renaissance scholars who, methodologically treating subjectivity as socially constructed (Fineman 1986), find themselves finding just what their supposedly conservative predecessors found: modernity (the Romantic deep self) in Shakespeare. Instead of being valorized, as in traditionally Romantic Shakespeare criticism, as something ahistorically natural (Hamlet's deep doubts confirm the *essential humanity we share* with Shakespeare), that self *remains* Romantically centred – not in spite of but *by* this methodological turn – as something historically found.

What these critics find, however, is not subjectivity as we know it – the condition of being epistemologically centred as a psychologically unified, developmentally coherent, and self-disciplined individual (Rosenau 1992: 42–50) – but features: features that only later produce – *combined* with other features and thus functioning in different ways – the effects we know as the modern subject. Aspects of what Foucault calls the 'Author function' (1977: 113–38), for example, certainly appear prior to the late eighteenth century, but, as I shall detail later, not until they are put into combination with narratives linking aesthetic depth and individual development, as well as with rewritten copyright laws, is that most familiar form of the subject – the Creative Author – in place. Attending historically and theoretically to these changing combinations must, I would argue, be a central task of a *historical* New Historicism, one which is most simply defined as occupying the current intersection of literary history and literary theory. Aware of itself as a kind of writing, a particular combination of features, that criticism would engage such signs as the dissolution of boundaries and the construction of a subject as local manifestations of an informing concern with boundary-making, classification, grouping as a process rather than a category – the problem, that is, of genre.

I link process to genre in order not to fall foul of what Derrida has called the 'law of genre' (1980). Arguing for the need and futility of generic labels, Derrida claims that we identify a work according to the 'mark of a genre' that it bears, but, since any such mark can also be found in any *other* genre, then we are left with a paradox: 'the re-mark of belonging does not belong'. The resulting 'law' is that the making of a class is necessarily the beginning of its unmaking. Faced with such an 'irony', one can either live within the law, and thus limit the analytic efficacy of genre, or venture into other territory. If, that is, we think of the study of genre not as a study of closed, essentialistic categories, but of the *process* of categorizing, then the sharing of marks can be seen not as a paradoxical violation of unchanging boundaries but as an index to the ways in which boundaries change over time.

To focus on process, in other words, is to enter the historical, addressing the issue of difference in the manner Derrida's law effaces – diachronically. Genres always share 'marks' because they exist only in competitive or complementary relationship to each other, and the system or hierarchy of genres constituted by those relationships is always subject to temporal change (for example, the 'rise' of lyric and the 'fall' of satire during the late eighteenth century). 'Genre concepts in theory and practice', points out Ralph Cohen, 'arise, change, and decline for historical reasons. And since each genre is composed of texts that accrue, the grouping is a *process* not a determinate category. Genres are open categories' (Derrida 1980: 64–5; Cohen 1986: 204).

To engage New Historicism as a kind of writing, and what is more to consider any 'kind' as an open category located at the temporal intersection of other kinds, are both enabling acts. They allow us: first, to establish the historicity of the category and thus allow it to be placed *in* the histories it helps to construct (enabling New Historicism to historicize itself); second, to illuminate the hierarchy that orders that openness and thus place the label 'New Historicism' within the category of new histories (enabling us to weigh New Historicism alongside other new historiographical priorities – a species within a genus); and third, to clarify what is at stake in occupying that intersection and thus to confront the issues of whether this is merely bad history or just the latest critical fad. We can begin by historicizing the first word in the label. The New Historicism should be understood as 'new' not in the Romantic terms of its 'originality', the author's 'creativity', or the profession's inevitable 'development'. It is new in that it is *form*ally innovative, for our place, in the last quarter of the twentieth century, is within an era of conceptual and thus generic transition. As we read and write, the interrelations among inherited forms of discourse are rapidly shifting. The function of literary history, for example, had been to help make the subject matter of English studies: history construed as developmental narrative – for instance, the 'rise of the novel' – canonized certain texts as 'literature'. But this process has, in turn, generated other needs. For the dispensing of the matter to be anything other than haphazard, it must be systematically ordered. Thus the institutionalization of English studies has been accompanied by a turn to the kind of writing we call 'literary theory', a form that seeks to provide us with a procedure for understanding problematic areas, not particular works, in literary study (Cohen 1975: 45, 57; Siskin 1988: 4).

Deconstruction and its various post-structuralist manifestations have often been mistakenly identified as *being* literary theory, the problematic area taken to be language in its synchronic indeterminacy, but they constitute only one version of what theory currently can be. When features of literary theory are mixed with features of literary history, the functions of both of those kinds are altered. Literary theory, with its turn from individual works to areas or groupings, is redirected by the historical features, emphasizing chronology, to highlight the problem of groupings over time. Literary history no longer performs its lyrical, and yet canonical, function of ordering literary highs (great authors and great works); instead, it functions theoretically, at our present moment of social, economic, and cultural change, to provide us with procedures for identifying and understanding precisely that problematic area in the production and circulation of discourse: literary change – that is, shifts over time in the ways we group and hierarchize (that is, theorize) texts.

New history *is*, then, theoretical; in fact, its increasing prominence in the hierarchy of scholarly genres is keyed to its increasingly theoretical nature. And, it counts among its most important proponents the writer whose works return always to issues of groupings over time, changing limits, classificatory problems, genre – the writer who charted the changing boundaries between normality and madness, studied the orders of things, situated the 'Author' as a 'means of classification', complicated the distinction between power and knowledge, detailed the historical transformation of punishment into discipline and sex into sexuality, and historicized the networks of difference, ethical and otherwise, that have defined changing selves. This is not to say that all new history must deal directly with Foucault, but it does explain why his name and work appear so often when new history is produced and discussed.[3]

Before pursuing Foucault's classificatory manoeuvres further, however, we need to move from historicizing 'new' to historicizing the nouns in our labels. 'Historicism' is a term that appears often within the open category of new 'history', presenting both a problem and an opportunity. The problem is that the word 'historicism' is, as Herbert Lindenberger has put it,

> loaded with historical baggage, for it evokes the great revolution in historical thought anticipated by Vico, brought to fruition by a succession of thinkers during the half century between Herder and Hegel, and institutionalized within German literary study early in the present century.

These historicists 'opted for the high road – high ceremony, high art, high politics', producing 'those larger narratives about the rise and fall of eras and about the crises, collisions, and dialectical movements that raise human actions to the level of drama' (Lindenberger 1990: 83; Lindenberger 1984: 22). The choice of the word 'historicism' by Stephen Greenblatt and others may thus be somewhat suspect in terms of taking on this baggage, but it does allow us to distinguish that writing as a kind – a subgenre along with the gendered Foucauldianism of Nancy Armstrong, the radical cultural studies issuing from the Essex conferences, and the interdisciplinary feminism of Mary Poovey – that is being produced within the discursive space I have labelled 'new history'. As such, we can argue about the efficacy of New Historicism's particular combination of literary historical and literary theoretical features without calling into question the entire enterprise of new history.

Those who do wish to call it into question often raise the spectre of arrogant literary critics mischievously crossing departmental boundary lines to do bad history. Fears of encroachment into professional specialities by imperialistic amateurs from another field have thus been used to suggest that this historical business in literary studies is just a fad, and that the adventurers will return to their camps – where they belong – as soon as their salaries are high enough. But no matter what motives we attribute to the new historians, the fad argument, in its assumptions about the proper separation of history and literature, is itself almost bizarrely ahistorical. We know from recent work on the history of both fields that the idea of an essential separation between the two is far more qualified for the label 'fad'. The first professor of English Literature in England was appointed only 164 years ago in 1828. He fought for disciplinary space and for students against the established mix that made up English studies at the time – rhetorical and philological studies increasingly focused on the vernacular language – by emphasizing a chronology of great works (see Court 1988). English literature as we know it, in other words, became a separate field of study *by mixing* with history. The separation of history is an even more recent story. According to Philippa Levine, its acceptance

> as a curricular subject worthy of separate academic attention was attended by a good deal of hostility. From its first tentative recognition in the 1850s a pamphlet war ensued as to its suitability for serious academic consumption and until the early 1870s it was not deemed a sufficient subject for exclusive study. It thus formed one element of a joint course with at least one other subject, a tendency which itself proved a major irritant.
>
> (Levine 1986: 136)

That other subject was, more often than not, literature. New history may also be irritating, but it is certainly not historically faddish to make the future of both English and history by using theory to mix the two.

Disciplinary Power

At stake in discussions of new history is its very label and the possibilities of new practice, the disciplinary future. By not psychologizing and so personalizing the shift in my work on *The Prelude*, we can begin to think about it as a change – occasioned by theory – within English studies, English being the institutional location (discipline) for the production of a particular kind of knowledge (commentary) about a particular object of knowledge (the Author). The authorial organization of the best-selling anthologies, such as the Norton, as well as of standard syllabuses in the UK and the USA, confirms the pervasiveness of this triad. When I made my hybrid 'Prelude', for example, the object I was knowing was Wordsworth-as-*oeuvre*: the Author as the Mastertext to which every individual text, including all the *Preludes*, ultimately refers. My comments, both the 'better' text and the editorial gloss, were generated by my sense of the 'truly' Wordsworthian; the judgements and meanings were, in David Simpson's formulation of knowledge production in English, 'adjudicated by reference to a biographical entity' (1982: xxvi). This type of knowledge earned, in the marketplace of our discipline, the previously mentioned grade, as well as professional advancement to postgraduate studies.

We find Foucault – or, actually, he finds us – at this intersection of knowledge production and professionalism. His work puts our professional forms of adjudication into history – and thus politicizes them – by theorizing disciplinarity. Two interrelated meanings of 'discipline' are crucial to his endeavour: discipline as a field of study connects to knowledge, while discipline as regimentation invokes power. Foucault erased the 'uncrossable line between the domain of knowledge, seen as that of truth and freedom, and the domain of the exercise of power' by turning to the historical moment in which Western societies were 'disciplined', in both senses of the term. In the eighteenth century, he found, 'the birth of the human sciences goes hand in hand with the installation of new mechanisms of power' (Foucault 1988: 106). Disciplines of knowledge such as psychiatry and criminology 'presuppose[d] and constitute[d] *at the same time*' (Foucault 1979a: 27; emphasis added) power structures such as hospitals and prisons.

The point is not that power and knowledge are the same, for, as Foucault himself remarked, 'if I had . . . made them identical, I don't see why I would have taken the trouble to show the different relations between them' (Foucault 1988: 264). It was in mapping the historical transformations of those relations that Foucault identified an extraordinary political shift: power came to be increasingly deployed during the eighteenth century through a 'yes' rather than a 'no'. Given the size and complexity of the modern state, observed Foucault,

> power would be a fragile thing if its only function were to repress,
> if it worked only through the mode of censorship, exclusion,

blockage and repression, in the manner of a great Superego, exercising itself only in a negative way. If, on the contrary, power is strong this is because, as we are beginning to realise, it produces effects at the level of desire – and also at the level of knowledge. Far from preventing knowledge, power produces it.

Such power has been relentlessly affirmative, responding, for example, to the contemporary 'liberation' of the sexual body not with a 'no' but with an 'exploitation of eroticisation, from sun-tan products to pornographic films . . . a new mode of investment which presents itself no longer in the form of control by repression but that of control by stimulation. "Get undressed – but be slim, good-looking, tanned!"' (Foucault 1980: 59, 57).

This power rewires our desires; it is *self*-disciplinary, in that it helps to make up the very self it disciplines as it 'induces pleasure, forms knowledge, produces discourse' (Foucault 1980: 119; Siskin 1988: 151–3). The proliferation of knowledge-bearing discourse over the past 200 years has thus been 'pleasurable', but – keeping in mind the political economy of knowledge I described earlier – it has not been 'free'. Since the 'truth' of any discourse 'isn't outside power, or lacking in power', it is, Foucault insists, 'a thing of this world: it is produced only by virtue of multiple forms of constraint'. The 'yes' of modern power, in other words, configures and delimits as it affirms and elicits: 'linked in a circular relation with systems of power which produce and sustain it, and to effects of power which it induces and which extends it'; truth, for Foucault, functions as a 'regime'. He argued that

> each society, has its regime of truth, its 'general politics' of truth: that is, the types of discourse which it accepts and makes function as true; the mechanisms and instances which enable one to distinguish true and false statements, the means by which each is sanctioned; the techniques and procedures accorded value in the acquisition of truth; the status of those who are charged with saying what counts as true.
>
> (1980: 131)

As classificatory 'system[s]' (1980: 133) – ones that set, for example, the boundary between 'true' and 'false' – these regimes, and the ways they change, have become the objects today of what I am calling 'new history': the analysis of discursive groupings over time. The new historical mix of the theoretical and chronological is now, I am suggesting, transforming the discipline of English in the very act of mapping earlier forms of disciplinary power.

Practice

The affirmative, even seductive, nature of that power is perhaps nowhere more evident than in the conclusion to *The Prelude*: 'what we have loved,/' asserts Wordsworth coercively, 'Others *will* love, and we will teach them how' (1850, XIV: 448–9; emphasis added). This assertion describes the triad of knowledge production in English I mapped out earlier. First, the repeated first-person plural centres the *Author* figures (the poets Wordsworth and Coleridge) as the initial objects of knowledge. Second, to know through the Author as the 'means of classification' is to delimit the 'what' as that which must be taught; the reader identifies with the Author through the paradoxical repetition of what Foucault calls *commentary* – each reader needs to 'say, for the first time, what has already been said, and repeat tirelessly what was, nevertheless, never said' (1972: 221). Third, by disciplining ourselves into this form of knowledge production we constitute English as a *discipline* defined by the repeated 'love' of literature.

For Foucault, all three – Author, Commentary, Discipline – are 'principle[s] of limitation' that constrain discourse, and thus configure regimes of truth, even as they further its proliferation (1972: 222). The point in using them to organize my practice upon *The Prelude* is *not*, I must emphasize, to condemn the text as bad, aesthetically or politically, compared to some unconstrained alternative or some 'real' truth, but to identify what configurations of power it may have helped to produce and may be continuing to naturalize. My purpose in this section, then, is to use these 'principles' to interrupt our repetitively gratulant understanding of *The Prelude* as a celebration of individual development and turn, instead, to the kinds of question I myself ignored twenty years ago. Each section title, then, refers to a 'natural' developmental step, the principle of limitation that helps us to rethink it, and the inquiry that rethinking makes possible.

Get a Job! (Author): What is The Prelude?

Wordsworth's decision that *The Prelude* be published after his death seems particularly strange to us today, in an era in which the absolute imperative of print is spelled out in the titles of our software programs – *PUBLISH IT!* We have followed that punctuation zealously, compensating for Wordsworth's delay by publishing every version of *The Prelude* we can identify: two-part, thirteen-book, fourteen-book, etc. I want to take a step back from this editorial abandon to begin to think about the question I posed earlier: what should we do with all of this stuff? We can begin by asking what Wordsworth was doing with it. What were the various versions of *The Prelude* to Wordsworth? Did they function for him in a way that made sense of non-publication? These questions, by mapping an intersection of literature and owner- ship, turn inevitably on the issue of the Author; new history practices on *The Prelude*, then, by placing it in a history of the Author- function.[4] This is not a matter of leaving the text behind, but of trying to recover what may have been behind the text – as well as left behind by previous criticism.

Wordsworth's birth corresponds almost exactly with the event commonly cited as the birth of modern copyright: the 1774 decision by the House of Lords in the case of *Donaldson v Becket*. The date requires qualification, however, since that decision did not detail a concept or mechanism of copyright, but allowed for the enforcement of the statute that did. The Statute of Anne had been enacted in 1709 but had been circumvented in practice and in lawsuits for 65 years. That span, like most 'spans' in our histories of the eighteenth century, has most frequently been written up as a 'rise' – this time, not of the novel or the middle class but of the Author. Certainly the century that ended with the 'creative geniuses' of Romanticism did see the consolidation of the Author function. However, to view the changes in copyright solely in terms of that consolidation is to risk misconstruing the actors and actions of the copyright story, thereby turning its climax into paradox: the *Donaldson* v. *Becket* decision that supposedly topped off the 'rise' of the author actually denied the author's claim to a perpetual common-law copyright in favour of the limited fourteen- year terms of the 1710 statute.

That statue, as Lyman Ray Patterson has observed, was not

> intended primarily to benefit authors. It was a trade-regulation statute enacted to bring order to the chaos created in the book trade by the final lapse in 1694 of its predecessor, the Licensing Act of 1662, and to prevent a continuation of the booksellers' monopoly.[5]
>
> (Patterson 1968: 143)

The 1662 Act had sustained that monopoly through the granting of perpetual copyrights to anyone who registered a work with the Stationers' Company; the only other form of copyright was the limited- term protection offered by printing patents granted for certain classes of works, such as those on law. The legislative activity that culminated in the Statute of Anne was thus primarily initiated by the stationers themselves in attempts to perpetuate the perpetual copyright after the 1662 Act had expired.

Parliament did respond by legislating copyright, but not of the duration desired by the petitioners: previous copyrights were set to expire after twenty-one years while new ones were limited to fourteen, with an additional term of the same length granted to authors still alive after the initial term. This extension was the highlight of the statute for authors, for its truly 'radical change', in Patterson's words, 'was not that it gave authors the right to acquire a copyright . . . but that it gave that right to all persons' (1968: 145). The legislative object, in other words, was not authors with rights but booksellers with a monopoly.

That monopoly required perpetual copyright not only to ensure ongoing profits from selling older, popular works; as perpetual property, the copyrights themselves could be treated as stocks sold at auctions (Belanger 1982: 15). Expiration dates would obviously negate their investment value. The booksellers thus reacted to the 1709 limits by ignoring them in practice and seeking in the courts a new conceptual basis for perpetuity. Whereas they had earlier used censorship laws as the stalking horse – their ongoing monopoly would help protect the kingdom against seditious works – the new strategy was to insist upon the common-law right of authors in having a natural right of property in their works. So weak was the position of authors in relationship to the monopoly in the eighteenth century, that, from the booksellers' point of view, a perpetual copyright for authors was a copyright in perpetuity for them.

Authors, that is, were a means to a specific economic end for the monopolists – a weapon wielded by the booksellers that their opponents managed to turn against them. An apparent victory for the booksellers in the case of *Millar* v *Taylor* (1769), in which the author's common-law right was upheld, was precisely the opportunity that the Lords needed to end the monopoly in two strokes. The questions posed to the twelve common-law judges who advised the House on *Donaldson* v *Becket* were structured such that the booksellers could be taken on their own legal ground. In the judges' advice and in the debate that followed, the author's right was affirmed, thereby bringing the monopoly within legal range, but so was the notion that the right was 'taken away by the Statute of Anne'.[6]

This was a crucial moment in the advent of the modern system of letters we call 'literature' (Kernan 1987: 283–7), but not primarily because the Author had risen. The redistribution of property involved more than the authorial. As Trevor Ross has so shrewdly noted, the canon of English literature, which had been designed rhetorically 'in accordance with the immediate needs of speakers and "makers" [poets]', became, after *Donaldson* v *Becket*,

> valued as public domain: as one contemporary account put it, 'the Works of *Shakespeare*, of *Addison, Pope, Swift, Gay*, and many other excellent Authors . . . are, by this Reversal [of *Millar* v *Taylor*] declared to be the Property of any Person.' Never before in English history had it been possible to think that the canon might belong to the people, to readers. From that moment, the canon became a set of commodities to be consumed; it became literature rather than poetry.
>
> (Ross 1990: 22–3)

This new world of literary commodities certainly opened up, in the long term, extraordinary financial and artistic possibilities for authors, but, in their being pawns in the struggle over monopoly, they had paid a price: 'Henceforth, an English author's "natural" right to his work was . . . perpetual and unlimited only so long as he never published it' (Amory 1984: 453).

We are back, of course, to Wordsworth's strange decision. I am not suggesting, with this sketch of copyright, that he withheld *The Prelude* to perpetuate his natural right to that work, but rather that both the decision and the right need to be considered within a more comprehensive set of socioeconomic and literary concerns. What the writer gained as Author was not just the opportunity to earn money from selling individual works. The demise of one type of monopoly in the making of the Author had engendered monopolistic possibilities of another kind – expert control, for example, over the commodification process itself – that also seemed worthy of protection in perpetuity. If we begin to think about the form such protection might take, the strangeness of Wordsworth's decision may begin to lessen. Don't all academics have a piece of writing that they never publish, at times allow to circulate, and always revise? At its most effective, it attempts to expand autobiography to epic dimensions by recounting supposedly heroic acts.

The Prelude is, quite simply, the most extraordinary résumé in English literary history. Wordsworth referred to it as a 'review' of what 'had qualified him for such employment', the 'such' referring to the writing of a long poem (*The Recluse*) that he considered 'the task of my life' (3 June 1805, in de Selincourt 1967– , I: 594–5). Its primary function then, was to present an individual's training and qualifications for performing his life's work: it 'conducts the history' of the candidate 'to the point when he was emboldened to hope that his faculties were sufficiently matured for entering upon the arduous labour which he had proposed to himself' (Preface to *The Excursion* (1814) in Owen and Smyser 1974, III: 5). This curriculum vitae-like detailing of personal identity turns maturation into a preoccupation with occupation: in this case, how to become, behave like, and perform as a professional poet. Such status is described in a now familiar sequence in which personal background (the influence of nature), formal education (Cambridge and books), and significant life experiences (the French Revolution) all contribute to the concluding epiphany of *professional* purpose I cited at the beginning of this section: 'what we have loved,/ Others will love, and we will teach them how'.

Work Hard! (Discipline): What does The Prelude (make us) do?

The Prelude concludes professionally in the sense isolated by the sociologist, Magali Larson: modern professionals, she observes, 'constitute *and control* a market for their expertise' (Larson 1977: xvi). What they own, then, is the right to define and exercise their expertise. Their specialization in depth *is* the property that, once earned, must be preserved beyond any statutory limits. This is the principle that is surfacing so frequently today in divorce proceedings; property settlements now increasingly turn upon assessing the value of the professional status – the right to labour, the productive capacity – achieved by one or both partners during the marriage.

Literary professionals certainly have their share of divorces, but we rarely read about the value of their specialized labour in today's gossip columns. Nor does it figure prominently in scholarly efforts by Larson and others to detail the advent of modern professionalism; they focus instead on medical doctors, lawyers and accountants. New history, however, by attending theoretically to historical shifts in the ordering of the disciplines, can tell some different tales: the production of literary knowledge, I would maintain, was crucial to that advent. Rather than focusing solely on that knowledge as something that was passively professionalized, we need to recognize that professionalization itself has a history, and central to its tale is the very labour – the production, circulation, and valorization of writing – that became literature's area of expertise.

Professionalization in that sense dates historically from corresponding changes in the division of labour – towards specialization – and in the organization of knowledge – towards narrow but deep disciplines. As they deepened, literature displaced philosophy from its central place among the other disciplines: poetry, claimed Wordsworth, is the 'breath and finer spirit of *all* knowledge' (Preface to *Lyrical Ballads* in Owen and Smyser 1974, I: 141; emphasis added). Unlike the older organization, in which every kind was a branch of philosophy, literature was centred in this new system as the specialization all of the others had in common – the *prerequisite* for entering them as autonomous professional fields.

'Men are men before they are lawyers', wrote John Stuart Mill (1867 Inaugural Address at the University of St Andrews; see Elliott 1972: 51), compressing the tale of specialization into its essential stages. It is important to be precise here: men cannot become lawyers until they are *first* made into men. One must specialize *from* a prior state of fullness. Mill, as we know from the *Autobiography*, understood himself to have been broadened by a literary experience: he required a heavy dose of Wordsworth prior to attaining professional success. 'Work without hope', in Mill's own words borrowed from Coleridge, was transformed into work with 'joy' (Mill 1924: 1070). The narrative of that transformation inscribes literary knowledge as a specialized prerequisite for the intellectual work of the modern professional.

The problem troubling both self and world in Mill was progress – not (and this is the crucial twist to the whole scenario) the failure to improve but the consequences of doing so: 'if the reformers of society and government could succeed in their objects . . . the pleasures of life, being no longer kept up by struggle and privation, would cease to be pleasures' (Mill 1924: 1072). Mill must make progress – professional success – and the social improvements it occasions make sense by linking it to pleasure: developmental change, to use to use the words from Wordsworth that head this essay, can be experienced as 'gratulant' when 'rightly understood' (1850, XIII: 389). Literature's job as a discipline was to produce the right kind of understanding. It helped, that is, to construct and naturalize new relationships between knowledge and power, underwriting the intellectual labour of what Mill called 'the most confirmed habit of analysis' with a guarantee of 'joy' – joy 'which had no connection with struggle or imperfection, but would be made richer by every improvement in the physical or social condition of mankind' (Mill 1924: 1073).

I emphasize that this was literature's job *as a discipline* in order to clarify how the work was performed. The reorganization of knowledge I described earlier occasioned a shift in the relationship between 'doctrine' and 'discipline' that turned upon the concept of property. Etymologically, doctrine, which the *Oxford English Dictionary* refers to as 'the property of the doctor, or teacher' had been 'more concerned with abstract theory, and "discipline" with practice or exercise'. But with the advent of specialization, as subject areas became rule-based fields of knowledge mastered through vocationally plotted educational schemes, the discipline itself became the doctrine – the property owned by the specialist. To *have* a profession, at the historical moment that the qualification was no longer being a gentleman but having a résumé, meant that what one possessed, as I noted earlier, was the right to exercise certain modes of knowledge production.

Mill, then, was not cured by Wordsworthian doctrine; he learned to discipline himself by producing knowledge within a particular discipline – literary knowledge. There are no quotations from the poet in the paragraphs describing Mill's recovery; they detail, instead, the intellectual work by which the poet was found and valued. First, the competition is winnowed away, Byron being cited and then rejected. Then Mill makes intra-Wordsworthian discriminations, turning from *The Excursion* and 'beautiful pictures of natural scenery' as he tries to focus only on 'the precise thing' of value. By assigning value, Mill himself makes what he says he discovered through Wordsworth: 'culture'. What is *in* Wordsworth, therefore, is not really the point; since culture is the repository of what pleases us, this literary ability to make culture provides the guarantee Mill requires – the ongoing presence of pleasure in all other forms of making.

The discipline of literature, as a means of thus *optimizing* production in the new system of knowledge, can be related generically and historically to the branch of philosophy devoted, under the old system, to optimizing capitalism: political economy. In fact, keeping in mind R.S. Crane's definition of taste as 'the capacity to receive pleasure from aesthetic objects' (Crane 1967: 104), literary knowledge as it appears in Mill, and in Wordsworth ('what we have loved,/Others *will* love'), is a political economy of taste. It attempts to encourage and rationalize social progress by measuring the *value* of things.

The comparison to political economy is valuable because it helps us to isolate the dual nature of literary study since the late eighteenth century. Like political economy in the work of David Ricardo, on the one hand, and Adam Smith, on the other, literature is concerned with both 'regulating [the] distribution' (see Clegg *et al.*, 1986: 6–13;

Ricardo 1819: iii) and maximizing the growth of that value. These are not just different emphases in literature but coordinated functions. The study of literature was institutionalized, as Ian Michael's recent survey of textbooks and curriculum has detailed, by combining what had been rhetorical instruction in the skills of literacy with the construction and appreciation of newly defined chronologies of 'great' works. The first regulates standards of literacy in order to distribute its skills hierarchically, while the second, as we just saw in Mill, employs canon-making to naturalize growth – the Wordsworthian desire for 'something evermore about to be'.

These functions correspond to the two conceptual categories that sociologists use to identify modern professionalism: 'technicality', which 'refers to the extent to which a systematic body of knowledge is' utilized in the justification of competence or expertise', and 'indetermination', which points to 'the bases of [an occupation's] mystique . . . the elements of its ideology [as they] underpin its monopolistic position and successful resistance to external authority' (Johnson 1977: 99). Literature, in its dual nature, maintains what sociologists term the professional 'ratio' between the two by insisting heavily upon the mystification of taste that is the canon (indetermination) while also deploying a systematic body of knowledge governing literacy (technicality).

That ratio is what professors of literature have *possessed* since *The Prelude*, a text that is both a 'masterpiece' of indetermination – something that is so much 'something evermore about to be' that, during Wordsworth's lifetime, as well as now, through our incessant editorial efforts, it never at any point just *is* – and, as a résumé, a document of technicality detailing the training necessary to master a required body of knowledge. To see *The Prelude* now as both, and thus as an embodiment of professional behaviour, is to begin to recognize literature's place *in* the history of professionalization and *as* the centred prerequisite.

Fall in Love! (Commentary): How does The Prelude do it?

If Wordsworth's emphasis at the end of *The Prelude* on 'what we love', and on the 'joy' it brings, seems too fuzzy and sentimental a prerequisite for deep professional work, we need only take a quick chronological detour to gauge how powerful an ideological prescription it turned out to be. A century after the first versions of *The Prelude*, on 1 July 1901, a group of workers met in Paris to organize a new union: the

Confederation of Intellectual Workers. And how was this class of labour defined? 'The intellectual worker', wrote William MacDonald in his 1923 description of the movement, 'works primarily from love of the task, from subtle but conscious joy in performance or achievement' (MacDonald 1923: 65). This is not simply a matter of whistling while you work, for what is at stake are the hierarchical differences between kinds of work and the criteria for who gets to do them. Both work and desire had to be rewritten before they could so naturally come together. From that which a true gentleman does not have to do, in the eighteenth century, work became the primary activity informing adult identity. The developing 'I' of the résumé came to define itself in terms of its happiness at work as certain kinds of work were valorized as worth doing for the sheer joy of doing them. The ideological circle was completed, of course, by the fact that the privilege and high pay attending that valorization actually made the job all the more lovable.

When, as practising new historians, we reclassify 'love' with 'work' in *The Prelude* (1850), the organization of the longer versions of the poem begins to make a new kind of sense. Previous critics have puzzled over both the turn in Book VIII[7] to a 'Retrospect' Wordsworth called 'Love of Nature Leading to Love of Mankind', and the concluding emphasis in Book XIV on 'intellectual love'. Without calling into question the psychological, philosophical and religious speculations of those critics (see *P*, 468–9), we can, when we see *The Prelude* as résumé, recognize how it helps to naturalize the division of labour into physical and mental by claiming, for the Poet's work of writing, the higher (and thus deeper) motivation of love instead of money. The raw material of that work – and the new object of knowledge of all of the then innovative disciplines of the human sciences – is, of course, what Wordsworth in Book VIII is naturally led to: 'man'.

The entire résumé, then, privileges 'intellectual love' as a kind of 'work' productive of a 'joy' that 'complete[s] the man' (1805, XIII: 185–202). *The Prelude*'s tale of masculine completion – love of nature, love of man, love of work – is the gendered counterpart of the marriage plots of nineteenth-century romances and domestic novels. In both cases, what is at stake is the socioeconomic order and one's place in it. Love, in the masculine version, is not just what works – it is work. The spatialization – falling in love – functions in both to idealize the completion of self as a parental- and class-transcendent act of knowledge production: in the feminine, a disciplined knowledge of self through the other, and, in the masculine, a knowledge of a discipline through the self. An intellectual worker 'falls' in love by 'deeply' specializing in a particular kind of work.

The Prelude produces the effect of 'depth' both thematically and formally – effects we must be careful to historicize rather than repeat. To employ them ourselves, especially those that seem most familiar, is to accept and reproduce in our own writing the assumptions about the organization of work in modern society that I have been detailing. M.H. Abrams, for example gives us a grip on *The Prelude* by isolating within it the 'typical Romantic design' of the 'spiral journey back home' (Abrams 1971: 183–7). The Foucauldian danger lies in how that typicality is cast; classified within a range of different philosophies (for instance, 'Neoplatonism', 'post-Kantian'), the spiral argument[8] gives *The Prelude* a grip on us, causing us, like Abrams, to lose sight of it as a work about the problem of work. To keep that social function in view, we need to recognize that the motif works (see Siskin 1988: 116–23) by spatializing value (of the individual) as depth (of imaginative self-knowledge). But 'depth' itself – of feeling, character, and meaning valorized in poems such as *The Prelude*, novels, and criticism – has, as I have been arguing, prescribed modern professionalism: as the metaphor of specialization (knowledge that is narrow but deep), depth has made common sense out of the very pattern of division of labour that rationalizes our professionalized society. The specific kind of professional labour that Foucault calls 'commentary' is thus an intellectual reenactment of *The Prelude*'s spiralling journey: the critical circling around a 'primary' text in which we return to it to say it again, but never in a fully repetitive nor fully adequate way.

Theory = Practice

This volume, by posing theory as something to be put into practice, authorizes ongoing spiralling; after all, practice means not only 'application' (of a theoretical 'approach') but also 'preparation' (for better fly-bys in the future – a prelude?). Now that I have spiralled around *The Prelude* yet again, twenty years after my undergraduate flight, the question is what has changed. Clearly the flight path has been altered: earlier, the multiple versions of the poem, cast psychologically as evidence of an Author's creative struggle, became the occasion for a series of aesthetic judgements aimed at producing and preserving the 'best' text; now, seen as the ongoing revisions of a résumé, the multiplicity of versions authorizes a historical and political analysis of modern professionalism, in which the revisions index a naturally increasing depth of specialization.

The other obvious difference is the turn away from traditional 'close' readings of individual passages. In related pieces of my project on professionalism, I do perform a significant amount of line-by-line work; one chapter traces changes in the georgic-descriptive in numerous eighteenth-century texts while another attends to the particularities of the Romantic remixing of the georgic, pastoral, lyric, and epic. In focusing on combinations of the first two in *The Prelude*, for example, as in the passage

> It was a splendid evening, and my soul
> Once more made trial of her strength, nor lacked
> Æolian visitations; but the harp
> Was soon defrauded, and the banded host
> Of harmony dispersed in straggling sounds,
> And lastly utter silence! 'Be it so;
> Why think of any thing but present good?'
> So, like a home-bound labourer I pursued
> My way beneath the mellowing sun . . .
>
> (1850, I: 94–102)

I read a prescription for two of the most important characteristics of the professional ideal. First, it presents professional work as desirable work – an edenic georgic. Since the pastoral is not offered as a separate source of happiness, the georgic activity with which it is intertwined is taken to be a means to that end. Second, the mixture naturalizes what many sociologists consider to be the distinguishing characteristic of modern professionalism: the claim to autonomy. When the domain of work is assumed to be a personal Eden, the professional assumes ethical sway over his or her own actions: the Wordsworthian phrase 'Be it so' signals the self-authorizing power of professionalism (see Siskin 1990: 314–16).

Even in these close textual encounters, however, the 'closeness' has a non-traditional purpose, for I attend to the texts not primarily as aesthetic objects or as Authorial products, but as sites for new historical inquiry into the work of discourse – including its aesthetic and psychological functions. Thus in my work in those chapters, and in the topical (copyright) and chronological (Mill) turns of this piece, I am not surrendering closeness. Rather, new history redefines the object of knowledge as it redefines the means of gaining proximity to it.

In that sense, a volume like this one can be understood as transitional.

We are still spiralling around the same object – *The Prelude* as an individual piece of literature – but there is mounting evidence that these particular theoretical spirals at this particular historical moment are already altering what is at our disciplinary centre. Michael Riffaterre, for example, finds that for traditional humanists the 'fear of theory' is 'very real', since theory has appeared 'alien' to the 'spirit' and 'entrenched habits' of the established disciplines. For Riffaterre, the imperative is to 'assuage' that fear by using theory to conserve, rather than question, the category of 'literature' by having it define 'literariness' as a 'timeless' quality of particular texts (Riffaterre 1990: 921–3).

What I share with Riffaterre, then, is the sense that theory's work now entails a rethinking of disciplinary boundaries; his rethinking, however, is a re-enforcement of the standard lines with an accompanying dose of the standard discipline, replete with appeals to such ahistorical categories as 'mankind', '*the* reader' (emphasis added), and 'objective fact' (Riffaterre 1990: 922, 923, 925). For me, theory's intersection with history, in what I have called 'new history', is an occasion for taking these modes of disciplinarity, and how they change, as a subject for professional inquiry. To do so is not to try to assume a stance outside of any disciplinary regime, but to recognize how, in acting professionally, 'we' configure the very regimes that, in turn, configure us. Only now are we beginning to see the ways that the professions themselves have, in the words of the sociologist, Dietrich Rueschemeyer, 'inform[ed] the dominant understandings' we have of them and of the conditions and consequences of the behaviours they authorize (Rueschemeyer 1986: 138).

The Prelude's ongoing power – the point with which I began this paper – is nowhere more evident than in the ways it has helped to authorize our current professional status. By putting that status into history I am not suggesting that we abandon it as bad but that we learn to negotiate it as dangerous. The 'political problem' now for intellectuals, argued Foucault, 'is not changing people's consciousness – or what's in their heads – but the political, economic, institutional régime of the production of truth' (1980: 133). What we *do* as students and scholars is produce knowledge and thus what we *can* do about 'the forms of power that transform [us] into its object and instrument' is to theorize alternative modes of knowledge production and thus different kinds of knowledge. 'In this sense,' pointed out Foucault, 'theory does not express, translate, or serve to apply practice: it is practice' (1977: 208). What is at stake, then, in placing *The Prelude* in a new history of professionalism and in pursuing its role in naturalizing the triad of Author, Commentary, Discipline, is more than just a difference in approach from my earlier method, but the spiralling 'approaches to it' model of knowledge production in English. In historicizing the object of knowledge, and therefore ourselves as knowledge producers, our theory as practice opens up possibilities for disciplinary change.

SUPPLEMENT

NIGEL WOOD: On page 106, you claim that a 'theoretical' literary history can provide for us procedures that help identify 'problematic' areas in the 'production and circulation of discourse' – both in the contemporary critical debate and also on the writing of the chosen period for the study. Could you provide some examples of how, *in the Romantic period*, discourse was produced or circulated anew?

CLIFFORD SISKIN: This essay, by addressing the strangeness of Wordsworth's decision that *The Prelude* be published after his death, complements my earlier work on the 'growth' of the poem. Together they describe one of the most striking examples of how discourse was produced and circulated anew at the turn into the nineteenth century. I go to great lengths (through close readings) in *The Historicity of Romantic Discourse* to detail how Wordsworth's poems are produced through specific strategies of interpretative revision. Since the end of all such revision is the poet's *oeuvre* – the transcendent signified for each of the parts – Wordsworth works throughout his career to produce two structures that will order his output: *The Prelude* and the system for classifying his poems detailed most fully in the Preface to the edition of 1815 (Owen and Smyser 1974, III: 26–9).

Seen in that light, the production of *The Prelude*, from fragments in two parts to fourteen books, can be explained without recourse to outlandish psychological claims. To offer egotism, for example, as the central issue raised by Wordsworth's decision to write about himself at a length 'unprecedented in Literary history' (de Selincourt 1967– , I: 586–7) is to miss the historical point: without a developmental model grounded in these revisionary strategies, the most egotistical person in the world would not – in fact, could not – *produce* that much writing about himself (Siskin 1988: 94–124, 143–4). My essay in this volume similarly obviates the need for ahistorical (and Romantic) psychological assertions about the *circulation* of such discourse – in the case of *The Prelude*, circulation without publication – by using the stories of copyright and professional expertise to identify the poem as an informally circulated résumé.

NW: How would you counter the New Critical objection to your project, that your refusal to 'enter' the text and discover its individual features by close reading is only so that your critical presuppositions may go unchallenged?

CS: Such an objection, of course, inevitably functions to relegitimate the 'presuppositions' of those who make it. Should our primary object of knowledge today be the individual 'text'? In what ways and for what purposes can we and do we 'enter' it? What are the functions of 'close'ness? How are they achieved? To what ends? For New Critical critics, the answers will amount, finally, to an insistence upon Foucault's trinity of Author, Commentary, Discipline. Their 'challenge', by denying the *dangerous* choices they have already made, is neither an objective demand for proof nor a call to meaningful debate, but a demand that pre-empts the possibility of significant difference.

NW: You describe your critical orientation as one near to 'spiralling', where you constantly tack and veer from the placing of the text historically alongside considering it as it has been read and so how it functions within our own culture. To what extent does this determine a new set of priorities when we now write criticism? And what may these be?

CS: 'Spiralling' is not *my* particular 'critical orientation', but the standard model of knowledge production in English – a model in which we continually orientate ourselves towards a centred object of knowledge: the individual piece of literature. However, the particular 'theoretical' spirals that I have been attempting do point to two new kinds of 'priorities'. In *The Historicity of Romantic Discourse*, I related the past to the present by focusing primarily on how standard interpretations of Romanticism were actually repetitions of what they were supposed to be interpreting. By pinpointing the Romantic nature of criticism written about the Romantics, I tried to initiate work that would not use Romantic distinctions (creative versus critical), values (spontaneity and intensity), and truths (development and the unconscious) to reproduce the psychologized 'reality' of the developmental self. I sought, instead, by putting them into the past, to facilitate the writing up of alternative behaviours, ones that might eventually be acculturated as newly 'natural' ways of thinking and acting.

That concern is certainly central to my essay in this volume as well, but my focus is less specifically on Romantic criticism of Romanticism and more on the priority of disciplinary change. I have tried to suggest how, for example, new interrelations among literature, history and sociology have enabled me to pursue the problem of professional power in ways that have not been available in any one of those fields. I should add that, even as I write this transitional spiral, its theory-as-practice is participating in institutional change. My university, like many others in the USA, is responding to changes in economic and public support by reconfiguring traditional disciplinary boundaries; in one such plan, the English Department as presently constituted will cease to exist. Figuring out what it did, what it does now, and what it should be doing is clearly a new priority not just for some, but for all of its members.

CHAPTER 4

'Answering Questions and Questioning Answers': The Interrogative Project of *The Prelude*

SUSAN WOLFSON

[The study of interpretation (hermeneutics) is of special interest to a volume of this kind, for it highlights the difficulties faced when the needs of practice test the validity of universal propositions, how the one can be reconciled to the many. At base, there is a procedural problem whenever we try to draw some scientific distinction between the perceiving subject (the reader) and the object of analysis (in this case, the writing in question). What constitutes both elements, or rather, what might give objective authority to the inter-preter, is also (not totally coincidentally) what *The Prelude* most obviously explores as well. The need to escape the 'perplexed' information derived from the eye's 'discoveries', and 'part/The shadow from the substance' in order to find the 'true dwelling' of, for example, rocks and sky (1805, IV: 250–8) is very much Wordsworth's own problematic in the poem. Susan Wolfson does not wish to endorse the Romantic solution to this problem: merely imaginative involvement until the divide between subject and object is obliterated. This attempt at a solution (if solution it be) ignores the process of reading and the fact that most texts anticipate, to a lesser or greater degree, a 'reader's' response and frame a strategy for interaction accordingly. There is more of a dynamic tension in this model than usually catered for in Romantic aesthetics.

Texts 'interrogate' the reader as a basic rhetorical ploy to engage attention but also sometimes to resist the apparently instinctive need for textual coherence as a reliable aid to intelligibility. In Catherine Belsey's *Critical Practice* (1980), the 'interrogative text' is characterized by its irreconcilable significances and rhetorical registers. It challenges unthinking *ideology*, that is, necessarily false or partial perspectives on the totality of contemporary social practices that answer some need for apologetic self-definition, by denying the privilege usually granted the subject (the fictional 'I') of the discourse. Either by local or more widespread structural irony, we are brought to distrust this first-person voice and seem, therefore, to be obliged to use the judgement to 'discover' the authentic 'author'. Such a search cannot find secure corroboration from the text, however, and so can only be resolved by a *critical* act of closure (deciding on what the author's intention 'must' have really been, and ignoring the text's figurative play). Belsey concentrates on a particular passage from *The Prelude* to illustrate Wordsworth's desire to create a continuity out of his past identity and that of the grown poet (1805, II: 326–37). Here, the transition between the narrative and meditation in the present tense is glossed over to the point where both 'selves' are deemed identical for an instant – and yet, as we read, we can note the rhetorical effort needed to accomplish this (Belsey 1980: 87).

Wolfson, on the other hand, finds this textual effect only a preliminary manoeuvre. Wordsworth's involvement of the reader is not just the working of some ideology of which he was ignorant, but, more positively, a perceived textual trope, where the distance between the two 'selves' is actually dramatized as well as pushed to some form of provisional narrative resolution. In her study of *The Questioning Presence* (1986), she finds a positive agenda for the multi-layered 'interrogative' text, where the 'possibility of new meanings and projects' can be tested: 'Indeterminacy is more often than not a consequence of Romantic inquiry than a premise' (Wolfson 1986: 31). In the work of Hans-Georg Gadamer modern hermeneutical theory becomes flexible enough to cater for this form of interplay between the writer and implied reader. In his *Truth and Method* (1960), he explores the ways in which both items in his title are *dissociated*, for the analysing subject often formulates a 'method' only so as to find a specified result. This is not the same as seeking after 'truth', and so he regards hermeneutics as a mediation between philosophy and science, so that we may be able to go beyond a restricted scientific horizon. Furthermore, art and its reading/viewing is actually a privileged arena for us to appreciate the workings toward truth. Drawing on Martin Heidegger's perception in his *Being and Time* (1927) that being is always time, that is, not open to full understanding through the deployment of ideal timeless structures of rationality, Gadamer finds prejudice an *aid* to the full understanding of temporal objects such as art. As Heidegger puts it, 'Whenever something is interpreted as something, the interpretation will be founded essentially upon fore-having [*Vorhabe*], foresight [*Vorsicht*], and fore-conception [*Vorgriff*]. An interpretation is never a presuppositionless apprehending of something presented to us' (Heidegger 1962: 191–2). Prejudice (*Vorurteil*) is not only inescapable, but a condition of understanding, and should not be denied, for it forms a fundamental part of any hermeneutical operation. Such preconception limits our approach conveniently – not in any fixed way, but rather to ensure intelligibility. Gadamer identifies the effect of such prejudging, a 'horizon' evidenced not only on a personal level, but also in a more general historical context. Understanding is often a self-conscious merging of this personal perspective with the historical horizon (a *Horizontverschmelzung*). As we become aware of our historical or personal prejudices, it is likely that they cease to have the same continued hold over us. This does not lead to the discontinuance of such horizons, but rather the creation of new ones. Past and present are mediated through our present horizon; we cannot break through by scientific means to some standing outside of time. In more practical terms, interpretation always seems to involve a form of dialogue with the past (*note: not* the passive cultivation of our first 'prejudiced' impressions), so that we strive always to open ourselves to a horizon initially foreign to our own personal and historical horizon: we recover a past text 'back out of the alienation in which it finds itself and into the living presence of conversation, whose fundamental procedure is always question and answer' (Gadamer 1975: 331; see Weinsheimer 1991: 24–40, and Bubner 1988: 98–102.)

Gadamer's general work on hermeneutics has been focused on literary study in particular by Hans Robert Jauss, especially in two works, *Toward an Aesthetic of Reception* and *Question and Answer*. In an influential essay in the former, 'Literary History as a Challenge to Literary Theory' (first published in 1970), Jauss tries to reintegrate aesthetic judgement into literary history, a form of study that could decline into chronologies or the proliferation of influence-studies. He accomplishes this by dwelling on the aesthetic *effects* of the work, and does not just hunt after authorial intention. This results in a fusion of history and aesthetics:

> The aesthetic implication lies in the fact that the first reception of a work by the reader includes a test of its aesthetic value in comparison with works already read. The obvious historical implication of this is that the understanding of the first reader will be sustained and enriched in a chain of receptions from generation to generation; in this way the historical significance of a work will be decided and its aesthetic value made evident.
>
> (Jauss 1982b: 20)

'Theory', buttressed by universal statements, is challenged by this inescapable historicity of response. This does not prevent Jauss, it should be pointed out, from constructing a theoretical model of his own, when he coins the term, 'horizon of expectations', to describe Gadamer's necessary 'limitation of vision'. This is often a specifically *literary* construction in Jauss's work, and works to recover some idea of the text:

> The psychic process in the reception of a text is, in the primary horizon of aesthetic experience, by no means only an arbitrary series of

merely subjective impressions, but rather the carrying out of specific instructions in a process of directed perception, which can be comprehended according to its constitutive motivations and triggering signals . . .

(1982b: 23)

A text is thus constituted in a process of reception as signals relayed to the reader.

In Jauss's recent *Question and Answer,* the emphasis is very much more on the dialogic reading relationship first charted by Mikhail Bakhtin and Gadamer. Texts do not merely supply answers to their own constructed questions (the basic satisfaction of all narratives), as they partake in a dialectic with the reader's set of predicted assumptions. Answers provoke ancillary and further questions, each exchange capable of newly synthesized responses that gradually take analysis away from the textual point of origin and those initial 'signals' to the reader's powers of provoked creativity. Readers, therefore, exist in a dramatic relationship with the text, eliding the authorial 'voice' with their own perceptions as a condition of understanding.]

NIGEL WOOD

Getting Started

> *'Quid enim tam commune quam interrogare vel percontari?'*
> *(What is more common than to interrogate or inquire?)*[1]

Using theories concerned with the hermeneutics of question and answer for a practical reading of *The Prelude* may seem redundant, for in crucial aspects this is self-evidently a poem in the interrogative mode: its composition originates in authorial self-questioning; its recollections are drawn to interrogative crisis; its autobiographical present protracts and replays these crises and, despite its designs of resolution, it habitually leaves its most critical questions unanswered, or answered with something less than full conviction and simplicity.[2] What recommends a review of *The Prelude* in light of theories of textual questioning is not so much the ease with which one can gloss the practices of a poem written over the first half of the nineteenth century with theories advanced in the second half of the twentieth. It is something closer to the reverse: the way *The Prelude*'s rich manifold of interrogative engagements strengthens the illumination, or, alternatively, tests the adequacy, of various theories of the interrogative; and, relatedly, the particular power of this poem to organize our experience of textual hermeneutics in the interrogative mode. Our chief points of reference in this experiment will be Hans-Georg Gadamer's brief but trenchant essay, 'The Hermeneutical Priority of the Question', in *Truth and Method* (1960; trans. 1975), Hans Robert Jauss's summary refinement of his critical theory and practice in *Question and Answer: Forms of Dialogic Understanding* (1982; trans. 1989), and, with more focus on issues of literary practice, John Hollander's *Melodious Guile* (1988; the chapters on 'Questions of Poetry', 'Poetic Answers' and 'Poetic Imperatives'), and Catherine Belsey's chapter on 'The Interrogative Text' in *Critical Practice* (1980). With various emphases, these theorists and critics examine the nature of interrogative exchanges within texts, between texts, and, beyond these, between texts and larger cultural discourses.

Before turning to their discussions, we should recall how fundamentally an interrogative project *The Prelude* was for its author and the initial ways this inflected his processes of composition. The interrogative origins are announced in rather strained tones when Wordsworth first reveals the existence of this project in his 1814 Preface to *The Excursion*. By this point, the poem had been in draft in thirteen books for nearly a decade, and in development for more than half a decade before that:

> —Several years ago, when the Author retired to his native mountains, with the hope of being able to construct a literary Work that might live, it was a reasonable thing that he should take a review of his own mind, and examine how far Nature and Education had qualified him for such employment. As subsidiary to this preparation, he undertook to record, in verse, the origin and progress of his own powers, as far as he was acquainted with them . . . and the result of the investigation which gave rise to it was a determination to compose a philosophical poem . . . having for its principal subject the sensations and opinions of a poet living in retirement. – The preparatory poem is biographical, and conducts the history of the Author's mind to the point when he was emboldened to hope that his faculties were sufficiently mature for entering upon the arduous labour which he had proposed to himself.
>
> (Owen and Smyser 1974, III: 5)

In its overt rhetoric, this review seems interrogative only by device: the author, we are told, asked himself a question about his preparation for certain employment and answered it in such a way as to consolidate his commitment; the question seems to have been generated by the answer, rather than the other way around, for the 'result' of his investigation is a 'determination' that was already predetermined as the rationale. In preparation, the author retires, and in retirement he decides that he is prepared; his initial 'hope' encourages a review that yields 'emboldened . . . hope'.[3] And what he finds himself prepared for is not labour in a new field – say, *The Recluse*, the other poem in this document also noted by absence – but more preparation by way of an account of the retirement itself.

For some readers, such as M.H. Abrams, this circularity of desire spells success:

> *The Prelude* . . . is an involuted poem which is about its own genesis – a prelude to itself. Its structural end is its own beginning . . . The conclusion goes on to specify the circular shape of the whole. Wordsworth there asks Coleridge to 'Call back to mind/The mood in which this Poem was begun.' At that time,
>
> > I rose
> > As if on wings, and saw beneath me stretch'd
> > Vast prospect of the world which I had been
> > And was; and hence this song, which like a lark
> > I have protracted . . .
> >
> > [1850, XIV: 381–5]
>
> This song, describing the prospect of his life which had been made visible to him at the opening of *The Prelude*, is *The Prelude* whose composition he is even now concluding.
>
> (Abrams 1971: 79–80)

This adroit reading nicely casts Wordsworth's characteristic self-reflexiveness on an epic scale: a 'prestructuring of the perfect', in Jauss's terms, in which 'the journey through the world' elevates 'the end (which is already determined at the beginning), or the latent order that comes to light along the way, to the level of mythic significance' (Jauss 1989: 14–15): 'Poetic fiction in which the progress of the narrative is actually a return to the beginning' depends on 'the presence of an unchanging picture, one that had been there all the time' (1989: 16). Jauss's project, unlike Abrams's, is not to explicate this pattern for the sake of endorsing it but to submit it to interrogation, using 'historical and literary hermeneutics together' to elucidate its 'fictional status'. His terms for this procedure emphasize its interrogative project: he means to show how the '*what* of the event is always conditioned by the perspectival *when* of its being perceived or reconstructed' and 'by the *how* of its representation and interpretation' (Jauss 1989: 26; emphasis in original).

This questioning to uncover the fictional, too, may seem a redundancy for *The Prelude*, however, for Wordsworth's text already engages this task. Passages such as the one Abrams cites above rarely inscribe a conceptual pattern without destabilizing its authority – sometimes soon after, sometimes nearly simultaneously – and to such a degree that other readers see Wordsworth's 'Conclusion' describing a different circle from the one Abrams describes, one returning the poet to the 'point at which he begins in self-doubt and questioning' (Bostetter 1963: 52). There are, moreover, complications to Abrams's design posed by history, both anterior and subsequent. In terms of the latter, and with increasing embarrassment after 1814, the self-affirming completion that Abrams reads is inconveniently contradicted by Wordsworth's inability to present *The Prelude* as the work he was thus emboldened to write, or perhaps, less boldly, substitute for *The Recluse*. In terms of the former, the passage which Abrams takes as epiphanic is haunted by its dialogic implication – its referential involvement –with voices in Genesis and *Paradise Lost*, an intertextual field which presses against the self-enclosed authority of Wordsworth's rhetoric of argument.

I will return to these complications later, showing how they shape the forms of interrogative dialogue that interest Jauss. For now, I wish to focus on Wordsworth's own evasive, but still legible, sense of himself being interrogated by his readers. The prospect of *The Recluse*, linked in the 1814 Preface to *The Excursion* by the negative 'of performances either unfinished, or unpublished,' as he himself puts it in the next paragraph (Owen and Smyser 1974, III: 6), may still be rationalized as work in progress; but the absence of *The Prelude* (already complete enough, or more than enough in Abrams's defence) bodes a deeper interrogative origin than the one represented in this Preface. The questions Wordsworth here denotes and contains in prepositional and adverbial phrases – '*how far* Nature and Education had qualified' him for his desired task; '*when* he was emboldened to hope that his faculties were sufficiently mature' – put their purchase on matters of degree and date while begging (and evading) questions of *whether* and *what*: whether the author really does feel himself qualified, and what kind of story he really wants to tell.

The elision is critical, because it was such questions, and not their (pre)determined answers, which gave the autobiography its initial charge in the late 1790s. Its earliest fragments of sustained composition begin *in medias res* with an obscurely weighted, but clearly important, petition whose mysterious emergence, repetition, and elaboration spell an urgency of expression in simultaneous competition with a desire to resist naming its cause:

> was it for this
> That one, the fairest of all rivers, loved
> To blend his murmurs with my nurse's song
> And from his alder shades and rocky falls
> And from his fords and shallows sent a voice
> To intertwine my dreams, for this didst thou
> O Derwent — travelling over the green plains
> Near my sweet birth-place didst thou beauteous stream
> Give ceaseless music to the night & day
> Which with its steady cadence tempering
> Our human waywardness compose[d] my thought
> To more than infant softness giving me
> Amid the fretful tenements of man
> A knowledge, a dim earnest of the calm
> That Nature breathes among her woodland h[?aunts]
> Was it for this & now I speak of things
> That have been & that are no gentle dreams
> Complacent fashioned fondly to adorn
> The time of unrememberable being
> Was it for this that I a four years child
> Beneath thy scars & in thy silent pools
> Made one long bathing of a summers day . . .
>
> (MS. JJ [Z^r–Y^v], in Parrish 1977: 123–4)

These questionings, rather than an invocation of the muse, launch the epic. As a substitution for this convention, they even suggest that poetic beginnings are interrogative inspirations. Insisting on transcription though the consequences seem indeterminate, Wordsworth's questioning articulates the interrogative 'passion' Gadamer describes: 'a question presses itself on us; we can no longer avoid it' (Gadamer, 1975: 330).

Yet however true this passion is experientially, in representing it, Wordsworth is alert to how both its textual mediation and intertextual affiliations subject it to scrutiny as well as expression. Poems 'containing questions explicitly assert their intertextual nature,' remarks Jonathan Culler, 'not just because they seem to request an answer and hence designate themselves as incomplete, but because the suppositions carried by their questions imply a prior discourse . . . already

in place, as a text or set of attitudes prior to the poem itself'
(1981a: 113–14). In the case of 'was it for this . . .?', this implication
is signalled, opaquely but insistently, by the metrically emphatic
pronouns. As Wordsworth's processes of composition gradually
disclose referents through an answering narrative, the question gets
conscripted, retroactively, as a rhetorical prelude to emerging self-
confidence. The syntax of interrogation, in this perspective, is
transformed from a sign of genuine inquiry for which there may be no
answer into a rhetorical figure of emerging declaration. Even its formula, with antecedents in Virgil, Ariosto, Milton, Thomson, Pope
(and its inevitable parody later in Byron), reveals how much the question already has a textual domain, and therefore a way to be troped as
an allusion, and resourceful application, to other such questioners in
similar crises.[4]

Gadamer, when he situates the passion for questioning in the
mediating and potentially enabling structures of 'historical consciousness', recognizes the value of such resources: 'the anticipation of an
answer itself presumes that the person asking is part of the tradition and regards himself as addressed by it' (Gadamer 1975: 340). In this
regard, tradition also offers the trope of question as invocation:
'was it for this?' yields textual place to a memory of the river, then
its voice, then its place, then images of the life that took place. Without
being answered directly, the question is elaborated in terms of positive
deflection. Inspiration comes, even in the earliest manuscript, as the
incantation of verse shifts from questioning to declaration. As if for-
malizing this access, the 1850 text even declines a question mark, which
now seems irrelevant (see 1850, I: 290). The verse turns away from the
vacancy implied by the present *this* and proceeds to recover, through
texts of memory and imagination, the *it* that bodes a providential
motive and agency for writing:

Nor less
~~For this~~ in springtime when on southern banks
          its
The shining sun had from his knot of leaves
Decoyed the primrose flower and when the vales
And woods were warm was I a rover then . . .
                              (Y^v, Parrish 1977: 113)

Ah not in vain ye beings of the hills . . .
                              (X^v, Parrish 1977: 109)
Ah not in vain ye spirits of the springs . . .
                             [W^r, Parrish 1977: 103]

I may not think

A vulgar hope was ^your's when ye employd
Such ministry . . .

For this when on the witherd mountain slope
The frost and breath of frosty wind had nippd
The last [autumnal?] crocus did I love
To ^{wander} range though half the night among the cliffs . . .

[W^v, Parrish 1977: 105]

In the two-part *Prelude* of 1799, the next substantial effort after MS. JJ, Wordsworth repeats and expands this emergent affirmative answering to the initial question's mysterious pronouns, *it* and *this*:

Not uselessly employed,

I might pursue this theme . . .

(1799, I: 198–9)

I would record with no reluctant voice . . .

(I: 206)

Nor with less willing heart would I rehearse . . .

(I: 234)

Nor is my aim neglected if I tell . . .

(II: 98)

These statements gain effect from their implicitly pointed opposition to the futile and elegiac mode of another interrogative trope and its tradition: 'ubi sunt?' – a question which evokes a past that cannot be recovered, leaving the present profoundly emptier and unrecompensed for such loss.

Yet for all this deft response, Wordsworth's syntax of denial and defence keeps in view the original question and so, by a paradoxical turn, makes *The Prelude* contest the authority of the answers it unfolds. Even his formulaic 'was it for this . . .?', which works in part to stabilize individual distress by troping a traditional crisis rhetoric, bears potentially reverse effects, for one of its prior voicings, in Milton's *Samson Agonistes*, aggravates the interrogative burden on Wordsworth's faltering poet. It appears in a father's address to a son chosen and nurtured, he was sure, for important work:

O miserable change! is this the man,
That invincible *Samson* . . .
For this did th'angel twice descend, for this

> Ordain'd thy nurture holy, as of a Plant?
> Select, and Sacred, Glorious for a while . . .
>
> (340–1; 361–3)

Samson answers with self-indictment rather than self-affirmation:

> Appoint not heavenly disposition, Father,
> Nothing of all these evils hath befall'n me,
> But justly; I myself have brought them on,
> Sole Author I, sole cause.
>
> (373–6)

Wordsworth's poet produces a more positive self-authorizing rhetoric:

> But wherefore be cast down,
> Why should I grieve? – I was a chosen son.
> For hither I had come with holy powers
> And faculties, whether to work or feel.
>
> (1805, III: 81–4)

But his verse is implicated in a lineage that includes Samson's voice. The troping of his question as exclamation bears a dissonance for the present poet in the past tense of its answering. Wherefore, indeed? This is a past confidence – one whose hyperbole and whose difference from the voice of the autobiographical present not only casts the historical integrity of the self into doubt, but ironizes the certainties proffered by this sort of catechism.

The difference abides in *The Prelude* as a latent force always potentially capable of exposing 'was it for this . . .?' as a question in the 'ubi sunt' mode, particularly when 'this' seems discontinuous with, even a betrayal of, 'it'. It is telling that the 1850 text, in retrospect of a hope-filled youth, expands its elegiac questioning. After recounting the ascent of Mount Snowdon, with its climax in the sudden revelation of the moon from behind the clouds – a scene Abrams and others, following Wordsworth's 'meditation', read symbolically as an emblem of psychic integration and empowerment[5] – Wordsworth does not end his poem, as he well might have. Instead, he persists interrogatively and disintegratively:

> Oh! who is he that hath his whole life long
> Preserved, enlarged, this freedom in himself?
> For this alone is genuine liberty:
> Where is the favoured being who hath held
> That course unchecked, unerring, and untired,

> In one perpetual progress smooth and bright? –
> A humbler destiny have we retraced,
> And told of lapse . . .
>
> (1850, XIV: 130–7)

Here, the implied 'ubi sunt' trope intensifies the question, making the lapse of youthful optimism seem epochal and historically inevitable. This resonance sounds even in its truncated 1805 version (which, while it stops at 'liberty', has a historical proximity to the crisis of Revolution that charges this word and 'freedom' more strongly).[6] The question that produces a confession of lapse is the reciprocal of the failure of questioning in one of these lapses: Wordsworth's record of how during the Terror, events, impressive but uninterpretable, seemed to place him before

> a volume whose contents he knows
> Are memorable, but from him locked up,
> Being written in a tongue he cannot read,
> So that he questions the mute leaves with pain,
> And half upbraids their silence.
>
> (1805, X: 50–4; cf. 1850, X: 59–63)

Soon after, 'Sick, wearied out with contrarieties', he says, he found himself 'Yield[ing] up moral questions in despair' (1805, X: 899–900; 1850, XI: 304–5).[7]

Theorizing the Interrogative

In recent decades, deconstructive approaches to a text's ways of organizing its meanings have found support in reception theory, which also decentred the text's authority by arguing for the production of meaning by the reader in terms of what Jauss has called a 'horizon of expectation'. This metaphor, from his now famous essay, 'Literary History as a Challenge to Literary Theory', refers to the linguistic, aesthetic, cultural, and literary norms (the 'horizon') against which a text is read and received. A text, Jauss proposes, has no totalizable, objective, stable meaning; it is a set of features to be negotiated by historically specific expectations, and it either proves legible within this horizon to the degree that it satisfies expectations, or exceeds it, with the effect of challenging, transforming, or even subverting normative values. As the title of his most recent work, *Question and Answer*, advertises, Jauss conceives of this dialogue between reader and text as a fundamentally interrogative one.

Jauss's refinement in some ways comes full circle to an original basis in the interrogative mode. His term 'horizon of expectations' is derived from Gadamer, his teacher at Heidelberg, who in *Truth and Method* used 'horizon of the question' to signify the implicit placement of any question 'within a particular perspective' which functions, not quite paradoxically, as a structure which 'is already an answer' of sorts (Gadamer 1975: 326–7). Although 'the logical form of the question, and the negativity that is part of it, find their fulfillment in a radical negativity' (325) this 'knowledge of not knowing', Gadamer argues, is constrained by the logic that informs the structure of the question, its 'presuppositions' of answerability (327; cf. Culler 1981a). Presuppositions also forecast the terms in which an answer is expected to emerge: 'an interpretation is determined by the question asked. Thus the dialectic of question and answer always precedes the dialectic of interpretation' (Gadamer 1975: 429). Although the linguistic and rhetorical resistances of Wordsworth's texts suggest that he is less confident of the status of the truth to be won from such a method, his compositional processes, as his initiating question, 'Was it for this . . .?' makes clear, act out the dynamic of presupposition Gadamer describes.

The Prelude dramatizes how reading, as the trope of generating a text as well as of interpreting it, in fact doubles this dialectic. Gadamer articulates the implicit theoretical stakes of Wordsworth's sense of autobiography as a textual interrogation of history – where questioning is understood as reading – that itself becomes a subject of critical interrogation. 'For an historical text to be made the object of interpretation', Gadamer contends, 'means that it asks a question of the interpreter. . . . To understand a text means to understand this question' (Gadamer 1975: 333). Correspondingly, interpretation becomes 'a process of questioning through which we seek the answer to the question that the text asks' (337); 'We must attempt to reconstruct the question to which the transmitted text is the answer'. Thus, 'the work of hermeneutics [is] a conversation with the text . . . whose fundamental procedure is always question and answer' (331).[8] This 'hermeneutical priority of the question has a comprehensive scope for Gadamer: 'the structure of the question is implicit in all experience. We cannot have experiences without asking questions.' Nor can we learn anything: 'the development of all knowledge [occurs] through the question', and dialectic, the structure of discovery and intellectual refinement, 'proceeds . . . by way of question and answer' (325–6).

This dialectic, Gadamer goes on to say, makes communication possible, not only between parties in the same historical moment but also, and suggestively for Wordsworth's interrogations, between past and present – the autobiographical past as well as literary tradition: 'that which is handed down in literary form is brought back out of . . . alienation . . . and into the living presence of conversation, whose fundamental procedure is always question and answer' (331). Through this handing down, 'the horizon of the question within which the sense of the text is determined' (333) expands historically, including within it other 'questioners' of the text who have preceded us (337). Such a hermeneutics is global in application: 'The logic of the human sciences is . . . a logic of the question' (333). 'A person who seeks to understand must question what lies behind what is said. He must understand it as an answer to a question . . . We understand the sense of the text only by acquiring the horizon of the question that, as such necessarily includes other possible answers' (333).

Complementing and developing the interrogative emphasis that Gadamer gave this interaction, Jauss's initial essay on reception aesthetics, 'Literary History as a Challenge to Literary Theory', stressed the interrogative role of reading: first, 'the specific disposition toward a particular work that the author anticipates . . . presuppose[s]' a perceivable 'opposition between fiction and reality, between the poetic and the practical function of language' – an opposition, Jauss suggests, that may 'be objectified by means of the hermeneutics of question and answer' (1970–1: 24). Second, reconstructing 'the horizon of expectations, in the face of which a work was created and received in the past enables one . . . to pose questions that the text gave an answer to' (1970–1: 28). Jauss's base of examination, like Gadamer's, is broadly cultural, but he diverges from him in arguing that readers' questions engender a critical operation as well as a reconstructive one. Interrogative reading, that is, is not simply prescripted by a text's immanent questions; it asks its own questions against the text's manipulation of answers and may call 'into question as a platonizing dogma of philological metaphysics the apparently self-evident claims that in the literary text . . . objective meaning, determined once and for all, is at all times immediately accessible to the interpreter' (1970–1: 28). By suggesting that the supposition of 'objective meaning' may be no more than a product of a certain kind of signifying practice eager to claim scientific basis for its assertions of truth – a process he cartoons as 'a platonizing dogma of a philological metaphysics' – Jauss meant to relativize the authority of such myths. His method was to resist the universalizing claims of their platonizing discourses by disclosing the historical foundation of the particular, and evolving, terms of a work's reception – how it was reviewed, written about, discussed, troped, parodied, and alluded to, both in its own age and in subsequent traditions of reading. Against assumptions that there is a 'right' reading to be arrived at through instruments of objective knowledge, he argued that a text's meaning is always in flux, constituted by its reception in a given social and historical moment and the accretion of these receptions in the history of reading. His theory is overtly dialogic: it not only places the text's meaning in a field of potential responses formed by the reader's horizon of expectations, but it also characterizes those expectations themselves as dialogic, influenced by the history of the way in which a text has been read.

Even so, there are aspects of Jauss's initial theorizing which, like Gadamer's hermeneutics, tend to presume a stable framework: with the right amount of methodological rigour, the text, its original horizon of inquiry, and the horizon of present interpretation may be brought into synthesis, even fusion; the judicious interpreter knows what constitutes the right kind of interpretive question, and, relatedly, assumes the ontological stability (if not the interpretive authority) of the anterior question determining the sense of the text.[9] *The Prelude* poses an interesting challenge to this faith for, as much as its management of questions and answers within the terms of its argument appears to share its orientation, its verbal texture persists in thwarting the legibility of a coherent interrogative motivation as well as the stability of its answering style. Wordsworth's sensitivity to 'other possible answers' remains an interference that results in continued and prolonged revisions, either to articulate the presupposed answers more securely, or to give the instabilities more play. A less determined and at times deconstructive questioning prompts him to reread his various textualizations of his life, a process of interrogation that was never able to fix *The Prelude* in final form. This instability also informs the poem's reception – from its first (posthumous) publication in 1850; through the contested discriminations of 'Wordsworths' in the second half of the century (roughly, Arnold's sense that the poem was anomalous to the character of Wordsworth's best work versus Bradley's sense that the 'perplexities' of this poem were 'most characteristic'); to the controversial introduction of the 1805 text by Ernest de Selincourt in 1926; ensuing arguments about which text, 1850 or 1805, is the authoritative one; the institution of a 'Two-Part *Prelude* of 1798–99' in the third and fourth editions of *The Norton Anthology of English Literature* (1974; 1979); to, most recently, the case for presenting three 'Authoritative Texts' in the Norton Critical Edition (1979): *The Prelude: 1799, 1805, 1850*.[10] In a way uncannily predicted by the compositional dynamics of the poem itself, its textual history, along with its history of interpretation and reception, are now integral aspects of the poem for its readers, part of their informed horizon of expectation.

Yet even as Jauss's initial essay stresses the importance of such perspectives in historicizing interpretation, it also, almost offhandedly, introduces a radical problem: the way a horizon is itself a product of reception (defined by 'pre-understanding', forms and themes 'already familiar', 'constitutive motivations', 'conventions', 'literary expectations' (1970–1: 23–4). For Paul de Man, this problem calls into question 'the impression of methodological mastery' in Jauss's claim that the horizon of expectation 'mediates between the private inception and the public reception of the work' (1986: xiii). That a horizon of reception is itself composed of 'received' ideas, de Man argues, destabilizes both historical and discursive difference. Correspondingly, if a question implies something already answered, behind every answer there is a motivating question. A Jaussian reader's question, de Man explains, may disrupt 'an answer that has become common knowledge', but in so doing it reveals that answer itself to have

> been an individual response to an earlier, collective question. As the answer metamorphoses into a question, it . . . reveals . . . a live background behind its background, in the form of a question from which it now can itself *stand out*. The question-and-answer structures are the abysmal frames that engender each other without end or *telos*.
>
> (1986: xiii)

These frames are 'abysmal' precisely because they subvert the possibility of any cognitive distinction between question and answer: in another version of the hermeneutic circle, questions are found, in the terms of their formulation, to imply their answers, and answers disclose backgrounds against which they are transformed into questions. We will soon look at how the interrogative schemes of *The Prelude* become such a whirl, a redundant energy vexing its own creation. For now, we may note (as some may have already), a typical deconstructive turn in de Man's analysis: an apparent synthesis of understanding demystified to reveal a process without closure, yet another 'rhetoric of temporality' that 'allows for no end, for no totality' (1983b: 222).[11]

For de Man, these abysmal frames coincide with the duplicitous generativity of the text itself; applied to reception theory, they loom within the historical instabilities of interpretation. Although Jauss's earlier work seemed to de Man not to be sufficiently interested in textual resistances, *Question and Answer* joins rigour to provisionality, moving closer to de Man's sense of free play: 'No fixed view ever prevails,' explains Wlad Godzich in his Introduction; 'each generation must read the texts anew and interrogate them from its own perspective and find itself concerned, in its own fashion, by the work's questions' (Godzich 1982: xii–xiii). These essays still show Jauss resisting de Man's effort to merge rhetoric with literature, especially on the point of the rhetorical and literary uses of questioning (1989: 84) – a crucial exception, as we shall see later – and still adhering to Gadamer's conception of the text as a voice in a dialogue. But he has relinquished his claim for the total recuperability of a text's original horizon of meaning: what our interrogations give access to, instead, is a sense of 'the *otherness* of the past at those moments when the question is rediscovered to which the text, within its historical horizon, was the answer' (Jauss 1989: 63; emphasis added). Historical knowledge is enmeshed in and problematized by 'the historicity of understanding itself' (1989: 198), and methodological awareness is a caution but no solution: with fuller attention to the issue that fastened de Man's attention, Jauss now elaborates the way that 'the meaning that a historically distant text can recapture for us does not emerge solely from the folds of the original horizon', but 'stems to an equal degree from the later horizon of experience belonging to the interpreter' (1989: 206).[12]

Wordsworth knew this already. His sensitivity to this epistemological bind, and his prediction of the theoretical impasse, emerges quite early on in *The Prelude*, when he confesses his frequent inability to say of his poem

> what portion is in truth
> The naked recollection of [past] time,
> And what may rather have been called to life
> By after-meditation.
> (1805, III: 645–8; cf. 1850, III: 613–16)

In passages such as this, Wordsworth verges on nullifying the difference between the one and the other. Even so, that the emergent syntactic form in which he expresses this apprehension is interrogative – 'what . . . And what' – helps us see the value of Gadamer's seminal, and influential, perception that texts are mobilized by, and as, interrogative dialogues. Indeed, Wordsworth's interrogative readings, both of a history conceived of as a text and of a text conceived as a history, constitute a peculiar, individual enactment of the dialogics of question and answer that Jauss puts at the centre of textual meaning.

Jauss begins *Question and Answer*, in fact, in a Wordsworthian spirit, with an extended discussion of the relation between the procedures of fiction and the understanding of reality (a territory charted by Hayden White).[13] Examining the fictive constructions that both communicate and underlie historical orders of meaning, Jauss means to show how historical writing is motivated in ways that open its authority to interrogation. Literature, he argues, offers an arena in which 'the system of answers given by a currently dominant worldview' may be subject to scrutiny of a particularly interrogative kind:

> Fictional actions can be used to test the religious truths or the ideas with which a theology or a philosophy answers ultimate questions, or . . . impudent questions can be asked . . . [as well as] the indirect forms constituted by the 'merely rhetorical,' the 'incorrectly posed' and even 'dumb' questions that cannot be answered by the system and are therefore destined to interrupt an unquestioning view of the world.
>
> (Jauss 1989: 71)

That Wordsworth understood the degree to which the historical project of autobiography was implicated with the procedures of fiction and the interrogative actions they enable is everywhere evident in *The Prelude*, even when he is speaking emphatically of answers revealed in the 'history' produced by the question, 'was it for this . . .?'. Consider this passage, near the end of the last book:

> And now, O Friend! this history is brought
> To its appointed close: the discipline
> And consummation of a Poet's mind,
> In everything that stood most prominent,
> Have faithfully been pictured; we have reached
> The time (our guiding object from the first)
> When we may, not presumptuously, I hope,
> Suppose my powers so far confirmed . . .
>
> (1850, XIV: 302–9)

The history ('faithful' though Wordsworth claims its picturing to be) is described in an explicitly aesthetic mode, as even his metaphor 'picture' implies: it has a hero (the 'Poet'), an overall design (a guiding object), and a narrative structure replete with a theme (discipline and consummation) and an appointed close. These poetics provide no better case in point for Jauss's observation that all historical narratives obey 'a law of fiction, namely, the Aristotelian requirement that a plot have a beginning, middle, and end', a structure that is 'always a more or less fictive arrangement' with hermeneutic agency, that of revealing the meaning of events (Jauss 1989: 31).

Jauss's claim that fictionalization is 'always at work in historical experience' (26) is embodied in the practice of *The Prelude*, which, at its most radical moments, wonders not whether history is mediated by fiction, but whether historical constructions can be differentiated from fictional ones. 'Through this retrospect', Wordsworth writes in the 1850 text, he has

> played with times
> And accidents as children do with cards,
> Or as a man, who, when his house is built,
> A frame locked up in wood and stone, doth still,
> As impotent fancy prompts, by his fireside,
> Rebuild it to his liking . . .
>
> (1850, VI: 286–94)

Not only does this analogy make explicit the constructedness of the story, but the figure of analogy itself doubles the gesture with a rhetorical construction. For Wordsworth, this play more often than not produces perplexity; for Jauss, the complicity of fiction and historical knowledge is critical resource. Jauss's aim is not to deny the possibility of history but to affirm the mutual interaction of '*res fictae*, the realm of poetry, and *res factae*, the object of history': 'Poetic fiction becomes the horizon of reality, and historical reality becomes the horizon of poetry' (1989: 27). His goal is to 'legitimat[e] the use of fiction in writing history', showing how its forms are crucial to any effort 'to lift historical experience from the diffuse events of historical reality (1989: 29), and to show in particular how the interrogative forms of fiction operate as a critical tool of knowledge.

Gadamer's and Jauss's hermeneutic of interrogation is not only predicted in the self-scrutinies of Romantic poems such as *The Prelude*; it has also, through modern continental routes, influenced or coincided with developments in linguistic and literary analysis. In the decade after *Truth and Method*, Emile Benveniste took the three basic kinds of statement – declarative, interrogative, and imperative – and the syntactic modalities from which they derive to describe three basic functions of social interaction: to impart knowledge; to obtain information; to give an order (Benveniste 1971: 110). Catherine Belsey takes up these distinctions to develop a general theory of textual modes, focusing on the social texts projected by the syntactic model. She defines textual modes chiefly by their practice upon the reader. The 'declarative text', epitomized in the discourse of 'classic realism', addresses a reader through a position of privilege which, she claims, mystifies itself as objective. The 'imperative text', formed in the more overt designs of propaganda and the sermon, gives instructions to its readers (Belsey 1980: 90–1).[14] In contrast to the guile of these two textual modes in 'effac[ing] contradiction' and keeping masked 'the ideology masquerading as truth' in various kinds of naturalized discourses, the 'interrogative text' disrupts their circuits of communication. It 'refuses a single point of view, however complex and comprehensive' and, instead, 'brings points of view into unresolved collision or contradiction' (92) – with the effect of putting into question both the reader's position as the stable receiver of discourse and the author's status as a unified subject. This effect is radically rhetorical, in so far as such a text invites readers 'to produce answers to the questions it implicitly or explicitly raises' (Belsey 1980: 90–1) and enlists them 'in contradiction'. Deconstructive criticism has a cooperative aim for Belsey: that of exposing the false coherences and plenitudes of ideology, and revealing, instead, its contradictions, its incompleteness and, above all, its 'mode of production, the materials and their arrangement in the work'. Thus revealed, 'the text is no longer restricted to a single, harmonious and authoritative reading. Instead it becomes *plural*, open to re-reading, no longer an object for passive consumption but an object of work by the reader to produce meaning' (103–4).

Belsey's exemplary critics for such practice are Roland Barthes (especially *S/Z*) and Pierre Macherey (especially *A Theory of Literary Production*). But it is ironic that her brief remarks on *The Prelude* so passively credit its internally proffered ideology over its ironic demystification. For *The Prelude* is a work which – in its collisions and contradictions, in its virtual thematizing of inevitable rereading, as well as in the bafflement that its plural texts pose to any reader's desire for a single authoritative reading – fulfils all her criteria, not only for an 'interrogative text' but also for the sort of critical reading she calls for. Yet in its representation in *Critical Practice*, this poem merely contrasts literature in which the subject is unfixed and decentred: it is unproblematically governed by its dominant agenda of ensuring 'a convergence' between its hero and its autobiographer, in order 'to create a unified identity which is intelligible as the product of past experience: what the poet *was*, we are to understand, is the source of what

he *is* . . . there is a clear transition from narrative to meditation in
the present tense' (Belsey 1980: 87). Certainly, as the embarrassed
text of Wordsworth's 1814 Preface reveals, this was the determination,
and there are more than a few passages in *The Prelude* itself that
trace this intention. But, within such designs, the poem's resistant
signs of textual and figural difference show that for its author 'what
the poet was' and 'what he is' are not the closed issues represented
in Belsey's declarative syntaxes. If *The Prelude*'s originating question
('was it for this . . . ?') generates an elaborately self-authorizing
text, there are numerous passages that, in turn, show the text
interrogating its conclusions: 'How shall I trace the history, where
seek/The origin of what I then have felt?' the poet explicitly asks
(and not just as a trope of introduction) in a draft of 1799 (II: 395–6),
using a past progressive tense that implies a continuity which the
very asking of the question belies; the 1805 text even retains the
question verbatim (1805, II: 365–6), though presumably the 1799
text had already produced some significant tracing. Asking may
prompt tracing, but tracing does not cease asking.

The interrogative involution is made more critical, in fact, by its
retracing, with a difference, another interrogative dialogue: Adam's
interview with Raphael in *Paradise Lost*. With wondering curiosity,
Adam ponders his origin: 'For Man to tell how human Life began/Is
hard; for who himself beginning knew?' (VIII: 250–1). His urbanely
rhetorical and self-answering tone belies a more genuine interrogative
desire. Knowing not 'who I was, or where, or from what cause' (270),
Adam entreats, 'How came I thus, how here?' (277). But not for long:
troping prelapsarianism itself, Milton takes these questions emphatically
into what Belsey would call a 'declarative text' and Jauss a 'catechistic'
one. Adam soon senses the answer: 'Not of myself; by some great
Maker . . . In goodness and in power preëminent . . . From whom I
have that thus I move and live,/And feel that I am happier than I know'
(278–82). Adam's 'Author' forthwith reveals Himself in and as answer
to all questions about the basis of his identity: 'Whom thou sought'st
I am' (316) – a closed chiasmus of questioner and respondent that forms
a marked contrast to the conditions of Wordsworth's postlapsarian self-
questioning. This allusive conversation between Wordsworth's text
and Milton's shows the degree to which Wordsworth depicts origin not
as the ground of permanence Milton portrays (at least at this lost,
mythic moment in history) for Adam, but instead as an elusive term of
desire for such a ground and its traceable history.

In the 1850 text, with the retrospect of a half century, Wordsworth comes a little closer to stabilizing some of his interrogative dramas with fleeting moods of Adamic faith. The question above, for instance, modulates its tone into the declarative – 'How shall I seek the origin? where find/Faith in the marvellous things which then I felt?' (II: 346–7). The initial question of 'how' succumbs to the answer implied by the alliance of faith and feeling that is patterned by alliteration, a dactylic variation, and chiastic syntax. At the same time, however, and with opposite effect, we see this alliance attenuated by a now closed past tense – 'felt' rather than 'have felt'. Textual archaeology shows the revision registering the inquiry in more urgent terms. This sort of intertextual reading was not possible for nineteenth-century readers, and our sense of *The Prelude* as a contradictory and unstable artefact is due, in no small part, to the work of scholars in collating the poem's several drafts and their palimpsests of revision. There are some occasions, nevertheless, when, even without reference to earlier texts, we can see the transparency of original, and still urgent, questions – and with the radical effects Belsey reserves for interrogative texts, namely, the refusal of 'a single privileged discourse which contains and places all the others' (Belsey 1980: 92). There is no more exact a case in point for this refusal than a passage from the 1850 text of *The Prelude* – one Wordsworth auditioned first in the 1799 drafts and felt compelled to retain every time he revised. Speaking in the autobiographical present, the poet interrupts his elegy for the 'eagerness of infantine desire' to confess,

> A tranquillizing spirit presses now
> Upon my corporeal frame, so wide appears
> The vacancy between me and those days,
> Which yet have such self-presence in my heart
> That sometimes when I think of them I seem
> Two consciousnesses – conscious of myself,
> And of some other being.
>
> (1799, II: 25–31)

In this syntax, the self is split into a speaking subject ('me') and textual object ('those days' of 'some other being'), and the divorce is radical, yielding not only an otherness of self, but its estrangement by vacancy. Moreover, even the speaking subject is disrupted, split not only into a historical subject, 'myself,' and a historicizing one, 'I', but yet another: the 'I' that writes them. The fissuring of the self into these several signs is a potent figure of how any claim to an integrated, unified centre of consciousness is an illusion susceptible to dispersal along a potentially infinite succession of signifiers.[15] The next time Wordsworth fixed this passage into his text, his only substantive revision was to change *heart* to *mind*, as if to concede the cognitive dilemma against the emotional faith in one's life as a coherent and legible text.

If Belsey's implied assumption that the real interrogative texts are produced by readers and critics rather than authors seems to limit what she can say about the composition of *The Prelude* in the interrogative mode, John Hollander's work reveals the flexible and complex ways in which poetry operates interrogatively and intertextually. Hollander shows, in other words, how authors may produce the sorts of complex and complicating works that Belsey assumes exist primarily in the domain of critical practice. Working independently of both Belsey and Benveniste, though in correspondence with their interests, he focuses three chapters of his most recent study, *Melodious Guile*, on the way three syntactic modes – questions, answers, and imperatives – inflect poetic composition, enter into its tropings, and develop its traditions (Hollander 1988: 110). His concern is with the way poetry exploits these discourses as tropes rather than deploys them as straightforward modes of communication (even in the 'philosophical question', he suggests, 'the literal integrity of the question is presumed and honored' (27)). In the case of the interrogative mode, for example, Hollander studies syntaxes that work for ends other, or more, than a direct and literal request for information. The 'rhetorical question' is one such, but 'its blatancy as device makes it less a trope than a scheme' (64). Hollander's greatest interest is the metaphorizing intensification he calls 'poetic questioning': 'poetry . . . always means . . . at best something else by the question it is asking. Its very mode of interrogation is itself a trope' (26). His previous book, *The Figure of Echo* (1981), looked at the ways in which poetic allusions operate as intertextual dialogues; *Melodious Guile* suggests that such dialogues are an 'aspect of poetic answer. One text answers a prior one as if that prior one had posed a question' (1988: 58). What for Gadamer is central to historical knowledge becomes for Hollander the basis of literary tradition. Questioning and answering, he proposes, operate not only in relation to each other but also across an intertextual field, with a sensitivity to powerful anterior figurings: 'Whether or not a prior poem has actually asked a question, a later one will assume that it has, and answer what it insists on interpreting as having been a figurative query' (57); such answering is 'figuratively so, because no actual question has been asked' (63). Even imperatives in poetry do their best work as tropes, in dialogue with traditions of invocation, incantation, envoi, and prayer: all these 'represent poetry's discourse with itself' (79), its self-consciousness about its cultural, linguistic, rhetorical, and formal terrains.

Especially valuable for thinking about Wordsworth as a perpetually questioning and revising reader of his life's text is Hollander's suggestion that 'poets as readers of their own poems' are 'tropes of audiences, and the very question of what is "appropriate response" is always being called into poetic question. This is obviously true of questioning one's own self' (29). Correspondingly, there are rhetorical answers and poetic answers, as well as literal ones. What Hollander terms the 'poetic' mode of answering is particularly relevant not only to Wordsworth but also to Jauss's theory of dialogic understanding. For Hollander, 'poetic answering' is implicitly 'intertextual', occurring when a poem

> treats an earlier one as if it posed a question, and answers it, interprets it, glosses it, revises it . . . In these terms, the whole history of poetry may be said to constitute a chain of answers to the first texts – Homer and Genesis – which themselves become questions for successive generations of answers.
>
> (56)

Hollander goes on to say that while such dialogues 'are of a different sort from those which occur between parts of the same poem', they 'may be related by the ways in which they trope, or make nonliteral, the rhetoric of answering' (56). In *The Prelude*, both kinds of action are in force. Wordsworth is clearly in dialogue with the questionings and answering style of certain powerful precursors such as Milton; at the same time, each revision puts him in a critical dialogue with his own previous texts, rehearing their questions and renegotiating their answers.

Interrogating the Text, With and Against Wordsworth

To see how even one discrete version of *The Prelude* enters into such dialogues, despite what Keats called the 'palpable design' of Wordsworth's poetry (Keats 1970, 1: 224), we may look at the interrogative composition of Book I. The architectonic seems a confident, stable structure of self-interrogation, beginning with questions and ending in answers. We note, first of all, that Wordsworth deliberately does not open this book, and the poem as a whole, with the questions that originally forced the autobiographical project into production (his sudden 'Was it for this . . .?'). Instead, he begins with declarations that subsume even interrogative syntax, troping it, as Hollander would put it, as a rhetoric of self-affirmation. The first thing we read is an epic invocation that does not petition a muse but already claims its inspiration:

Oh there is blessing in this gentle breeze,
That blows from the green fields and from the clouds
And from the sky; it beats against my cheek,
And seems half conscious of the joy it gives.
O welcome messenger! O welcome friend!
. . .
Now I am free, enfranchised and at large,
May fix my habitation where I will.

(1805, I: 1–10)

By the 1850 text, the figuration of the breeze as spiritual inspiration is heightened by its having a 'mission' (1850, I: 5). Wordsworth turns this confidence to a series of enthusiastically projected questions:

What dwelling shall receive me, in what vale
Shall be my harbour, underneath what grove
Shall I take up my home, and what clear stream
Shall with its murmurs lull me to my rest?
The earth is all before me . . .

(1805, I: 11–15)

Wordsworth's way with interrogative syntax here is a familiar one, for which the Renaissance rhetorician, George Puttenham, provides a fine gloss:

There is a kinde of figurative speach when we aske many questions and looke for none answere, speaking indeed by interrogation, which we might as well say by affirmation. This figure I call the *Questioner* or inquisitive.

(Puttenham 1970: 220)

Wordsworth's inaugural questions breezily assume this figure. Despite their seeming expansiveness and their openness to the unknown, they already, and quite self-consciously, assume some matters: there is a receptive dwelling, a vale affording the safety implied in the metaphor of harbour, a hospitable grove, and a world of rest and nurture; only the precise realization is in suspense. The intent of questioning is not to worry about 'what?' but to affirm 'Shall'.

Yet this rhetorical confidence is already destabilized in Wordsworth's textural figuring, specifically the risky extension of response into a Miltonic allusion: as readers long have noted, the answering prospect, 'The earth is all before me,' casts the hero of the autobiography in the place of Adam and Eve at the close of *Paradise Lost*:

> The World was all before them, where to choose
> Thir place of rest, and Providence thir guide:
> They hand in hand with wand'ring steps and slow,
> Through *Eden* took thir solitary way.
>
> (XII: 646–9)

In its optimistic register of calculation, the allusion supplies Wordsworth's solitary hero with the provident guidance guaranteed to Adam and Eve. But the echo is more complexly scripted with important counter-intimations: Adam and Eve are entering postlapsarian history in which their 'wand'ring' is prone to error – a latency in the unnamed Latin synonym (*errant*) against which Milton has been playing throughout the poem. Wordsworth's echo thus not only forecasts providence, it also brings into play a script of failure and alienation. Although his hero's voice does not pause over this double legacy, Wordsworth's sense of it inflects the voicing of his next question which, though still cast in a rhetoric of affirmation, bears a more hesitant tone, and as a consequence, an ambiguous sense:

> Whither shall I turn,
> By road or pathway, or through open field,
> Or shall a twig or any floating thing
> Upon the river point me out my course?
>
> (1805, I: 29–32)

Is this one more expression of confidence, or a real question? While a 'course' is claimed as a sure possession (a sense heightened in the 1850 text by the conversion of the 'open' field into a 'trackless' one: there to be tracked), the multiplication of options seems less a sign of expansive liberty than of a map of too much, potentially unproductive, wandering. At issue in this tonal shift is an emergent and more genuine questioning about a course of life: a desired entry into what the poet soon names as the 'holy life of music and of verse' (1805, I: 54). The word 'verse', in fact, unpacks the question 'Whither shall I turn?' with another Latin punning that tropes the question as 'What shall I write?' – a question that soon enters the verse as the heretofore unexplicated pretext of the earlier manuscript's 'Was it for this?'

What has happened over the course of this seemingly stage-managed performance in interrogative figures – a masquerade, in Belsey's terms, if ever there was one, of 'coherence and plenitude' (Belsey 1980: 104) – is a contradictory eruption of a more authentic uncertainty, a 'gap' between the affirmative intention and the sensation of experiential uncertainty, or worse, inability. De Man is particularly attentive to this sort of interrogative instability, one in which grammar and rhetoric not only diverge from but oppose one another, 'the same grammatical pattern engender[ing] two meanings that are mutually exclusive' (1979b: 9). Wordsworth's question, 'whither . . . my course', seems at first, and in consequence of its preceding questions, another trope of declaration. But the subsequent verse applies a competing meaning, a genuine expression of what is not known: what course of life, what course of writing. Book I remains preoccupied with this issue – the 1850 text names it explicitly as 'contradiction' (238) – and brings it to a climax in the poet's confession, after a prolonged bout of writer's block, of feeling himself 'Unprofitably travelling towards the grave,/Like a false steward who hath much received/And renders nothing back' (1805, I: 269–71). The simile evokes the parable of the talents that was so important to Milton's self-interrogation.[16]

This latent alliance of Wordsworth's self-representation with the occasion of Milton's self-interrogation provokes and reintroduces the poem's historically originating question:

> Was it for this,
> That one, the fairest of all rivers, loved
> To blend his murmurs with my nurse's song . . .[?]
> (1805, I: 271–3)

An intermediate version, still with mysterious pronouns, launched 'The Two-Part *Prelude* of 1798–99', and there, as we have seen, the question not only generated composition, but that composition, over the course of the verse, yielded a scheme of tentatively affirmative answering. Recovering both that textual past and the biographical past towards which the initial pronoun had pointed, Wordsworth places this question in 1805's Book I at the head of a new verse paragraph (1805, I: 271). So situated, it gains new force, working at once as a critical consummation of a now disclosed, preceding narrative of distress and as a sudden, rhetorical conscription of the interrogative mood into a moment of electrically condensed self-reading. 'Was it for this?', that is, now bears a hortatory rhetoric as well as a self-interrogating one, and with this double charge infuses the rehearsal of crisis in Book I with a sense of imminent self-possession. With 'this' implying a destiny or determination, the question seems to require only an unpacking of 'it' to inspire the present. This is the reading John Ogden gives this pivotal moment: even the syntax 'serves to interweave past and present, as the first pronoun points forward to the following recollection of the past, while the next pronoun points backward to the present vexation that the poet has just reviewed and re-experienced' (Ogden 1978: 371-2). The question bears the terms by which it may be answered, and beyond this, made structurally essential to the project at hand.

There is no better illustration than this moment in Book I of Gadamer's argument that sudden realizations emerge from an interrogative structure. 'Sudden thoughts', he argues, 'do not come entirely unexpectedly':

> They always presuppose . . . questions. The real nature of the sudden idea is perhaps less the sudden realisation of the solution to a problem than the sudden realisation of the question that advances into openness and thus makes an answer possible. Every sudden idea has the structure of a question.
>
> (Gadamer 1975: 329)

This structure is cannier in Book I than we may at first realize, for not only do the immediate terms of 'Was it for this . . .?' bear the latent access Ogden identifies for us, but the terms of its elaboration evoke the confident questioning at the head of Book I. The river remembered is not just the one of historical memory (the scene of boyhood play), but the one of the opening lines: 'what sweet stream/Shall with its murmurs lull me to my rest?' Unlike the suspended composition of the 1799 drafts, the scheme of Book I provides a restorative context, diverting the question from its original crisis mode into a narrative mode prescripted as provident.

The patient counsel that Milton's questioner strains to hear as he thinks of the parable of the talents has already paid off for Wordsworth, specifically through a 'rhetorical' or 'tropological' operation on questioning itself.[17] In this context, not only are the suppositions borne by questions already in place and evident in the event of the poem itself, but they give an early audition to the deconstructive circularity of question and answer rehearsed in the 1814 Preface. We might say that if the dramatized sequence of Book I has the question provoke the poetic project, the discursive requirements of the project produce, and even determine, the question – shaping it with what Wordsworth himself calls at its close 'a theme/Single and of determined bounds', namely, his desire to tell 'the story of [his] life' (1805, I: 667-9). 'Was it for this?', latently intentional in its first asking, now participates in a staging of self-discovery in which questioning, to use Jauss's terms, seems to abide within 'the horizon of the known and the secure': it is pointed, however provisionally, toward 'a solid answer' and serves, implicitly, 'in magistral dialogue, to transmit some doctrine', even extending, in some rehearsals, 'to catechetical interrogation' and towards 'a closed doctrinal system of answers' (1989: 73–5).

These terms may seem quite restrictive, but we can see how Wordsworth's reiteration of 'Was it for this?' in the direction of 'determined bounds' enacts such an extension, for in each reasking (not only in the initial MS JJ but also, more elaborately, in subsequent manuscripts), the question is increasingly textualized and increasingly implicated, in its very asking, with the question-begging intentionality of 'for this'. This intentionality emerges forcefully in the last verse paragraph of the 1805 text, whose images as well as rhetoric are cast in implicit answer to the book's initial questions of vocation:

> One end hereby at least hath been attained—
> My mind hath been revived—and if this mood
> Desert me not, I will forthwith bring down
> Through later years the story of my life.
> The road lies plain before me. 'Tis a theme
> Single and of determined bounds, and hence
> I chuse it rather at this time than work
> Of ampler or more varied argument,
> Where I might be discomfited and lost,
> And certain hopes are with me that to thee
> This labour will be welcome, honoured friend.
>
> (1805, I: 664–74)

Wordsworth has audibly composed this coda within the book's interrogative theme. Earlier he recounted his longing 'To brace [him]self to some determined aim' and for a subject that 'may be singled out with steady choice' (1805, I: 171); now he 'chuse[s]' a 'theme/Single and of determined bounds'. With 'the earth . . . all before me', he had wondered, 'Whither shall I turn,/By road or pathway . . .?'; now he claims, the 'road lies plain before me'.

And yet, in dialogue with these signals is a contradictory tone of doubt, apology – and, in effect, a persistent questioning of the answers being proclaimed: 'at least' suggests an accommodation by necessity rather than a sure resolution; the qualification, 'if this mood desert me not', especially in view of the darker moods that prompt self-inquiry, bears a question and virtually predicts a negative answer. The road not chosen – 'the work of ampler or more varied argument' – not only is cast in terms of higher endeavour, but is rejected by an explicit sensation of inadequacy: in this field, the poet says, 'I might be discomfited and lost'. And finally, even the reception by the audience designated for this account – Coleridge, the 'honoured Friend' (1850, I: 647) who had been urging Wordsworth to write the major philosophical poem of the age – is tendered with a certain amount of hesitant hope and uncertain result. For he, as Wordsworth was all too aware, regarded the auto-biography as a diversion from or a stall against the more worthy project of writing the first and finest philosophical poem of the age.[18]

These interrogative stirrings are even more evident in the penultimate paragraph of Book I – originally the last of 1799's First Part. Here Wordsworth discloses a series of belated confessions whose import, despite the book's design of resolution, recalls the interrogatives never quite contained by the book's schemes of answering:

>   I began
> My story early, feeling, as I fear,
> The weakness of a human love for days
> Disowned by memory— . . .
>   . . .
> Nor will it seem to thee, my friend, so prompt
> In sympathy, that I have lengthened out
> With fond and feeble tongue a tedious tale.
> Meanwhile my hope has been that I might fetch
> Invigorating thoughts from former years,
> Might fix the wavering balance of my mind,
> And haply meet reproaches too, whose power
> May spur me on, in manhood now mature,
> To honorable toil. Yet should these hopes
> Be vain, and thus should neither I be taught
> To understand myself, nor thou to know
> With better knowledge how the heart was framed
> Of him thou lovest, need I dread from thee
> Harsh judgments if I am so loth to quit
> Those recollected hours that have the charm
> Of visionary things, and lovely forms
> And sweet sensations, that throw back our life
> And almost make our infancy itself
> A visible scene on which the sun is shining?
>   (1805, I: 641–63)

The question, 'need I dread from thee/Harsh judgments . . .?' is scarcely audible amid all these premises and qualifications, its interrogative impulse so stifled, that its rhetoric seems to shift, almost effortlessly, into that of a confident conscription of sympathy. Yet the dread of harsh 'judgments', in being named and confessed, retains the grammatical model of the question against the oppositely tuned rhetorical one. This grammatical literalism finds allies in the tentative locutions of 'might', 'Might', 'haply', 'May'. The effect is to unfix and set wavering the verse by resummoning, if not exactly revoicing, 'Was it for this . . .?': in their suggestion of an incompletely realized response to a present deficiency of 'Invigorating thoughts' and the still unrealized event of 'honorable' toil, they trace the figure of a premature 'balance' of mind. When the poet goes on to admit as much, conceding that his hopes might prove 'vain', he attempts to subsume the confession into a question troped for Coleridge's endorsement of the poem clearly underway: the prolonged 'if' clause attenuates and absorbs the question to such a degree that by the time one reaches the question mark, its force as punctuation has been rendered irrelevant by the declarative defence.

And yet the interrogative syntax retains a cognitive force, because Book I does not conclude here: Wordsworth retests and opens up the whole question of 'judgment', indeed of 'harsh judgments', in the remarkably qualified claims of the final paragraph. If the book opens with a set of questions that function more rhetorically than interrogatively, turned into metaphors of confident expectation, this last grammatically identifiable question about Coleridge's reception works inversely. It is advanced in the rhetorical mode as declaration, resisting that containment. When it returns nearly verbatim, in the 1850 text, it substitutes an affirmative denial – 'I began/My story early – *not misled, I trust,*/By an infirmity of love . . .' (1850, I: 612–14, emphasis added) – but the effect is equivocal. Not only is the question still there, but the preliminary denial – by its very existence, by the litotes that keeps visible the matter to be denied ('misled'), and by its punctuation with a subjective plea – makes legible its motivation, subtracting thereby as much as it adds.

To read this way is to read against the self-affirming design of the autobiography and to discern a competing action, one that continually deconstructs answers to reveal the questions by which they are motivated and which resist settling. This is a double operation, in which the reader not only heeds the text's answers to the questions it has represented, but also 'enquire[s] . . . about the questioner and his meaning, to which the text is, perhaps, only the imagined answer' (Gadamer

1975: 335). This is not a matter of critiquing Wordsworth's text from a position of superior insight but of appreciating how much the activity of his text, despite the constraints of its argument, generates such competition. For Geoffrey Hartman, in fact, *The Prelude*'s key questions trope this practice. In a narrative whose 'dominant emphasis' is on scenes of 'dissonance-resolution', Hartman proposes, the 'this' of 'was it for this . . .?' invites attention as a 'metalinguistic' reference to a recurrent turbulence which has now taken the form of an incessant questioning', namely, 'Was it for this kind of questioning . . .?'. This reading of inwrought rhetorical self-reference enacts with a vengeance Gadamer's claim that 'the real and basic nature of a question [is] to make things indeterminate' (Hartman 1990: 338).[19]

This indeterminacy, as well as the rhetorical self-consciousness Hartman describes, emerge most dramatically, and paradoxically, in those passages of *The Prelude* where Wordsworth is advancing a design of interrogative closure, for it is here that the deconstructive tendencies of his imagination are also, characteristically, activated. On these occasions, questions such as 'need I dread from thee/Harsh judgments . . .?' or 'Where is the favoured being?' contrast the blithely rhetorical appropriation of questions in the 'glad preamble' (Wordsworth's later phrase for the poem's opening lines), by generating the sorts of semiotic instability de Man describes when he finds it impossible to decide whether, in the question that closes Yeats's *Among School Children* ('How can we know the dancer from the dance?'), the grammatical model or the rhetorical mood prevails. This is not a case of a figural meaning cancelling a literal meaning (as in the textbook paradigm of 'the rhetorical question'), but of linguistic events in which

> Rhetoric radically suspends logic and opens up vertiginous possibilities of referential aberration . . . two entirely incompatible readings can be made to hinge on one line, whose grammatical structure is devoid of ambiguity, but whose rhetorical mode turns the mood as well as the mode of the entire poem upside down . . . The two readings have to engage each other in direct confrontation, for the one reading is precisely the error denounced by the other and has to be undone by it.
>
> (de Man 1979b: 10, 12)

Applying these terms to Wordsworth's closing questions, we may say that their grammar provokes harsh 'judgments' while the rhetoric denies the possibility; that his grammar searches for a better lost self while his rhetoric defends his present character. The autobiographical argument, that is, is working in two contradictory directions, exemplified figurally by the tensed confrontation of its possible inter-rogative modes.

Such contests between rhetoric and grammar have radical implica-tions, for as Jauss observes, they invite 'a rhetorical interrogation of the literary text . . . that inevitably uncovers the latter's self-contradictory nature, and demonstrates the naïveté of all interpretations that try to locate the meaning of a text in the concordance of signs and meanings' (1989: 84). Jauss's concern is to save a place for literary hermeneutics amid this radical instability, and he does so by making a case for the reader's dialogue with, rather than defeat by, the text's interrogatives – even in such perverse forms as the de Manian rhetorical question. Echoing Hollander's case for poetic questioning, Jauss proposes the category of the 'lyric' or the 'poetic' question. Neither literal nor rhetorical, this mode of asking is projected not to win an answer but to sustain the process of inquiry, 'searching further by asking more'. If literal questioning, following Gadamer, is a dialectic of knowledge, 'the negation of the known . . . is commensurate with the lyric question' (Jauss 1989: 84–5). One instance, of interest to both Jauss and Hollander (Hollander 1988: 37–40) is 'Ubi sunt?', a trope felt implicitly everywhere in The Prelude and heard explicitly at a few key moments. A literal answer, Jauss says, would only be the most banal of responses; a poetic answer takes the question as an evocation whose function is to open 'the closed horizon of the known and unquestionable to the ques-tionable situation of the human being poised between life and death' (Jauss 1989: 86–7).

Jauss concedes that the lyric question is 'predominantly monologic' even when 'question and answer are split into two speaking roles, or when the poem fabricates a dialogue with itself', because such dialogues remain 'within the subjectively experienced world . . . an "I" seems to be speaking only to itself, as if it had no listeners' (1989: 91). As we have seen, Wordsworth contains much of the poetic questioning of The Prelude, no matter how indeterminate in issue, within such monology; and its radically private mode – withheld from public scrutiny and addressed to, but not really in dialogue with, its reader-Friend – cooperates. Even so, the poem's intertextual conversations reveal how this lyric questioning can become uncertainly dialogic, not only in con-versations with precursor texts, but in its risky situation of the reader as a critical audience – one whose interpretation may not be entirely governed by the autobiographer's own orchestration of questions and answers.

I conclude this essay, therefore, by returning to the scene Abrams privileges in his reading of *The Prelude*: its last explicitly punctuated question, in the fourth to last stanza of the Conclusion:

> Having now
> Told what best merits mention, further pains
> Our present purpose seems not to require,
> And I have other tasks. Recall to mind
> The mood in which this labour was begun,
> O Friend! The termination of my course
> Is nearer now, much nearer; yet even then
> In that distraction and intense desire,
> I said unto the life which I had lived,
> Where art thou? Hear I not a voice from thee
> Which 'tis reproach to hear? Anon I rose
> As if on wings, and saw beneath me stretched
> Vast prospect of the world which I had been
> And was; and hence this Song, which like a lark
> I have protracted, in the unwearied heavens
> Singing, and often with more plaintive voice
> To earth attempered and her deep-drawn sighs,
> Yet centring all in love, and in the end
> All gratulant, if rightly understood.
>
> Whether to me shall be allotted life,
> And, with life, power to accomplish aught of worth,
> That will be deemed no insufficient plea
> For having given this story of myself,
> Is all uncertain . . .
>
> (1850, XIV: 371–94)

The autobiographer rehearses a seamless transition between question and response: deliberately reviving the poem's originating questions, which are now history, he represents their positive agency of revelation and inspiration. We note, however, that his question is not so much answered as reviewed in a strategy of omniscience, an evasion that haunts the conditional on which the paragraph concludes – 'if rightly understood' – and pressures the contained, but darkly indeterminate, motions of interrogation that initiate the next, and ante-penultimate, paragraph of the entire poem: 'Whether . . . aught of worth . . . no insufficient . . . all uncertain'. This strain makes the primary texture of

verse in the Conclusion one of transparently suppressed authentic questioning in competition with the bold display of questioning troped in
the rhetoric of affirmation – a competition aggravated by the historical
perspective of the 1850 text, which gives more poignancy to the images
of early expectation and subsequent termination.

The persistent interrogative force of these textual figures and their
immediate contexts against the rhetoric of answering is further enhanced,
and complicated, by the poem's allusive dialogue with precursive texts.
The autobiographer's double petition, 'I said unto the life which I had
lived,/Where art thou? Hear I not a voice from thee/Which 'tis
reproach to hear?' (XIV: 379–81), at once tropes and revises the second
question in biblical history. It is addressed by God to Adam, initiating
an interrogation in which Adam is forced to confess his fault:

> And the LORD God called unto Adam, and said unto him,
> Where *art* thou?
> And he said, I heard thy voice in the garden, and I was afraid,
> because I *was* naked; and I hid myself.
> And he said, Who told thee that thou *wast* naked? Hast thou
> eaten of the tree, whereof I commanded thee that thou shouldest
> not eat?
> And the man said, The woman whom thou gavest *to be* with
> me, she gave me of the tree, and I did eat.
> And the LORD God said unto the woman, What *is* this *that*
> thou hast done? And the woman said, The serpent beguiled me,
> and I did eat.
>
> (Genesis, 3: 9–13)

For Jauss, this primary cultural moment of interrogation is the paradigm
of all 'authoritarian question-and-answer', not only in the archaic world
of myth and legend, but 'extend[ing] well into the social history of the
modern era' (1989: 52). Yet the initial question, he suggests, is
rhetorically indeterminate: God may be speaking ironically, for he
clearly knows where Adam is and why he is hiding; but he may also
be speaking in sympathy with Adam's embarrassment. The ambiguity
arises, Jauss argues, 'from a function of the question-and-answer that
is already aesthetic'. On the one hand, the authoritarian structure
'highlights the theological function of question and answer'; on the
other, the textual 'priority of question and answer, which implies the
precedence of dialogic or monologic discourse, produces a division of
understanding' (1989: 53). The rhetorical ambiguity of God's questioning, even in this apparently authoritarian drama, puts into play a

'literary hermeneutics' that 'pluralizes, and thus stands in opposition to singularizing hermeneutics . . . countering a dominant monologic discourse' (1989: 54). For Jauss, this counteraction is equivalent to critical reading: a reader develops new answers that differ from those presented in the overt structure of the text. This dialogue, in which the text poses a question to the reader's understanding and the reader opposes (or at least wonders about the construction of) the authority of the text's answer, Jauss contends, is an 'aesthetic event . . . repeated in the reception history of all the great myths' (1989: 57): unlike 'a theological hermeneutics that grants an original superiority to the question posed . . . by the text – that is, posed to one's understanding of oneself ("Adam, where art thou?")', an 'aesthetic hermeneutics . . . gives priority to the interpreter's questions – through which the text's answer is constantly revised' (1989: 66).[20]

Jauss's discussion of how this scene of interrogation in Genesis shifts slightly between a theological hermeneutics and an aesthetic hermeneutics helps to illuminate the complexity of Wordsworth's manoeuvring around his allusion. There are two readers: Wordsworth is reading his poem within a grid of an originating question and a revealed logic of answering style; but he is exhorting at least one other reader, which he constructs as its 'Friend' – namely, Coleridge, a historically real Other whose gratulant reading, at least for three decades, could be given a script but could not be prescripted. Certainly by the 1830s, Coleridge was no longer a reader, and 'Friend' had become a general rhetorical category, a figure constructed as a timeless guarantor of Wordsworth's own desire – or, in the term made famous by Stanley Fish's study of *Paradise Lost*, the 'ideal reader'.[21] With the benefit of Jauss, however, we see that texts assume different characters for different readers, and Wordsworth's very effort to determine a script – in Belsey's terms, 'to align the position of the reader with that of the omniscient narrator who is looking back on a series of past events' (Belsey 1980: 77) – suggests his awareness of these sorts of vagaries. As we have seen, Belsey thinks of *The Prelude* as this kind of unproblematic text, in contrast to the interrogative text that brings various 'points of view into unresolved collision or contradiction' (92). There are aspects of this passage that coincide, almost too easily, with this view of *The Prelude*. Like the God of Genesis, Wordsworth's poet asks 'Where art thou?' – somewhat preposterously, for his answer predicates the question. Moreover, the passage seems calculated both to evoke and boldly to reverse the drama of Genesis. Instead of an authoritarian hierarchy, this is an internal dialogue of self-questioning, and the answer, far from justifying an expulsion from Paradise, is self-authorizing and self-elevating, virtually reversing biblical history by returning the self in gratulant closure to harmony with heaven.

Yet this textual conversation with Genesis, once activated, is not securely contained for readers who, while they may appreciate the surrogate position of 'Friend' offered to them by the poem's author, are inclined to refuse this as the single privileged position, and along with it, the authority of 'the Author' over the interpretation of his text – especially when the text presents contradictions and collisions of meaning. Such readers may ironize the text in ways that Wordsworth's risky evocation of Genesis enables – and perhaps provokes, to the degree that he himself was motivated by a desire to criticize his favoured ideology of 'all gratulant' and press harder at the interrogative reserves of 'if rightly understood'. For once we recall Genesis, we may read ironically, ascribing to the autobiographer the evasions and failings against which he means to claim his ascendance. The Adamic drama, having been provoked by allusion, persists as a shadowy countertext, haunting the verse.

It also involves an anterior and parallel scene of questioning, the first one in biblical history, in fact. This is the serpent's relativizing, and thus implicit questioning, of God's authority: 'and he said unto the woman, Yea, hath God said, Ye shall not eat of every tree of the garden' (Genesis, 3:1). Wordsworth's answering action, 'Anon I rose,/As if on wings, and saw beneath me stretched/Vast prospect of the world . . .', oddly implicates this moment, by a detour through the greatest English interpretation of Genesis, *Paradise Lost*, where Milton prefigures this temptation in Eve's Satanically inspired dream:

> Forthwith up to the Clouds
> With him I flew, and underneath beheld
> The Earth outstretcht immense, a prospect wide
> And various . . .

> (V: 86–9)

In the palimpsest of Wordsworth's drama of question and answer is an incipiently errant Eve – in Jauss's terms, a horizon beyond the circuitous harmony of the autobiographer's overt design of self-reading. The intertextual field transforms the autobiographer's closed dialogue into one which, in Jauss's terms, 'serves to reopen the horizon of the questionable' (1989: 118) – especially the questionable authority of the poem's chief voice of interpretation. The effect is to bring the reader's questioning into play as an agent of different interpretation – a capacity

Jauss claims is one of the particular legacies of the Enlightenment, whose progressive 'dialogization' of discourse 'even forced its way into the conventionally monologic genres of literature and rhetoric' (1989: 119) and from which Jauss derives his own project, 'to reestablish the dialogic reciprocity between the text and the present, the inter-preted and the interpreter, through the interplay of question and answer' (1989: 205–6; cf. Jauss 1970–1: 44).

It may be that such recurring contradictions, between Wordsworth's affirmative self-reading and the undermining of those readings his text also produces, expose *The Prelude* as yet another of those Romantic poems whose interrogations, so Belsey argues, are 'unable to theorize the inadequacy of its concept of subjectivity (and committed, indeed, to experience as against theory)' (1980: 23). Whether or not we agree about these limitations, we can still see how much any commitment to theory requires the resource of interrogative texts such as *The Prelude*. Although I have not done so in this essay, there is nothing to prevent a wider application of Wordsworth's interrogative dialectics to the sociohistorical forces shaping both notions of subjectivity and attitudes about history as they are represented in, or excluded from, his auto-biography. Certainly, for the wide-ranging cultural dialogics explored by Jauss, and even for the desire of Belsey 'to seek out the process of production of the text: the organization of the discourses which consti-tute it and the strategies by which it smoothes over the incoherences and contradictions of the ideology inscribed in it' (1980: 129), there is no better practical exploration than *The Prelude*. Here is a text whose interrogative composition is repeated in the attention it continues to solicit from its readers – from Wordsworth himself, to his prescripted Friend and subsequent friendly, and unfriendly, readers, to his modern critical interrogators.

SUPPLEMENT

NIGEL WOOD: Jauss's thesis in *Question and Answer* should be familiar to those who have read Freud or Jameson (*The Political Unconscious*). Freu-dians tend to see interpretation of texts as an analysis of the instigating initial disorder for which the text is some form of compensation and Jameson's 'ideology' is an imaginary fictive resolution of deeply felt con-tradictions. Where does Jauss differ from either of these two positions?

SUSAN WOLFSON: To answer this question with appropriate nuance would require another essay. Briefly and reductively, it seems to me that Jauss is more interested in the conscious processes of critical reading, whereas Jameson and Freud understand texts and readers to be unconsciously motivated – the former positing as collective what the latter locates in individual psyches. The work of analysis for them is the work of recovering what is denied, repressed in the conscious structures of description – for Freud, anxiety, for Jameson, the historical contradictions of social existence. Jauss, too, understands texts as deeply motivated, but has confidence that a process of reading as questioning can not only discern this motivation but also resist manipulation by its dominant discourses. To identify the horizon of the question for Jauss means to release oneself from the closed structure of its knowledge and to activate new ways of understanding. Jauss makes fundamental claims for the aesthetic mode – what he calls 'the dialogic structure of poetic discourse' (1989: 57) – in enabling this deconstructive work. Whereas for Freud, Jauss himself argues, the return of the repressed produces anxiety, in the mediated realm of the aesthetic, it 'provides a peculiar pleasure' (1989: 58).

NW: Would it be an oversimplification of your (and Hollander's) distinction between the 'textual' and the 'rhetorical' to claim that the latter can be referred to an author's conscious intention whereas the former always tends to elude it?

SW: These terms have slippery careers in contemporary theory. I locate them less in terms of intention, which is itself a slippery matter, than of effect. To call a question 'textual' is to view it as embedded in the interpretive structures of writing and reading, and to situate it in relation to other texts (especially those that question) – in short, to understand it as a literary as well as a socially communicative event. To call a question 'rhetorical' (in the old sense of a 'rhetorical question') is to understand it as a trope within a design whose intention is not interrogative: such a question opposes its grammatical and syntactic form (interrogative) to its gesture (a soliciting of assent; a provoking of attention, and so forth) that is not fundamentally inquisitive. These two senses – the question as a textual event, and the susceptibility of its form to rhetorical troping – both inform my understanding of how questions operate as poetic figure. As a poetic figure, a question bears affiliations to literary traditions of questioning and, therefore, a capacity to trope (to evoke and require reading within) these traditions. Some of these tropings involve questions put into play for purposes that are not interrogative; and some enhance an interrogative gesture by the amplifications of other texts.

NW: I would like to hear more about the lead Belsey's comments on page 162 give you in locating this question-and-answer syndrome in a more detailed manner within the Romantic period. How could we say that the Romantics had an inadequate 'concept of subjectivity' and where else can we find it exemplified in the period?

SW: Belsey's charge against Romanticism is that its inability to theorize the inadequacy of its concept of subjectivity left it strung between an alien social and material existence and an increasingly phantasmic belief in subjective autonomy. This theoretical inability (or really, impasse), for her, is legible in the 'absence' that constantly appears at the centre of its poetics of subjective presence, and its telling sign is the elegy or interrogation that usurps the quest for wholeness. She cites the questions that close Keats's 'Ode to a Nightingale' as a case in point. The irony for her is that when these questions imply a subjectivity capable of transcending its social and historical moment, 'refusing the real conditions' of existence, they write a version of that 'liberal humanism which is the ideological ally of industrial capitalism' (Belsey 1980: 123).

No one would disagree with Belsey that the Romantic quest for wholeness and unity of consciousness failed more than it succeeded, and many before her, increasingly with the influence of deconstructive close readings, have attended to the rhetoric of absence, doubt, and questioning in its poetry. Romantic poetry is everywhere implicated with these questionings, as well as ones that destabilize claims to authority. My own book on Wordsworth and Keats treats some of these occasions; Hollander's chapters offer fine readings of poems by these two as well as by Blake. Those who desire a preliminary curriculum might study: 'The Thorn', 'We Are Seven', 'Anecdote for Fathers', 'Ode: Intimations of Immortality', and Book I of *The Excursion* by Wordsworth, Coleridge's *Rime of the Ancient Mariner*, Blake's *Songs of Innocence* and *Songs of Experience*, Shelley's 'Alastor', 'The Sensitive Plant', 'Ode to the West Wind', and 'To a Sky-lark', Keats's 'Isabella', 'La Belle Dame sans Merci', 'Ode on a Grecian Urn', 'Ode to a Nightingale', 'To Autumn'. My resistance to Belsey's remarks has to do with her cartoon of liberal humanism: Romantic poetics does not turn its questions as completely away from the social and material world as she claims, but remains alert to such desire and its implication in the very conditions it would escape.

NW: Is this self-referentiality of *The Prelude*, where Cambridge or the Alps are just items in an autobiographical landscape, true of all texts, or is there some point in gathering some historical contextual information about such references?

SW: The Alps and Cambridge, and even London, have such symbolic functions in *The Prelude* as places of crisis that one almost suspects that these proper names are merely contingent, place-markers in an internalized quest romance. Yet because representation, displacement, and repression are such critical manoeuvres in Wordsworth's poetics of autobiography – and because these gestures themselves at times emerge as subjects of critical contemplation in the poem – it is always worth investigating other accounts of these places in order to get a sense of Wordsworth's difference, and even of the way his text may acknowledge or disclose its special constructedness. Marjorie Levinson's book on *Wordsworth's Great Period*

Poems is exemplary of this contextualizing procedure (as well as of the limitations of not attending carefully enough to the texts in some instances). A more nuanced reading of Wordsworth's texts within their historical contexts is to be found in Manning. Other critics worth reading to learn about the value of situating *The Prelude* in relation to historical contexts are Alan Liu (1989b), and David Simpson (1987).

Endpiece

NIGEL WOOD

According to De Quincey in his *Tait's Edinburgh Magazine* piece on Wordsworth in February 1839, the 'commencement of Wordsworth's entire self-dedication to poetry as the study and main business of his life' can be dated from 1794–5 (De Quincey 1970: 183). If accurate, this is a significant point at which to find one's vocation. The shock for Wordsworth when France declared war on England on 1 February 1793, may be deduced from his *Letter to the Bishop of Llandaff*, written during February and March. The execution of Louis XVI on 21 January had provoked a staunch protest from Bishop Richard Watson, plus a banal piece of patriotism in praise of the British Constitution. Published alongside a reprint of his sermon on 'The Wisdom and Goodness of God in having made both Rich and Poor', the conjunction of revisionist zeal and comfortable complacency nettled Wordsworth considerably – and yet, the letter was unsent and unpublished. It is quite likely that his publisher, Joseph Johnson, albeit publisher of William Godwin, Horne Tooke and Joseph Priestley, was a more prudent judge of the times. Thomas Paine had just been tried in his absence for seditious libel (December 1792) for the temerity to oppose hereditary succession in his *The Rights of Man* (Part 1, 1791; Part 2, 1792). Like the 1805 and other versions of *The Prelude*, the *Letter*'s unpublished state points to many likely areas of unknowable privacy about the early, radical Wordsworth. Revision was a fact of life as well as his art, and yet Wordsworth was hardly alone. In May 1792, the Proclamation against seditious writing made many utter republican sentiments in private.

The other consideration that might have made Wordsworth pause was the changing French situation. Loyalist uprisings, especially involving the Vendean armies, gave the lie to his confidently expressed belief that all 'twenty-five millions of men were convinced of the truth' of the regicide (Owen and Smyser 1974, I: 32). History did not quite provide the platform for confident assertion. Freedom-loving subjects could 'submit without repining to the chastisements of providence . . . But when redress is in our own power and resistance is rational, we suffer with the same humility from beings like ourselves . . .' (Owen and Smyser 1974, I: 36). The opposition to the nobility and even a limited monarchy has a ring of the summer of 1789 – and yet the *Letter* only exists in fair copy in the Grasmere collection (MS. Prose 1). Perhaps this is a potent reminder that the private Wordsworth who knew his audience when it was composed of Dorothy, Sara and (the early) Coleridge could sense a fragility of communication when addressing a less well-defined public. For De Quincey, Wordsworth's road to Damascus was Morecambe Sands, where, on hearing of Robespierre's death, he shouted 'anthems of thanksgiving for this great vindication of eternal justice', while solacing his indignation by 'turning away from politics to studies less capable of deceiving his expectations' (De Quincey 1970: 183; cf. 1805 X: 531–66). It may seem inevitable that, for the poet of sincere simplicity, the private, confessional mode of *The Prelude* was inescapable, and yet, as Marilyn Butler recognizes, this internalizing of response (so dramatically enacted in *The Prelude*), this

> intellectual and spiritual journey [enacted] in terms of the poet's own experience, is also a national epic, since it explicitly weighs the social, secular ideology sustaining the Revolution against the ideology of the conservative powers, which focused more and more effectively upon the emotional appeal of traditional religion.
>
> (Butler 1981: 67)

In the 1790s the political was pervasive; where there was almost lyric grace or a few apparently ungeneric 'Lines', allegorical expectations were still high.

There is a consonance in any case between the acceptance of private destiny in *The Prelude*, and the indispensably subjective reporting of such crucial historical events. For example, it is not just a narrative detail, a functionally redundant circumstance that is presupposed by the needs of an autobiographical faithfulness of recall, that Wordsworth is forced to regard the Revolutionary momentum as commotion and noise. Without a secure share in the French language, Wordsworth is the mute traveller, this despite the 'personal wish/To speak the language more familiarly' (1805, IX: 36–7) when setting out from London. In the metropolis, Wordsworth lived 'obscurely . . ./Not courting the society of men' (1805, IX: 20–1) while 'in the midst of things' (1805, IX: 23). 'Looking as from a distance on the world' does not disfranchise him, as 'False preconceptions were corrected thus,/ And errors of the fancy rectified' (1805, IX: 24, 26–7). Subjectivity is the condition of greater perception, and, when this is breached in *The Prelude*, when the rush of sense perception is described as disturbing this secure (textual) tranquility, he protects himself by withdrawal into a constructed interior drama. The Paris of Book IX is a near neighbour to the London of Book VII, not to the London that precedes it chronologically. From lines 40 to 62 the first acquaintance with Paris forms a catalogue of disconnected items, where Wordsworth stares and listens 'with a stranger's ears' to the 'hubbub wild' of 'hissing factionists' among other 'ant-like swarms/Of builders and subverters' (1805, IX: 55–9). The allusion to Milton's Chaos, that 'universal hubbub wild/Of stunning sounds and voices all confused' (*Paradise Lost*, II: 951), is hardly surprising; this music of humanity is hardly still for a second, until Wordsworth finds himself in the 'open sun' (1805, IX: 64) in the dust of the Bastille.

In the picking up of a stone 'in the guise/Of an enthusiast' he tries to treat it like a religious 'relick' (1805, IX: 66–7), yet the outward observance of homage to what he feels should stir him does not satisfy. The 'various objects' he calls up in remembrance to denote 'the temper of [his] mind as then it was' lack the capacity to summon history quite so well as a painting, Charles le Brun's baroque Mary Magdalene. This 'single picture merely, hunted out/Among other sights' crystallizes and abstracts the movement of history. This symbol owes little to the metonymic logic of the narrative as it has to be 'hunted out', and yet there is another logic at work here. The potential profanity of the failed worshipper at the altar of revolutionary success, with little faith in his 'relick', is consistent with the choice of the tearful Mary Magdalene. Here the Anglican Wordsworth (of 1804–5, of course) confronts the devotional Catholic image, with its highly wrought 'painterly' style, and finds its artifice curiously apposite – but to what end? We had been promised a glance at the temper of Wordsworth's mind (sad at the proleptic death of Revolutionary hope? a love that is profane (Annette Vallon?)), and yet its mimetic accuracy does not turn out to be its eventual function. The le Brun gives delight and supplies recompense for 'the traveller's pains' (1805, IX: 72–80); we are encouraged to entertain the notion that it discloses a desire of Wordsworth's rather than a facet of his thought or situation at this time.

On the stage of history, Wordsworth feels like an actor that has missed his cue. This is no misfortune as he feels 'unconcerned/Tranquil almost, and careless as a flower/Glassed in a greenhouse, or a parlourshrub' during a violent storm (1805, IX: 87–9). Just as the currents of history are brought into view by the le Brun, they are simultaneously abjured by an aesthetic image that supplies the reader with no connection between the first person and the stirring events that are witnessed, yet not quite comprehended.

Those critics interested in returning Wordsworth to history (however defined) are divided over his apparent evasion of consistent political or even cultural interests. As Butler has pointed out, his paradoxical stature is based on the realization that, just as we may discover a historical interest in his more private modes, there are also 'Small islands in the midst of stormy waves' (1805, X: 441), individual tales of moral excellence that have a recuperative value (and fixity) even during the most tempestuous of times. This is the distinctive project of *The Prelude* and yet it differs in emphasis rather than sentiment from the *Salisbury Plain* poems, *Descriptive Sketches* or *An Evening Walk*. Increasingly, Wordsworth's historical imagination, in David Simpson's phrase, is a poetry of 'displacement', in that the subjective and intersubjective are simultaneously associated in the search for a *form* to express them. When the new history refuses to observe generic distinctions between the literary and the non-literary the aim is to rediscover the imaginative or figurative as a 'social practice' in its material influence on the motivations for action, and also to highlight the (presumably temporally produced) structures shared by fictional and non-fictional work. For Simpson, this method takes account of the intersubjective tropes of contemporaneous writing, but is less enabling when the subjective or individual features of writing are to be considered (see Simpson 1987: 10–21).

It is imperative to realize that the discovery of allusion or context does not guarantee its interpretative validity. Alan Liu, in his invaluable study of Wordsworth's 'sense of history', also chooses the Bastille and Magdalene passages as his entry into Book IX. Wordsworth scans the recent scene of stirring history as a tourist, happening on the le Brun in 1791 when he visited Paris's Carmelite convent. As one of the art treasures seized in 1792, this icon of soon-to-be-violated beauty is reminiscent of the interpolated Grande Chartreuse monastery passage of the 1850 *Prelude* (1850, VI: 420–88). Liu's painstaking recreation of the exact provenance of this image, its likely first context which determines certain kinds of seeing, concludes with the idea that the painting is a projection of Wordsworth's hopes for peaceful revolution, the liberation, 'not with the pike thrusts of violence, but with the soft, fluid undulations of a necklace spilling from a box, of clouds rolling through a window, or of the clothes, hair, tears, and body of a woman flowing out of old constraints' (Liu 1989b: 368). In short, he recovers its mimetic force as it no longer comes to resemble a turning away to the privacies of artistic pleasure, but, on the contrary, reads its code of liberation through beauty as very much a non-political comment: 'The search for a "relick" at the Bastille leads him directly to the Carmelite convent; the tour through France becomes a pilgrimage toward a Madonna's beauty bypassing historical reality' (Liu 1989b: 369). Certain awkward details need to be stressed here. Firstly, a Mary Magdalene is not a Madonna (far from it, but Liu does note this in another context (1989b: 371)). Le Brun's *Repentant Magdalene* is ravished by conscience as much as (not more than, note) the Burkean sublime, as Liu would have it. Secondly, the fuller narrative context provides at the very least an alternative function for this detail. As I read the turn to the icon of exquisite beauty I find it stages the drama of withdrawal in a contrastive process where the various broken shards of Bastille walls and the serpentine hissing of political agitation meet the simplicities of contemplative pleasure. This, too, is a *historical* gesture, in that it is inscribed within a precise historical moment; the 'evasion' is a response to events that have public weight and validity. The energy of the Baroque style may project the image and involve the viewer in the personal drama of repentance, yet the point of the contrast with the incomprehensible Parisian street scenes is that the frame, ensuring its artistic unity perhaps, is regarded as the *ne plus ultra* of even the most pyrotechnic of readings. Revolutionary reality is bad art. When Liu proceeds to contextualize the le Brun further, he finds that the young Wordsworth had probably misread the sublime beauty of the image, and thus 'the beauty of the revolution' (Liu 1989b: 369). Was Wordsworth a bad reader of the painting, or just not interested in (or lacking immediate narrative function for) the admittedly fascinating wealth of possibilities that Liu discovers? This is the victory of context over text. There is more force to the depiction of framed and comprehensible art if the image does extend to embrace the sensibilities of the spectator. Not only is this a reading of Wordsworth's own gaze at the le Brun that is more consistent with the contours of Book IX's narrative, it also helps to produce a reading of the work where Wordsworth's *dramatic* presentation of events is seen to leave open the possibility of self-irony.

The practical consequences of textualizing 'context' have been explored in Wordsworth criticism of the last decade or more. If we elide text and context too completely we are no longer able to retain some discrimination as to *which* contextual items are operative in our encounter with the text. Context is boundless; the point about the recourse to history and the search for contextual information is to rescue texts from such frameless incomprehensibility. Otherwise we may be left with shards that we try to pocket up yet at the same time find mute in any but the private associations with which we try to transform them.

This view is not designed to represent any informing *ethos* for the collection. For Philip Shaw and Jon Cook the historical status of *The Prelude* implies two-way traffic between a text and history. Put simply, the superficially apolitical description of landscape, for Shaw, exhibits a response to the hidden historical forces that have shaped it. Cook's detailed reading of the sometimes abrupt transitions in the narrative reminds us of the experimental risks that Wordsworth felt he was taking. Casting off from the security of writing within a recognized genre, he explores possible discontinuities in the self. In the essay by Susan Wolfson the dialogue between reader and text, which is an integral part of the search for meanings that are not centrally located, implicitly undermines a faith in a stable 'text'. More operative is the 'horizon' of possibilities activated in the process of reading, a process whereby our full answers to the staged questions of a text can invalidate the determining authority of the original question. In such a fashion do texts take on an autonomy that is not grounded on historical fact alone. For Clifford Siskin the rules of our critical discourse produce *The Prelude*. The desire to break through the hermeneutic circle to the 'text', apparently freed from the doubt of relativity, is itself the false promise of the critical enterprise. For example, command over the text often impels the professional student and academic to reify (treat as a discoverable object) *a* text of the poem, when, in fact, that is a false historical proposition, as *The Prelude* takes in several tributary manuscripts and editorial interventions.

There has been an attempt to render the *practice* of theory for the needs of this series an open and neutral programme, and yet *The Prelude* provides certain challenges to the concentration on individual texts that is one of its organizing features. To find a central 'text' of *The Prelude* involves preliminary critical choice. What comes to light when we concentrate on the several versions of *the poem* is the *fact* of its multiple existence, how the process of its creation permeates the internal testimony of the verse as well as all considerations of its poetic context. Perhaps what we are left with is some object of study that is not just the nominal effect of the reading public's need to have a convenient reading text. It could be that we are in fact inescapably studying a 'context' for the various forms of the poem as we read closely. The study of the single 'text' has a powerful redeeming feature, however, in that the inevitable questions this emphasis will pose for the reader are some form of guarantee that we actually come to be acquainted with the *reasons* we discover for our answers.

Notes

Introduction

1 Gittings ascribes the strength of the anti-Wordsworth sentiments to
Haydon's 'megalomaniac tendencies' which drove him to cap Leigh Hunt's
gossip about the meeting (Gittings 1968: 251). See also Gill 1990: 326–8;
and Jack Stillinger's 'Wordsworth and Keats', in Kenneth R. Johnston and
Gene W. Ruoff (eds), *The Age of William Wordsworth: Critical Essays on
the Romantic Tradition* (New Brunswick, NJ, 1987), pp. 172–6. Haydon
recounts another critical meeting on 3 January 1818, when Keats called
around to Mortimer Street on an impulse only to be kept waiting while
Wordsworth dressed for dinner with John Kingston, the deputy comp-
troller of the Stamp Office. Keats was apparently much dismayed at Wordsworth's stiff collar, frilled dress-shirt and silk stockings – all to impress a
civil servant (Haydon 1960–3, II: 175).

2 Coleridge suspected that the sentiments of Wordsworth's Preface to his
Poems (1815) had been very much his own. Indeed, *Biographia Literaria* was
planned for 1815 publication, but grew to have broader aims, that is, to
provide an apology for Coleridge's whole literary career. In Chapter XXII,
therefore, he emphasizes the areas where he and Wordsworth part company in aesthetic matters. The poet of the *Lyrical Ballads* has an inconstancy
of style and an attitudinizing matter-of-factness that veers into redundant
circumstantial details. Overall, there is a bathos that derives from providing
low life with dramatic grandeur (see 1983, II: 119–42).

3 The very opposite to Coleridge's opinion. See his letter to Richard Sharp
of 15 January 1804: Wordsworth is 'the first and greatest philosophical

poet, the only man who has effected a complete and constant synthesis of thought and feeling and combined them with poetic forms' (Coleridge 1956–71, II: 1034).

4 See Owen 1985b: 5–10, plus: 'The reading text of the "final" version of *The Prelude* in this edition is an eclectic one' (1985b: 11) and 'The reading text in this edition is an editorial construct . . .' (Owen 1985b: 19). See also *P*, 525–6, for some indication of those changes probably made by Wordsworth's executors.

5 In the second edition to de Selincourt 1926: xlvii. Darbishire lays great store by Coleridge's gift to Lady Beaumont of 'the first two parts of the biographical, or philosophical-biographical Poem to be prefixed or annexed to the Recluse' (26 March 1804; 1956–71, II: 1104).

6 The fullest account is in Reed 1991, I: 11–15. For a comprehensive study of the construction of the 1805 version of *The Prelude*, see Johnston 1984: 100–18. For a sceptical view of the existence of this 'Five-Book' version, see Jarvis (1981).

7 Hirsch's procedure here has been perceptively challenged by William Ray, who distrusts the narrowing of meaning promoted by the constant recourse to some constituting whole that subsumes its parts (Ray 1984: 98–103):

> To the extent that Hirsch's fragmentation of meaning never considers how an individual trait in an individual reading might subvert the whole meaning of the work and even the whole class of which the work seems to be a member, it can be thought of as conservative. What it conserves is the text of literary history, the set of classes presumed to furnish us our initial intuitions (intrinsic genre guesses) as well as the narrower subsets that help us refine those intuitions.
>
> (Ray 1984: 99)

8 See the mention in the 1799 Second Part of:

> these times of fear,
> This melancholy waste of hopes o'erthrown,
> . . . 'mid indifference and apathy
> And wicked exultation, when good men
> On every side fall off we know not how
> To selfishness, disguised in gentle names
> Of peace and quiet and domestic love . . .
>
> (478–84)

a virtually direct versification of Coleridge's thoughts in his letter of advice in September 1799 (see p. 6).

9 William Godwin's *Enquiry Concerning Political Justice, and its Influence on Morals and Happiness* (1793) engages Burke's *Reflections* in a protracted dialogue; for example, Book III, Chapter vii questions the very basis on which we owe or choose to give obedience to superior temporal powers:

Man is in a state of perpetual mutation. He must grow either better or worse, either correct his habits or confirm them . . . By its very nature positive institution has a tendency to suspend the elasticity and progress of mind. Every scheme for embodying imperfection must be injurious.

(Butler 1984: 160)

10 It also ought to be pointed out that the 1850 version has been regarded as a more finished and regular piece. For a general survey of the precedural problems, see Gill (1983), and Stillinger (who champions the retention of interest in the later Wordsworth). For a staunch rejection of the 1850 version, see Wordsworth 1982: 328–31. See also the debate in *The Wordsworth Circle* (1986), and the exchange between Jeffrey Baker and Robert Young in *The Wordsworth Circle* (1982).

11 Recent textual criticism has addressed this problem in ways that show a break with romantic individualism. See Jerome McGann's *A Critique of Modern Textual Criticism*:

Authority is a social nexus, not a personal possession; and if the authority for specific literary works is initiated anew for each new work by some specific artist, its initiation takes place in a necessary and integral historical environment of great complexity . . . [involving] the conventions and enabling limits that are accepted by the prevailing institutions of literary production.

(1983a: 48)

12 A full account can be found in Stephen Gill's *Wordsworth: The Prelude* (Cambridge, 1991), pp. 94–8. See also Lee Erickson, 'The Egoism of Authorship: Wordsworth's Poetic Career', *Journal of English and Germanic Philology*, 89 (1990), 37–50.

13 For example, David Punter's *The Romantic Unconscious: A Study in Narcissism and Patriarchy* (1989), where this self-regard

validates our claims to an emotionality which, we sense, is being exiled by the blast furnaces outside the windows of our fantasies; because, even more peculiarly, it gives us the belief that, if we have nothing else to call our own, at least we are privileged with an inalienable and individual set of fantasies . . .

(p. 13)

14 I would not wish to give the impression that both Levinson and Simpson are identical in their readings of Wordsworth, or that they stimulate a distaste of his poetry because of this process of 'displacement', which occurs pervasively in all kinds of expression – indeed, any critical project that warrants a full rendition of 'Reality' is a procedural impossibility.

Levinson is critical of writers such as Harold Bloom, Geoffrey Hartman and Paul de Man who have 'seized as their Wordsworthian truth the great epistemological and ontological arguments of the poetry' which leads to a narrowing of 'an already idealized canon' so as to rule out 'properly historical interrogations' (Levinson 1986: 6–7). The alienation from nature is so deeply felt by Wordsworth that it appears as some 'Other', 'ominous in its meaninglessness': 'more simply, Mind discovers its power to impress itself . . . upon the landscape and thereby to annihilate that first and miniatory gaze which fixes man as the intruder. Nature objectifies man who thereby finds his subjectivity, with which he then endows Nature'. The relation is not achieved by a perception of continuity, but rather 'catastrophe' (Levinson 1986: 124–5; see David Ferry's review in *Studies in Romanticism*, 30 (1991), 113–20, and the Introduction to Levinson *et al.* (1989: 1–17).

Simpson's awareness of the mind's perception (as opposed to the corporeal eye) leads him to investigate the conjunction of 'intention' and 'desire' in poetic perception, and also to find some link with the social aspect of expression (Simpson 1982: xi–xxvii; on *The Prelude*, see especially 49–68). Though directed less to analyses of *The Prelude*, Simpson's *Wordsworth's Historical Imagination* (1987) can be fruitfully applied to the poem. His 'materialist approach' always insists 'on going beyond and behind the surface of language to discover a system of energies that are not to be conjured away into merely additional fictions and substitutions. Mirror upon mirror is *not* all the show' (Simpson 1987: 19).

15 In my summary of recent critical positions I have not made much of Geoffrey Hartman's contribution, mainly for the sake of illustrating those alternative expressions of the 'idealist' and 'historicist' positions. Hartman's *Wordsworth's Poetry, 1787–1814* (1964) is hard to place within this argument. His concern with 'the individual poem, the sequence of the poems, and the generic relation of poetry to the mind' (Hartman 1987b: ix) is formalist in that it attends to questions of genre, yet its basic premise that literary genres can be equated with transindividual habits of thought does attempt to place *The Prelude* in the *spiritual* world:

> *The Prelude* tells us what lies behind fiction: the hope that the hopes of man can be wedded to this earth . . . his trust in Nature remains a trust in the human mind, which finds inexhaustible rewards in the world, and is renewed by natural rather than supernatural means . . . his abiding bitterness at England's betrayal is due to the fact that it deprived many of his generation of [an] ordinary food of hope ['supernatural' ideals], that it forced them toward violent schemes and vain imaginings.
>
> (Hartman 1987b: 259)

See also Hartman's 'A Poet's Progress: Wordsworth and the *Via Naturaliter Negativa*' (1962, rep. *P*. 598–613) and 'Words, Wish, Worth' (in Hartman 1987a: 90–119). From Hartman's perspective, Wordsworth's 'displacement' of history is no evasion.

16 See the note to the passage in, *P*, 142, and the text of the original lines in Beth Darlington's contribution to Jonathan Wordsworth (ed.), *Bicentenary Wordsworth Studies* (Ithaca, NY, 1970), pp. 433–7.

17 The act in question is/was Gilbert's Act 1782 (22 Geo. III.c.83), where parishes were permitted to combine for more effective policing of the poor and destitute. Only the infirm were to be committed to the workhouse. The able-bodied were to be found work with wages supplemented from parish poor rate. 'Guardians' administered this relief, usually with swingeing directness. The 'Speenhamland' system of 1795, named after the justices in Speenhamland, Berkshire, aimed to supplement wages on a sliding scale dictated by the prevailing price of bread. Both were open to local abuse, and were to create a permanently deprived underclass, 'thankful' for instituted (not instinctive) charity. See also Robin Jarvis, 'Wordsworth and the Use of Charity', in Copley and Whale 1992: 200–17.

18 For a more comprehensive account of the political context, see Emsley 1979: 22, 54 and 81.

19 For examples of how this can be brought to practice, see Onorato 1971: 100–15; Rzepka 1986: 31–71, and Ellis 1985: 17–34.

20 This is given focus in Jacobus 1989: 14–16. See Young 1979, and, for a less Lacanian emphasis, see Stoddard 1985.

1 Paul de Man and Imaginative Consolation

1 The first scholarly text of the 1805 *Prelude* was edited by Ernest de Selincourt. His text is based upon two manuscripts of the poem, divided into thirteen books, and written out in 1805–6, one by Wordsworth's sister Dorothy, the other by his sister-in-law, Sarah Hutchinson. Wordsworth began writing the poem early in 1798. He worked on it throughout his stay in Germany in 1799. An early version of the poem, the two-part *Prelude*, completed in 1799, includes material from the first two books of the 1805 *Prelude*, but also contains material included in Book XI of the 1805 text. After a short break Wordsworth returned to work on the poem early in 1804 and completed its thirteen books by May 1805. He revised the poem on many occasions after the completion of the 1805–6 manuscript versions, and a number of subsequent manuscript texts survive, including one written up between 1817–19, another in 1832, and yet another in 1839. A complete text of the poem was published shortly after Wordsworth's death in 1850.

2 For some of the argument here, see Abrams 1953; Abrams 1971; Aers *et al.* 1981; Marilyn Butler 1981; and McGann 1983b.

3 For Johnson's strictures on metaphysical wit, see his life of Cowley. The relevant excerpt can be found in an accessible edition in *Samuel Johnson: Selected Writing*, ed. P. Cruttwell (Harmondsworth, 1968) pp. 403–6.

4 For the distinction between fancy and imagination see Coleridge's *Biographia Literaria*, first published 1817, especially Chapters IV, XII, XIII (1983, I: 69–88; 232–306.); and Wordsworth's 1815 Preface to *Poems, including Lyrical Ballads* published in two volumes. (Owen and Smyser 1974; III: 26–39).

5 Coleridge wrote extensively about symbolism. For this particular quotation see 1972: 30. For MacLeish, see his essay 'In Challenge, not Defense', in *A Time to Speak* (Boston, 1941), p. 4.

6 For Coleridge's disturbance, see 1983, II: 139–41.

7 De Selincourt gives the manuscript identification A2 to the passage about the Chartreuse monastery. This makes it a correction to the 1805 manuscript identified as A. According to de Selincourt, 'the whole account of Wordsworth's impressions at the Chartreuse had its inception at Coleorton, and arose out of a conversation with Coleridge after reading this book to him on his visit there (Dec. 1806 – Feb. 1807)' (De Selincourt 1926: 539). In the Norton edition of *The Prelude*, Wordsworth, Abrams and Gill do not print the lengthy account of the Chartreuse monastery as part of the 1805 text. They note the anticipation of the passage in *Descriptive Sketches*, but argue that 'Wordsworth did not compose for *The Prelude* an account of the "convent" of Chartreuse, the Carthusian monastery near Grenoble, until 1816/1819' (*P*, 208). At the least the passage cannot be unproblematically assimilated to the 1805 text, as de Man seems to do.

2 Romantic Space

1 Elisée Reclus was a late nineteenth-century social geographer. Due to his involvement in the Paris Commune and his active support of the anarcho-communist movement, he was exiled to Switzerland, from where he produced his major works as well as numerous articles on political subjects for journals such as *Le Révolté* and *La Liberté*. A brief but very useful commentary on Reclus can be found in Ross 1988: 90–4, 98n.

2 Oddly enough, Marxist historians owe their distrust of 'spatial fetishism' to the idealist philosophy of Immanuel Kant. To sum up very briefly, space, for Kant, is not 'a real ground of things' but a purely 'formal condition' (Kant 1989, II: 65). As such, it belongs 'to the *a priori* realm of consciousness (i.e. of the "subject") and par[takes] of that realm's internal, ideal – and hence transcendental and essentially ungraspable structure' (Lefebvre 1991: 2). In line, therefore, with the general trend of post-Cartesian thought, Kantian space can be defined as 'mental space': unchanging, universal and absolute. Its existence cannot be deduced from the empirical 'finality' of objects in the world, what Kant refers to in a classic example as the 'order and regularity in the trees, flower-beds, and walks in the garden'. For Kant these are external things that 'to be cognized must

be given empirically', reduced, in other words, to objects of historical consciousness. A concept of space on the other hand, if it is to be defined as an 'intellectual finality' (that is, as transcendental), must be given 'according to [an internal] principle . . . a form of intuition which . . . is only found in ourselves, and found *a priori* as a representation' (Kant 1989, II: 9). In this manner, through the negative relation of unattainability – 'something lying beyond' – mental space can function as a category without itself being implicated in the structures for which it stands as a presupposition. As a result, therefore, physical space ceases to be of any concern to either philosophical Idealism or Marxism.

3 See, for example, Kristin Ross on the Communards' levelling of the Colonne Vendôme (Ross 1988: 5–8).

4 For more on this concept see Lefebvre 1971.

5 The quote is from Foucault, 'Of Other Spaces' (1986: 22). In *Postmodern Geographies*, 16–21, Soja argues convincingly that space was always at the heart of Foucault's concerns.

6 I have adopted these terms from Harold Rosenberg (1982). For an application to a reading of Romantic space, see Geoffrey Ward, 'Byron's Artistry in Deep and Layered Space' in Beatty and Newey 1988: 191–225. See also the analysis of Thomson's 'Spring' in Barrell 1988: 108–18.

7 Heidegger's space centres on the identity of the home, or shelter with being: 'Dwelling is the basic character of Being in keeping with which Mortals exist' ('Building Dwelling Thinking', in Heidegger 1971: 160). The relationship between Heidegger's and Wordsworth's concern with Being and Dwelling has been fruitfully explored by Geoffrey Hartman (see especially 'Wordsworth before Heidegger', in 1987a: 194–206). The translation of Collin's verdict is Gabriel Josipovici's, in his introduction to Blanchot 1982: 16.

8 'The passage concerned was transcribed by DW [Dorothy Wordsworth] in the manuscript commonly known as 18A (DC MS. 16)' (Owen 1985b, 115).

9 For a more detailed and favourable reading of Bachelard, see Jamie Brassett, 'The Spaced-out Subject' in Shaw and Stockwell, 146–58. Brassett's Ph.D. thesis, as yet unpublished, provides a rigorously Deleuzean structure for the study of social space.

10 Lefebvre's position on language and the body is very similar to Bakhtin's. In brief, Bakhtin's theory of language as social discourse is developed as a counter-response to the mental abstractions of Saussure's *la langue*. Rather than examining a fixed, invariable system of grammatical rules, dialogism looks at the ways in which the rules are actually used: the concrete circumstances in which words are exchanged, modified and adapted by speakers (see Bennett 1979: 75–82).

Bakhtin's materialist reading of the sign is linked to his treatment of the body which he divides into 'classical' and 'grotesque' forms. In the classical body, the accent is on self-completion, abstraction and isolation. As such, it represents state power in its purest, most abstract form. By contrast, the grotesque body is incomplete, multiple and collective. If the classical body stresses discipline and hierarchy, the grotesque body emphasizes the irrational and anarchic. At large in the social space of the street, or carnival, it poses a threat to any form of elitist self-representation. See Bakhtin's *Rabelais and His World* (1984). See also the later work of Michel Foucault, e.g. 1979a and 1981-7. An interesting discussion of the body in literary and artistic representations is offered in Barker 1984.

11 See especially Clark 1984 and Barrell 1986.

12 See Benjamin's essay, 'Surrealism', in Benjamin 1978: 179.

13 There are a number of possible sources for the descriptions of the panorama exhibit. The Norton *Prelude* (*P*, 240, n. 5) notes that Wordsworth may have visited Thomas Girtin's *Eidometropolis*, a view of London painted from · Blackfriars' Bridge and put on show in 1802. Owen (1985b: 143) proposes the influence of J.P. De Loutherbourg's *Eidophusikon* (1782) with its depiction of 'the Rising of the Palace of Pandemonium' from *Paradise Lost*. It seems, however, that Wordsworth arrived too late in London to view this work. A more likely source is Robert Barker's *London from the roof of the Albion Mills*. This famous panorama, which was displayed in Castle Street and then Leicester Square from 1791 to 1796, coincides with Wordsworth's sojourns from 1791-2.

   For more on the history of panaroma exhibitions see Hyde 1988.

14 See especially the opening of *Trivia*, Book I:

> Through Winter Streets to steer your Course aright,
> How to walk clean by Day, and safe by Night,
> How jostling Crouds, with Prudence, to decline,
> When to assert the Wall, and when resign,
> I sing . . .
>
> (I: 1-5)

The going gets much tougher by Book III, but, in the midst of the city's conflagration, the perceiving subject is still the spectator/bystander. I intend to examine the relationship between Augustan and Romantic space in a subsequent paper.

3 Working *The Prelude*

1 See my analysis of the Romantic function of the *oeuvre* in Chapter 5 of Siskin 1988: 94-124. Arguments regarding the Romantic nature of traditional criticism of the Romantics can also be found in McGann 1983a.

2 This question haunts all of literary studies now that the Cornell Wordsworth project, and other reclamations of past writing, have provided us

with so many versions of so many texts. The object of critical knowledge and the modes of knowing it – the organic unity and the ways it has been appreciated and/or interpreted – are no longer self-evident. What are we supposed to do with all of this material? We need theory to rethink the classification of writing called 'literature' and the forms of work that classification authorizes.

3 The historian, Lynn Hunt, has observed, for example, that the proliferation of new scholarship on the history of the body is due to three factors: 'feminism, Foucault, and interdisciplinary studies' (Heller 1991: A8).

4 The point of speaking historically about the Author as a 'function' that is 'far from immutable' ('We can easily imagine a culture where discourse would circulate without any need for an author' (Foucault 1977: 138)) is not, as Foucault emphasizes and his less able critics insist, to deny that it exists; rather, it is to clarify its importance as a way of classifying and working with discourse. 'Of course,' wrote Foucault,

> it would be ridiculous to deny the existence of individuals who write, and invent. But I think that, for some time, at least, the individual who sits down to write a text, at the edge of which lurks a possible *oeuvre*, resumes the functions of the author. What he writes and does not write, what he sketches out, even preliminary sketches for the work, and what he drops as simple mundane remarks, all this interplay of differences is prescribed by the author-function.
>
> (1972: 222)

For critics to find meanings only through this prescription is to leave whole categories of meanings and discursive functions unexplored. The meanings of poetry, for example, can be sought, as David Simpson points out, 'as much in the interrelations of the language of poetry with the languages of contemporary argument and expression as in the corporate identity of the Author' (1982: xxvi).

5 In addition to Patterson, the following sources are also useful in tracking the history of copyright: Rose 1988; Rogers 1989; Walters 1974; Belanger 1982; Feather 1984; Woodmansee 1984; Meyers and Harris 1985; Plant 1965; Wiles 1957, and Ross 1990.

6 The questions are reprinted in Patterson 1968: 175.

7 In Siskin 1988, I inquire generically into the fourteen-book *Prelude* as a sonnet; Book VIII would then contain the turn from octet to sestet (122).

8 For an exploration of how 'ironic spirals' map our 'complex cultural plane', see Livingston 1990.

4 'Answering Questions and Questioning Answers'

1 Quintilian, *Institutio Oratoria*, 9.2.6. I am indebted to Hollander's study for bringing Quintilian's consideration of the issue to my attention. The two verbs of this question on questions produce slightly different emphases of energy and intensity: *interrogare* denotes the simply interrogative mood, *to ask*, but also extends into the more coercive and insistent force of *to interrogate*, especially in a judicial proceeding; *percontari* (derived from *contus*, a pole used for sounding), although it, too, means *inquire, interrogate, question*, is pointed towards a more freely investigative sense.

2 I have worked out the basic lines of this approach to *The Prelude* in two chapters of *The Questioning Presence*; in a subsequent essay (1990), I considered, with attention to the interrogative textures of other poems, the implications of some recent New Historicist critiques of Wordsworth's ·poetry. The concern of this present essay is to elaborate my continued thinking about *The Prelude* in relation to important general discussions of interrogative poetics.

3 My attention to the fictionalizing of 'result' in this passage is indebted to Vogler 1971: 16–17.

4 A note in the Norton critical edition of *The Prelude* (*P*, 1) refers to 'correspondence in *TLS*, April–September 1975' which details these antecedents. Jonathan Wordsworth gives the Miltonic formula fuller consideration in Wordsworth 1982: 36–7 and 420 n. 3. The 'allusively evocative' character of this question and its reference to a specific rhetorical tradition – with a particular concentration on Virgilian instances and resonances – has been given a full explication by John Hodgson.

5 The passage can be found at 1805, XIII: 1–119 and 1850, XIV: 1–129. Abrams identifies a tripartite structure: 'a process of mental development which, although at times suspended, remains a continuum', followed by 'a crisis of apathy and despair', and then the mind's recovery of an 'integrity which, despite admitted losses, is represented as a level higher than the initial unity' as a result of 'the critical experiences it has undergone' (Abrams 1971: 77). The moonlight's flash 'upon the turf' (1805, XIII: 39–40) contributes to a 'total scene' which is 'the perfect image of a mighty mind' (1805, XIII: 69) 'in its free and continuously creative reciprocation with its milieu' (Abrams 1971: 78).

6 Oh, who is he that hath his whole life long
Preserved, enlarged, this freedom in himself?
For this alone is genuine liberty.
Witness, ye solitudes, where I received
My earliest visitations (careless then
Of what was given me), and where now I roam,
A meditative, oft a suffering man . . .

(1805, XIII: 120–6)

7 Wordsworth's representation of this crisis as a collapse of questioning gains a kind of epochal resonance from the fact that, as Jauss reports, the French Revolution was ushered in by a plethora of documents cast in the mode of catechistic, didactic questioning and easily remembered answers (1989: 78–9). Among these was a 1787 translation of Rousseau's *Contrat social* into an explicitly titled *Catéchisme* of questions and answers.

8 Culler, as we have seen, makes a similar point about the intertextual character of presuppositions. A full consideration of this issue is offered by Michel Meyer, who contends that 'the interpretation of literary texts consists first of all in reading the questions embodied in them' and second, that reading itself is 'a questioning process' (Meyer 1983: 7). Meyer resists Gadamer's claim, however, 'that the questions that give access to textual meaning must be found either in the text and/or in the author and argues that there 'is no necessary or intrinsic adequation between an author's questions and the textual answer that arises from them' (1983: 165).

9 In his introduction to *Toward an Aesthetic of Reception* (1986 esp. xvff.), de Man offers an interesting critique of this early phase of Jauss's reception aesthetics, in particular, its resistance to examining 'linguistic factors that threaten to interfere with the synthesizing power of the historical model' (1982: xvii): 'characteristic' of Jauss's method, de Man argues, is his 'lack of interest, bordering on outright dismissal, in any considerations derived from . . . the "play" of the signifier, semantic effects produced on the level of the letter rather than of the word or the sentence and which therefore escape from the network of hermeneutic questions and answers' (1982: xix).

10 For overviews of this history of reception, see *P*, 522–4 ('1850 versus 1805'); 541–64 ('The Early Reception'); and 567–85 (Jonathan Wordsworth's argument for the value of 'The Two-Part *Prelude* of 1799'). Jonathan Arac's essay, 'Bounding Lines: *The Prelude* and Critical Revision', contextualizes the debates about *The Prelude* typified in the 1960s and 1970s by the divergent readings of Geoffrey Hartman and M.H. Abrams in relation to the different nineteenth-century senses of Wordsworth presented by Arnold and Bradley. Arnold's *Memorial Verses* (1850) celebrates a Wordsworth whose,'soothing voice' (1979: 35) in the 'iron time' (43) of the 1850s 'spoke, and loosed our heart in tears' (47): 'Wordsworth's healing power' is one 'to make us feel' and to 'put . . . by' the 'cloud of mortal destiny' (67–8). This predisposition makes him discount the rather different effects of reading *The Prelude* in his Preface to the *Poems of Wordsworth* (1879) see Arnold (1979b). Bradley's essay, 'Wordsworth', quotes Arnold in order to 'dissent' from his 'picture' of Wordsworth (Bradley: 107–9) and to focus attention on a poet beset, especially in *The Prelude*, by 'perplexity', 'apprehension' (132) and 'visionary feeling' of a 'peculiar tone' (135).

11 De Man's articulation of this rhetoric of temporality in this essay emerges,

in fact, from his quarrel with how Gadamer's hermeneutics 'makes the valorization of symbol at the expense of allegory coincide with the growth of an aesthetic that refuses to distinguish between experience and the representation of this experience' (1983b: 188).

12 For Jauss's critiques of Gadamer on this point, see (1970–1: 30–2; his Preface to 1982a: xxxvi; and 1989: 200–7, 213–14.

13 White describes one of the devices of history as 'explanation by emplotment': 'Histories (and philosophies of history as well) combine a certain amount of "data", theoretical concepts for "explaining" these data, and a narrative structure for their presentation. . . . they contain a deep structural content which is generally poetic' (White 1973: ix–x).

14 Cf. Meyer: 'Literature raises questions through textuality' and its practices 'provide answers that suppress the "questionhood" of the ideas invoked. . . . As a result, texts have an ideological bearing, either by rais-
· ing questions that ideologies are reluctant to acknowledge as questionable or by raising questions whose answers reinforce ideologies by exemplifying them' (Meyer 1983: 113); 'Quite obviously, this process enables the logic of ideology to meet the challenge of answering all questions while never itself being questioned as an ideology' (102). Jauss, in a nice turn of phrase that emphasizes reception, calls this 'culinary', or 'entertainment', art, in which all problems are solved 'in an edifying manner as predecided questions' (1970–1: 25).

15 For my thinking about this paradox of multiplying and infinitely regressing selves, I am indebted to an unpublished essay by Ronald Levao.

16 The Norton editors refer Wordsworth's damning self-description to the parable of the talents (Matthew, 25: 14–30), which, as Wordsworth is acutely aware, is also Milton's point of reference in the interrogative dialogue that structures Sonnet XIX, 'When I consider how my light is spent'.

17 These suggestive terms are Culler's (1981b: 183).

18 In October 1803, Coleridge is pleased to report to Thomas Poole that Wordsworth 'has at length yielded to my urgent & repeated – almost unremitting – requests & remonstrances – & will go on with the Recluse exclusively – A Great Work' (1956–71, II: 1013). His confidence was clearly premature: by May 1815 (a year after the *Excursion* and its faintly apologetic Preface), he politely tells Wordsworth himself that he 'looked forward to the Recluse, as the *first* and *only* true Phil. Poem in existence (1956–71, IV: 574); when he published *Biographia Literaria* in 1817, his anticipation had acquired an elegiac tone: 'What Mr. Wordsworth *will* produce, it is not for me to prophesy: but I could pronounce with liveliest convictions what he is capable of producing. It is the FIRST GENUINE PHILOSOPHICAL POEM' (1956–71, II: 155–6).

19 Although he appreciates the thesis of R.G. Collingwood that 'one can understand a text only when one has understood the question to which it

is an answer', Gadamer suggests that Collingwood uncritically credits authorial intention as the 'answer' to be discovered, finding it 'methodologically unsound to differentiate between the question to which the text is imagined to be an answer and the question to which it really is an answer' (Gadamer, 335). In terms of how we read *The Prelude*, we might say that Collingwood represents the method most forcefully advanced by M.H. Abrams, in which Wordsworth's self-reading provides the paradigm for critical interpretation.

20 Later in this study, Jauss takes up Genesis 3 as an extended case study of the aesthetic application of question and answer, showing how a scene which appears to answer 'an elementary question in advance and for all time to come . . . acquires an enigmatic narrative complexity' (1989: 95) which generates and responds to 'a whole series of other questions, because the mythic event, in serving as answer, constantly generates new questions' (1989: 96–7).

21 See especially Fish's account of Milton's 'harassment' of the reader (1967: 38–56) and his manipulation of her/his guilt (1967: 142–57).

References

Unless otherwise stated, place of publication is London.

Abrams, M.H. (1953) *The Mirror and the Lamp: Romantic Theory and the Critical Tradition.* Oxford.

Abrams, M.H. (1971) *Natural Supernaturalism: Tradition and Revolution in Romantic Literature.* New York.

Aers, David, Cook, Jon and Punter, David (1981) *Romanticism and Ideology: Studies in English Writing, 1765–1830.*

Althusser, Louis (1971) *Lenin and Philosophy and Other Essays*, trans. Ben Brewster.

Amory, Hugh (1984) *De Facto* copyright? Fielding's *Works* in partnership, 1769–1821, *Eighteenth-Century Studies*, 17: 449–76.

Arac, Jonathan (1979) Bounding lines: *The Prelude* and critical revision, *Boundary*, 7: 31–48.

Arac, Jonathan (1987) *Critical Genealogies: Historical Situations for Postmodern Literary Studies.* New York.

Armstrong, Isobel (1981) Wordsworth's complexity: repetition and doubled syntax in *The Prelude*, Book VI, *Oxford Literary Review*, 4: 20–42.

Armstrong, Nancy (1987) *Desire and Domestic Fiction: A Political History of the Novel.* New York.

Arnold, Matthew (1979a) *Arnold: The Complete Poems*, ed. Kenneth Allott; 2nd edn, Miriam Allott.

Arnold, Matthew (1979b) *Poetry and Criticism of Matthew Arnold*, ed. A. Dwight Culler. Boston, MA.

Bachelard, Gaston (1969) *The Poetics of Space*, trans. Maria Jolas. Boston, MA.

Baker, Jeffrey (1982) Prelude and prejudice, *The Wordsworth Circle*, 13: 79–86.

Bakhtin, Mikhail (1984) *Rabelais and His World*, trans. Helene Iswolsky. Bloomington, IN.

Barker, Francis (ed.) (1982) *1789: Reading, Writing, Revolution: Proceedings of the Essex Conference on the Sociology of Literature, July, 1981*. Colchester.

Barker, Francis (1984) *The Tremulous Private Body: Essays on Subjection*.

Barrell, John (1986) *The Political Theory of Painting from Reynolds to Hazlitt: 'The Body of the Public'*. New Haven, CT.

Barrell, John (1988) *Poetry. Language and Politics*. Manchester.

Barthes, Roland (1977) *Image – Music – Text*, trans. and ed. Stephen Heath.

Bate, Jonathan (1991) *Romantic Ecology: Wordsworth and the Environmental Tradition*.

Beatty, Bernard and Newey, Vincent (eds) (1988) *Byron and the Limits of Fiction*. Liverpool.

Belanger, Terry (1978) From bookseller to publisher: changes in the London book trade, in Richard G. London (ed.) *Book-Selling and Book Buying: Aspects of the Nineteenth-Century British and North American Book Trade*. ACRL Publications in Librarianship, (40) Chicago.

Belanger, Terry (1982) Publishers and writers in eighteenth-century England, in Isabel Rivers (ed.) *Books and Their Readers in Eighteenth-Century England*. Leicester.

Belsey, Catherine (1980) *Critical Practice*.

Bender, John (1989) 'New Historicism and the Enlightenment', unpublished manuscript.

Benjamin, Walter (1978) *Reflections: Essays, Aphorisms, Autobiographical Writings*, trans. Edmund Jephcott. New York.

Bennett, Tony (1979) *Formalism and Marxism*.

Benveniste, Emile (1971) *Problems in General Linguistics*. Miami, FL.

Bialostovsky, Don (1989) Wordsworth's dialogic art, *The Wordsworth Circle*, 20: 140–7.

Bialostovsky, Don (1982) *Wordsworth, Dialogics and the Practice of Criticism*. Cambridge.

Bishop, Jonathan (1959) Wordsworth and the 'Spots of Time', *Journal of English Literary History*, 26: 45–65.

Blanchot, Maurice (1982) *The Siren's Song*, ed. Gabriel Josipovici and trans. Sacha Rabinovitch. Brighton.

Bloom, Harold *et al.* (1979) *Deconstruction and Criticism*.

Bostetter, Edward E. (1963) *The Romantic Ventriloquists: Wordsworth, Coleridge, Shelley, Keats, Byron*. Seattle, WA.

Bradley, A.C. (1920) Wordsworth, in *Oxford Lectures on Poetry*.

Brennan, Matthew C. (1987) The 'ghastly figure moving at my side': The discharged soldier as Wordsworth's shadow, *The Wordsworth Circle*, 18: 19–22.

Brinkley, Robert A. (1981) The incident in the Simplon Pass: A note on Wordsworth's revisions *The Wordsworth Circle*, 12: 122–4.

Browning, Robert (1981) *Robert Browning: The Poems*, ed. John Pettigrew, supp. and completed by Thomas J. Collins, 2 vols. Harmondsworth.

Bubner, Rüdiger (1988) *Essays in Hermeneutics and Critical Theory*, trans. Eric Matthews. New York.

Butler, Marilyn (1981) *Romantics, Rebels and Reactionaries: English Literature and its Background, 1760–1830*. Oxford.

Butler, Marilyn (ed.) (1984) *Burke, Paine, Godwin, and the Revolution Controversy*. Cambridge.

Byron, George Gordon, Lord (1980–1) *The Complete Poetical Works*, ed. Jerome McGann. Oxford.

Chandler, James K. (1984) *Wordsworth's Second Nature: A Study of the Poetry and Politics*. Chicago.

Clark, T.J. (1984) *The Painting of Modern Life: Paris in the Art of Manet and his Followers*. Princeton, NJ.

Clegg, Stewart, Boreham, Paul and Dow, Geoff (1986) *Class, Politics and the Economy*.

Cohen, Ralph (1975) Literary theory as a genre, *Centrum*, 3: 45–64.

Cohen, Ralph (1986) History and genre, *New Literary History*, 17: 203–18.

Coleridge, Samuel Taylor (1956–71) *Collected Letters of Samuel Taylor Coleridge*, ed. Earl Leslie Griggs, 6 vols. Oxford.

Coleridge, Samuel Taylor (1969) *Coleridge on Shakespeare*, ed. Terence Hawkes. Harmondsworth.

Coleridge, Samuel Taylor (1972) *Lay Sermons*, ed. R.J. White. Princeton, NJ.

Coleridge, Samuel Taylor (1983) *Biographia Literaria, or Biographical Sketches of my Literary Life and Opinions*, ed. James Engell and W. Jackson Bate, 2 vols. Princeton, NJ.

Collin, Françoise (1971) *Maurice Blanchot et la Question de l'Ecriture*. Paris.

Copley, Stephen and Whale, John (eds) (1992) *Beyond Romanticism: New Approaches to Texts and Contexts 1780–1832*.

Court, Franklin E. (1988) The social and historical significance of the first English Literature Professorship in England, *Publications of the Modern Language Association of America*, 103: 796–807.

Crane, R.S. (1967) *The Idea of the Humanities and Other Essays, Critical and Historical*. Chicago.

Culler, Jonathan (1981a) Presupposition and intertextuality, in *The Pursuit of Signs: Semiotics, Literature, Deconstruction*. Ithaca, NY.

Culler, Jonathan (1981b) Story and discourse in the analysis of narrative, in *The Pursuit of Signs*. Ithaca, NY.

Culler, Jonathan (1988) *Framing The Sign: Criticism and its Institutions*. Oxford.

de Man, Paul (1979a) *Allegories of Reading: Figural Language in Rousseau, Nietzsche, and Proust*. New Haven, CT.

de Man, Paul (1979b) Semiology and rhetoric, in *Allegories of Reading*. New Haven, CT.

de Man, Paul (1983a) *Blindness and Insight: Essays in the Rhetoric of Contemporary Criticism*, 2nd rev. edn. Minneapolis, MN.

de Man, Paul (1983b) The rhetoric of temporality, in *Blindness and Insight*, 2nd rev. edn. Minneapolis, MN.

de Man, Paul (1984) *The Rhetoric of Romanticism*. New York.

de Man, Paul (1986) Introduction in Hans Robert Jauss, *Toward an Aesthetic of Reception*, trans. Timothy Bahti. Minneapolis, MN. (Reprinted in *The Resistance to Theory*. Minneapolis, MN, 1986.)

De Quincey, Thomas (1970) *Recollections of the Lakes and the Lake Poets*, ed. David Wright. Harmondsworth.

de Selincourt, Ernest (ed.) (1926) *The Prelude, or Growth of a Poet's Mind*. Oxford.

de Selincourt, Ernest (ed.) (1967–) *The Letters of William and Dorothy Wordsworth*, 2nd (enlarged) edn rev. Chester L. Shaver, Mary Moorman and Alan G. Hill, 7 vols. Oxford.

Derrida, Jacques (1980) The law of genre, trans. Avital Ronnell, *Critical Inquiry*, 7: 55–81.

Derrida, Jacques (1987) *The Truth in Painting*, trans. Geoff Bennington and Ian McLeod. Chicago.

Dreyfus, Hubert and Rabinow, Paul (1983) *Michel Foucault: Beyond Structuralism and Hermeneutics*, 2nd edn. Chicago.

Elliott, Philip (1972) *The Sociology of the Professions*. New York.

Ellis, David (1985) *Wordsworth, Freud and the Spots of Time: Interpretation in The Prelude*. Cambridge.

Emsley, Clive (1979) *British Society and The French Wars, 1793–1815*.

Engell, James (1989) *Forming the Critical Mind: Dryden to Coleridge*. Cambridge, MA.

Feather, John (1984) The commerce of letters: The study of the eighteenth-century book trade, *Eighteenth-Century Studies*, 17: 405–24.

Feather, John (1985) *The Provincial Book Trade in Eighteenth-Century England*. Cambridge.

Fineman, Joel (1986) *Shakespeare's Perjured Eye: The Invention of Poetic Subjectivity in the Sonnets*. Berkeley, CA.

Fish, Stanley (1967) *Surprised by Sin: the Reader in Paradise Lost*.

Foucault, Michel (1972) *The Archaeology of Knowledge and the Discourse on Language*. New York.

Foucault, Michel (1977) *Language, Counter-Memory, Practice: Selected Essays and Interviews by Michel Foucault*, ed. Donald F. Bouchard. Ithaca, NY.

Foucault, Michel (1979a) *Discipline and Punish: The Birth of the Prison*. New York.

Foucault, Michel (1979b) What is an author?, in J.V. Harari (ed.) *Textual Strategies: Perspectives in Post-Structuralist Criticism*. Ithaca, NY.

Foucault, Michel (1980) *Power/Knowledge: Selected Interviews and Other Writings 1972–77*, ed. C. Gordon. Brighton.

Foucault, Michel (1981–7) *The History of Sexuality*, 3 vols. Harmondsworth.

Foucault, Michel (1986) Of other spaces, trans. Jay Miskoweic, *Diacritics*, 16: 22–7.

Foucault, Michel (1988) *Politics, Philosophy, Culture: Interviews and Other Writings 1977–1984*, ed. Lawrence D. Kritzman. New York.

Gadamer, Hans-Georg (1975) *Truth and Method (Wahrheit und Methode)* trans. G. Baden and J. Cumming. New York.

Gaskell, Ronald (1991) *Wordsworth's Poem of the Mind: An Essay on The Prelude*. Edinburgh.

Gay, John (1974) *Poetry and Prose*, 2 vols, ed. Vinton Dearing and Charles E. Beckwith. Oxford.

Gill, Stephen (ed.) (1975) *The Salisbury Plain Poems of William Wordsworth*. Ithaca, NY.

Gill, Stephen (1983) Wordsworth's poems: The question of text, *Review of English Studies*, 34: 172–90.

Gill, Stephen (1990) *William Wordsworth: A Life*. Oxford.

Gittings, Robert (1968) *John Keats*. Harmondsworth.

Godzich, Wlad (1982) Introduction, in Hans Robert Jauss, *Aesthetic Experience and Literary Hermenentics*, trans. Michael Shaw. Minneapolis, MN.

Green, Nicholas (1990) Rustic retreats: visions of the countryside in mid nineteenth-century France, in Simon Pugh (ed.) *Reading Landscape*. Manchester.

Greenblatt, Stephen (ed.) (1988a) *Representing the English Renaissance*. Berkeley, CA.

Greenblatt, Stephen (1988b) *Shakespearean Negotiations: The Circulation of Social Energy in Renaissance England*. Oxford.

Hamilton, Paul (1986) *Wordsworth*. Brighton.

Haney, David P. (1981) The emergence of the autobiographical figure in *The Prelude*, Book 1, *Studies in Romanticism*, 20: 33–64.

Hartman, Geoffrey (1987a) *The Unremarkable Wordsworth*.

Hartman, Geoffrey (1987b) *Wordsworth's Poetry, 1787–1814*. Cambridge, MA.

Hartman, Geoffrey (1990) 'Was it for this . . . .?:' Wordsworth and the Birth of the Gods, in Kenneth R. Johnston *et al.* (eds) *Romantic Revolutions: Criticisms and Theory*. Bloomington, IN.

Hayden, John O. (ed.) (1977) *William Wordsworth: The Poems*, 2 vols. Harmondsworth.

Haydon, Benjamin Robert (1960–3) *The Diary of Benjamin Robert Haydon*, ed. Willard B. Pope, 5 vols.

Hegel, G.W.F. (1975) *Aesthetics: Lectures on Fine Art*, trans. T.M. Knox, 2 vols. Oxford.

Heidegger, Martin (1962) *Being and Time*, trans. John MacQuarrie and Edward Robinson. New York.

Heidegger, Martin (1971) *Poetry, Language, Thought*, trans. Albert Hofstadter. New York.

Heller, Scott (1991) The human body and changing conceptions of it draw attention of humanities and social-science scholars, *The Chronicle of Higher Education*, 12 June: A4, A8–9.

Hirsch, E.D. (1967) *The Validity of Interpretation.* New Haven, CT.

Hodgson, John (1991) 'Was it for this . . . ?': Wordsworth's Virgilian Questionings, *Romans and Romantics (Texas Studies in Language and Literature)*, 33: 125–36.

Hollander, John (1981) *The Figure of Echo: A Mode of Allusion in Milton and After.* Berkeley, CA.

Hollander, John (1988) *Melodious Guile: Fictive Pattern in Poetic Language.* New Haven, CT.

Hyde, Ralph (1988) *Panoramania!*

Jacobus, Mary (1989) *Romanticism, Writing and Sexual Difference: Essays on The Prelude.* Oxford.

Jameson, Fredric (1991) *Postmodernism, or, The Cultural Logic of Late Capitalism.*

Jarvis, Robin (1981) The five-book *Prelude*: A reconsideration, *Journal of English and Germanic Philology*, 80: 528–51.

Jauss, Hans Robert (1970–1) Literary history as a challenge to literary theory, trans. Elizabeth Benzinger, *New Literary History*, 2: 7–37. (Reprinted as ch. 1 of Jauss (1982) *Toward an Aesthetic of Reception.* Minneapolis, MN).

Jauss, Hans Robert (1982a) *Aesthetic Experience and Literary Hermeneutics*, trans. Michael Shaw. Minneapolis, MN.

Jauss, Hans Robert (1982b) *Toward an Aesthetic of Reception*, trans. Timothy Bahti. Minneapolis, MN.

Jauss, Hans Robert (1989) *Question and Answer: Forms of Dialogic Understanding*, ed. and trans. Michael Hays. Minneapolis, MN.

Johnson, Terence (1977) The professions in the class structure, in Richard Scase (ed.) *Industrial Society: Class, Cleavage and Control.* New York.

Johnston, Kenneth R. (1984) *Wordsworth and The Recluse* New Haven, CT.

Kamuf, Peggy (1986) Monumental de-Facement: on Paul de Man's *The Rhetoric of Romanticism*, *Comparative Literature*, 38: 319–28.

Kant, Immanuel (1989) *The Critique of Judgement*, trans. James Creed Meredith. Oxford.

Keats, John (1970) *Letters of John Keats*, ed. Robert Gittings. Oxford.

Kernan, Alvin (1987) *Samuel Johnson and the Impact of Print.* Princeton, NJ. (Published in the UK as *Printing Technology, Letters and Samuel Johnson*).

Kishel, Joseph F. (1981) Wordsworth and the Grande Chartreuse, *The Wordsworth Circle*, 12: 82–8.

Klancher, Jon (1989) English Romanticism and cultural production, in H. Aram Veeser (ed.) *The New Historicism.* New York.

Kramer, Lawrence (1987) Gender and Sexuality in *The Prelude*: The question of Book Seven, *Journal of English Literary History*, 54: 619–38.

Kristeller, Paul O. (1965) The modern system of the arts, in Kristeller (ed.) *Renaissance Thought II*. New York.

Larson, Magali Sarfatti (1977) *The Rise of Professionalism: A Sociological Analysis*. Berkeley, CA.

Lefebvre, Henri (1971) *Everyday Life in the Modern World*. Harmondsworth.

Lefebvre, Henri (1991) *The Production of Space*, trans. Donald Nicholson Smith. Oxford.

Lehan, Richard (1990) The theoretical limits of the new historicism, *Journal of New Literary History*, 21: 533–54.

Levao, Ronald (1971) 'Above *Tintern Abbey*: The Subject as Object in Wordsworth's Poetry', unpublished paper.

Levine, Philippa (1986) *The Amateur and the Professional: Antiquarians, Historians and Archaeologists in Victorian England, 1838–1886*. Cambridge.

Levinson, Marjorie (1986) *Wordsworth's Great Period Poems*. Cambridge.

Levinson, Marjorie, Butler, Marilyn, McGann, Jerome and Hamilton, Paul (1989) *Rethinking Historicism: Critical Readings in Romantic History*. Oxford.

Lindenberger, Herbert (1964) *On Wordsworth's Prelude*. Princeton, NJ.

Lindenberger, Herbert (1984) Toward a new history in literary study, in Richard Brod and Phyllis Franklin (eds) *Profession 84*. New York.

Lindenberger, Herbert (1990) *The History in Literature: On Value, Genre and Institutions*. New York.

Liu, Alan (1989a) The power of formalism: The new historicism, *Journal of English Literary History*, 56: 721–71.

Liu, Alan (1989b) *Wordsworth: The Sense of History*. Stanford, CA.

Livingston, Ira (1990) 'Wheel Within Wheel: A Cultural Physics of Irony', unpublished dissertation.

MacDonald, William (1923) *The Intellectual Worker and His Work*.

McFarland, Thomas (1982) Wordsworth on man, on nature, and on human life, *Studies in Romanticism*, 21: 601–18.

McFarland, Thomas (1992) *William Wordsworth: Intensity and Achievement*. Oxford.

McGann, Jerome (1983a) *A Critique of Modern Textual Criticism*.

McGann, Jerome (1983b) *The Romantic Ideology: A Critical Investigation*. Chicago.

McGann, Jerome (ed.) (1985) *Historical Studies and Literary Criticism*. Madison, WN.

McGann, Jerome (1988) *The Beauty of Inflections: Literary Investigations in Historical Method and Theory*. Oxford.

McMaster, Graham (ed.) (1972) *Penguin Critical Anthology: William Wordsworth*. Harmondsworth.

Manning, Peter J. (1990) *Reading Romantics: Texts and Contexts*.

Martin, Philip W. (1991) Romanticism, history, historicisms, in Kelvin Everest (ed.) *Revolution in Writing*. Milton Keynes.

Meyer, Michel (1983) *Meaning and Reading*. Amsterdam.

Meyers, Robin and Harris, Michael (eds.) (1985) *Economics of the British Book-Trade, 1605–1939.* Cambridge.

Michael, Ian (1987) *The Teaching of English from the Sixteenth Century to 1870.* Cambridge.

Mill, John Stuart (1924) *The Autobiography of John Stuart Mill.* New York.

Milton, John (1971) *Complete Poetical Works,* ed. John Carey and Alastair Fowler.

Norris, Christopher (1985) *The Contest of Faculties: Philosophy and Theory after Deconstruction.*

Noyes, Richard (1968) *Wordsworth and the Art of Landscape.* Bloomington, IN.

Ogden, John T. (1978) Was it for this?, *The Wordsworth Circle,* 9: 371–2.

Onorato, Richard, J. (1971) *The Character of the Poet: Wordsworth in 'The Prelude'.* Princeton, NJ.

Owen, W.J.B. (1985a) The descent from Snowdon, *The Wordsworth Circle,* 16: 65–73.

Owen, W.J.B. (ed.) (1985b) *The Fourteen Book Prelude.* Ithaca, NY.

Owen, W.J.B. and Smyser, Jane Worthington (eds) (1974) *The Prose Works of William Wordsworth,* 3 vols. Oxford.

Parrish, Stephen (1977) *The Prelude, 1798–1799, by William Wordsworth.* Ithaca, NY.

Patterson, Lyman Ray (1968) *Copyright in Historical Perspective.* Nashville, TN.

Plant, Marjorie (1965) *The English Book Trade: An Economic History of the Making and Sale of Books,* 2nd edn.

Poovey, Mary (1988) *Uneven Developments: The Ideological Work of Gender in Mid-Victorian England: Women in Culture and Society.* Chicago.

Pugh, Simon (ed.) (1990) *Reading Landscape: Country – City – Capital.* Manchester.

Punter, David (1989) *The Romantic Unconscious: A study in Narcissism and Patriarchy.* Hemel Hempstead.

Puttenham, George (1970) *The Arte of English Poesie.* Columbus, OH. (1589; facsimile rep. ed. Edward Archer (1906))

Quintilian (1921) *Institutio Oratoria,* trans. H.E. Butler, 4 vols. Cambridge, MA.

Rader, Melvin (1967) *Wordsworth: A Philosophical Approach.* Oxford.

Ray, William (1984) *Literary Meaning: From Phenomenology to Deconstruction.* Oxford.

Reed, Mark L. (ed.) (1991) *The Thirteen-Book Prelude by William Wordsworth,* 2 vols. Ithaca, NY.

Ricardo, David (1819) *On The Principles of Political Economy and Taxation,* 2nd edn.

Riffaterre, Michael (1990) Fear of theory, *New Literary History,* 21: 921–38.

Roe, Nicholas (1988) *Wordsworth and Coleridge: The Radical Years.* Oxford.

Rogers, Deborah D. (1989) The commercialization of eighteenth-century English literature, *Clio,* 18: 171–8.

Rollins, H.E. (1948) *The Keats Circle: Letters and Papers, 1816–1879*, 2 vols. Cambridge, MA.

Rose, Mark (1988) The author as proprietor: *Donaldson v. Becket* and the genealogy of modern authorship, *Representations*, 23: 51–85.

Rosenau, Pauline Marie (1992) *Post-modernism and the Social Sciences: Insights, Inroads, and Intrusions*. Princeton, NJ.

Rosenberg, Harold (1982) *The Anxious Object*. Chicago.

Ross, Kristin (1988) *The Emergence of Social Space: Rimbaud and the Paris Commune*. Minneapolis, MN.

Ross, Marlon (1986) Naturalizing gender: woman's place in Wordsworth's ideological landscape, *Journal of English Literary History*, 53: 391–410.

Ross, Trevor (1990) 'How "Poesy" became "Literature": Making and Reading the English Canon in the 18th Century', unpublished manuscript.

Rueschemeyer, Dietrich (1986) *Power and the Division of Labour*. Stanford, CA.

Rzepka, Charles J. (1986) *The Self as Mind: Vision and Identity in Wordsworth, Coleridge, and Keats*. Cambridge, MA.

Sawicki, Jana (1988) Identity politics and sexual freedom: Foucault and feminism, in Irene Diamond and Lee Quinby (eds) *Feminism and Foucault: Reflections on Resistance*. Boston.

Schapiro, Barbara (1987) Wordsworth's visionary imagination: A new critical context, *The Wordsworth Circle*, 18: 137–45.

Shaw, Philip and Stockwell, Peter (eds) (1991) *Subjectivity and Literature from the Romantics to the Present Day: Creating the Self*.

Shelley, Percy Bysshe (1977) *Shelley's Poetry and Prose*, ed. Donald H. Reiman and Sharon B. Powers. New York.

Simpson, David (1982) *Wordsworth and the Figurings of the Real*.

Simpson, David (1987) *Wordsworth's Historical Imagination: The Poetry of Displacement*. New York.

Sinfield, Alan (1981) Against appropriation, *Essays in Criticism*, 31: 181–95.

Siskin, Clifford (1988) *The Historicity of Romantic Discourse*. Oxford.

Siskin, Clifford (1990) Wordsworth's prescriptions: romanticism and professional power, in Gene W. Ruoff (ed.) *The Romantics and Us: Essays on Literature*. New Brunswick, NJ.

Soja, Edward W. (1989) *Postmodern Geographies: The Reassertion of Space in Critical Social Theory*.

Stelzig, Eugene L. (1987) Coleridge in *The Prelude*: Wordsworth's fiction of alterity, *The Wordsworth Circle*, 18: 23–27.

Stillinger, Jack (1989) Textual primitivism and the editing of Wordsworth, *Studies in Romanticism*, 28: 3–28.

Stoddard, E.W. (1985) Flashes of the invisible world: reading *The Prelude* in the context of the Kantian sublime, *The Wordsworth Circle*, 16: 32–7.

Stoddard, E.W. (1988) All freaks of nature: The human grotesque in Wordsworth's city, *Philological Quarterly*, 67: 37–62.

Thomson, James (1981) *The Seasons*, ed. James Sambrook. Oxford.

Turner, John (1986) *Wordsworth: Play and Politics. A Study of Wordsworth's Poetry, 1787–1800.*

Veeser, H. Aram (ed.) (1989) *The New Historicism.* New York.

Vogler, Thomas A. (1971) *Preludes to Vision: The Epic Venture in Blake, Wordsworth, Keats, and Hart Crane.* Berkeley, CA.

Waiting for the Palfreys: The Great Prelude Debate, *The Wordsworth Circle* (special issue), 17: 1–38 (including Herbert Lindenberger (2–5) and Norman Fruman (7–14) for the 1805 version; J. Robert Barth (16–20) and Jeffrey Baker (22–4) for 1850).

Walters, Gwyn (1974) The booksellers in 1759 and 1774: The battle for literary property, *Library*, 5th series, 29: 287–315.

Ward, Geoffrey (1988) Byron's artistry in deep and layered space, in Bernard Beatty and Vincent Newey (eds) *Byron and the Limits of Fiction.* Liverpool.

Weinsheimer, Joel (1991) *Philosophical Hermeneutics and Literary Theory.* New Haven, CT.

Weiskel, Thomas (1976) *The Romantic Sublime: Studies in the Structure and Psychology of Transcendence.* Baltimore, MD.

White, Hayden (1973) *Metahistory: The Historical Imagination in Nineteenth-Century Europe.* Baltimore, MD.

Wiles, R.M. (1957) *Serial Publication in England Before 1750.* Cambridge.

Williams, Raymond (1977a) *The Country and the City.*

Williams, Raymond (1977b) *Marxism and Literature.* Oxford.

Wolfson, Susan (1984) The illusion of mastery: Wordsworth's revisions of 'The Drowned Man Of Esthwaite', 1799, 1805, 1850, *Publications of the Modern Language Association of America*, 99: 917–54.

Wolfson, Susan (1986) *The Questioning Presence: Wordsworth, Keats, and the Interrogative Mode in Romantic Poetry.* Ithaca, NY.

Wolfson, Susan (1990) Questioning 'The Romantic Ideology': The case of Wordsworth, *Revue Internationale de Philosophie*, 44: 429–47.

Woodmansee, Martha (1984) The genius and the copyright: economic and legal conditions of the emergence of the author, *Eighteenth-Century Studies*, 17: 425–48.

Woodring, Carl (1970) *Politics in English Romantic Poetry.* Cambridge, MA.

Wordsworth, Jonathan (1977) The Five-Book *Prelude* of Early Spring, 1804, *Journal of English and Germanic Philology*, 76: 1–25.

Wordsworth, Jonathan, Abrams, M.H. and Gill, Stephen (eds) (1979) *The Prelude: 1799, 1805, 1850: Authoritative Texts, Context and Reception, Recent Critical Essays.* Norton Critical Edition, New York.

Wordsworth, Jonathan (1982) *The Borders of Vision.* Oxford.

Young, Robert (1979) The eye and progress of his song: A Lacanian reading Of Wordsworth's *Prelude*, *Oxford Literary Review*, 3: 78–98.

Young, Robert (1982) Reply to 'Prelude and Prejudice' by Jeffrey Baker, *The Wordsworth Circle*, 13: 87–8.

Further Reading

1 Paul de Man and Imaginative Consolation

Marilyn Butler, *Romantics, Rebels, and Reactionaries* (Oxford, 1981)
   A lucid and informative introduction to the cultural and political contexts which helped shape the writing of Wordsworth and his contemporaries.

Jacques Derrida, *The Ear of the Other* (New York, 1985)
   A fascinating discussion of the conditions for autobiographical writing. The main focus is on Nietzsche, but Derrida's argument can be carried over into a reading of *The Prelude*.

Geoffrey Hartman, *Wordsworth's Poetry, 1787–1814* (New Haven, CT, 1964)
   This study places *The Prelude* in the context of Wordsworth's poetic development. Hartman's close readings of Wordsworth's poetry are unparalleled for their acuity and depth.

Geoffrey Hartman, *The Unremarkable Wordsworth* (1987)
   A collection of Hartman's essays on Wordsworth. A valuable complement to *Wordsworth's Poetry*, this collection has some perceptive accounts of the complex temporal structures of Wordsworth's poetry, and its relation to the work of Hegel and Heidegger.

David Simpson, *Wordsworth and the Figurings of the Real* (1982)
   Good detailed readings of particular poems, following through the political and philosophical implications of the interplay of differing perceptions in Wordsworth's poetry.

Gayatri Chakravorty Spivak, 'Sex and History in *The Prelude*', in *In Other Worlds, Essays in Cultural Criticism* (1987)
 Develops a psychoanalytic and deconstructive reading of the text, which draws out the anxieties about gender and politics at play in Wordsworth's acts of self-definition in *The Prelude*.

2 Romantic Space

Maurice Blanchot, *The Space of Literature*, trans. Ann Smock (Lincoln NB, 1989)
 A useful corrective to Bachelard's 'happy space' and to Lefebvre's spatial materialism. Although Blanchot is concerned with mental or imaginary space, there is nothing comforting about this thesis: 'in the world things are transformed into objects in order to be grasped, utilized, made more certain in the distinct rigour of their limits and the affirmation of a distinct homogeneous space. But in imaginary space things are transformed into that which cannot be grasped' (141).

Jamie Brassett, 'Cartographies of Subjectification: For the Subject of a Material Space'. University of Warwick PhD thesis (1992)
 Brassett's thesis is a challenging exploration of political space in Kant (1989), Bachelard (1969) and Deleuze (1989).

Gilles Deleuze and Felix Guattari, *A Thousand Plateaus: Capitalism and Schizophrenia*, trans. Brian Massumi (1989)
 Deleuze and Guattari present two distinctive though interrelated models of material space. The first is 'striated space': the space of the state which is fixed, ordered and reterritorialized. The second is 'smooth space': nomadic space which is decentred, deregulated and revolutionary.

Jacques Derrida *et al.*, *Deconstruction 2, Architectural Design*, 58 (1989), 1–97
 This includes an interview with Derrida as well as essays by deconstructive architects such as Robert Eisenmann and Daniel Libeskind. The aim is to solicit the privilege accorded to Kantian and Heidegerrian 'architectronics'.

Alice Kaplan and Kristin Ross, 'Introduction' in *Everyday Life*, Yale French Studies 73 (Fall, 1987), 1–4
 A useful introduction to the work of Lefebvre.

Henri Lefebvre, *Le Droit à la ville* (Paris, 1968); 'Reflections on the Politics of Space', trans. M. Enders, *Antipode*, 8 (1976), 30–7
 Two works by Lefebvre that anticipate and look back on *The Production of Space*.

For a more detailed bibliography of works on social space see Soja 1990: 249–57.

3 Working *The Prelude*

Nancy Armstrong, *Desire and Domestic Fiction: A Political History of the Novel* (Oxford, 1987)
By gendering Foucault's history of power, Armstrong brilliantly rewrites and links the rise of the novel and the rise of the middle class.

Ralph Cohen, 'History and genre' *New Literary History*, 17 (1986), 203–18
Precise formulations and examples turn this essay into the most effective formulation of Cohen's theory of genre.

Michel Foucault, *The Archaeology of Knowledge and The Discourse on Language* (New York, 1972)
This volume as a whole is the most systematic elaboration of Foucault's theory of discourse; the appendix on language is a particularly concise and accessible elaboration of his premises.

Michel Foucault, *Power/Knowledge: Selected Interviews and Other Writings 1972–1977*, ed. Colin Gordon (New York, 1988)
By masterfully manipulating the genre of the 'interview', Foucault both describes and enacts the concept of power/knowledge.

Terence Johnson, 'The Professions in the Class Structure', in Richard Scase (ed.), *Industrial Society: Class, Cleavage and Control* (New York, 1977), 93–110
By synthesizing and critiquing earlier work, Johnson produces the most useful sociological analysis of professionalism in terms of class.

Alvin Kernan, *Samuel Johnson and the Impact of Print* (Princeton, NJ, 1987)
Kernan provides a practical and quotable history of the construction of the modern concept of 'literature' in the eighteenth century.

Lyman Ray Patterson, *Copyright in Historical Perspective* (Nashville, TN, 1968)
Patterson assembles a very informative history of the origins of copyright.

Dietrich Rueschemeyer, *Power and the Division of Labor* (Stanford, CA, 1986)
Rueschemeyer's sociological inquiry helps us to rethink the history of work by refusing to naturalize the division of labour.

4 'Answering Questions and Questioning Answers'

Jonathan Culler, 'Presupposition and Intertextuality' (1976), in *The Pursuit of Signs: Semiotics, Literature, Deconstruction* (Ithaca, NY, 1981), pp. 100–118
Culler argues that the significance of a work, indeed the possibility of its significance, depends on its relationship to a body of discourse that is already

in place. Verbal constructs are therefore intertextual and involve presuppositions. Poems containing questions make this involvement explicit in
two ways – not just because a question is to be completed by a reader,
but also because the framing of a question bears the suppositions of a prior
discourse.

Jonathan Culler, 'Story and Discourse in the Analysis of Narrative' (1980), in
The Pursuit of Signs, pp. 169–87
    Culler deconstructs the assumed priority of event to discourse (the presenta-
tion of the events), by showing how various narrative and discursive requirements produce the events that are reported. Implied, but not stated, is the sort
of application to questioning and answering that 'Presupposition and Intertextuality' performs: an uncertainty whether a question leads to an answer, or
whether a question is generated by presuppositions about an answer.

Geoffrey Hartman, '"Was it for this . . . ?": Wordsworth and the Birth of
the Gods', in Kenneth R. Johnston *et al.* (eds), *Romantic Revolutions: Criticism
and Theory* (Bloomington, IN, 1990), pp. 8–25
    Hartman shows how the unsettled question of identity in *The Prelude* is
implicated with questions about the sources of inspiration: 'from what depth
of otherness do they come, and what do they imply about the relation of mind
to nature, even of human existence to other-than-human modes of being?'

John A. Hodgson, ' "Was it for this . . . ?": Wordsworth's Virgilian Questionings', *Romans and Romantics* (*Texas Studies in Language and Literature*) 33,
(1991), 125–36
    Hodgson examines the embedding of this inaugural question in an intertex-
tual field of 'antecedent and precedent, an allusive context that finely grounds
Wordsworth's persistent questionings'. He ranges from classical to contemporary texts.

John Hollander, *Melodious Guile: Fictive Pattern in Poetic Language* (New Haven,
CT, 1988)
    In a study concerned in its larger terms to show how poems write parables
about their poeticalness, Hollander examines how questions and answers
exceed their semantic function to becomes figures, metaphors, tropes. Like
Culler, he locates questioning and answering in an intertextual domain and
studies their mutual implication.

Susan J. Wolfson, 'Questioning "The Romantic Ideology": The Case of
Wordsworth', *Revue Internationale de Philosophie*, 44 (1990): 429–47
    This essay shows how Wordsworth's texts use questions to contest and frac-
ture from within the ideological certainties and strategies of evasion which certain New Historicist critics attribute to them.

Susan J. Wolfson, *The Questioning Presence: Wordsworth, Keats, and the Interrogative Mode in Romantic Poetry* (Ithaca, NY, 1986)

Three chapters of this book study the interrogative character of *The Prelude*: one on the poem's interrogative origins, and one each on how these origins inflect the organization of its first and last books, its Introduction and Conclusion. The larger project of the book is to contrast the poetics of questioning that characterize Keats and Wordsworth and to show how these contrasts illuminate the central tensions of Romantic poetics.

Index

A CRITICAL AND CULTURAL THEORY READER

Antony Easthope and Kate McGowan (eds)

The 'death of literature' and the rise of post-structuralist theory has breached the traditional opposition between the literary canon and popular culture, both in principle and in academic practice. There is therefore a growing need for a collection of essays and extracts required for the study of both high and popular culture together. Covering 'Semiology', 'Ideology', 'Subjectivity', 'Difference', 'Gender' and 'Postmodernism', this reader contains essential writing by Saussure, Barthes, Lacan, Kristeva, Foucault, Derrida and Cixous, as well as material for the study of popular culture. It concludes with a section of 'Cultural Documents' with extracts from Leavis, Adorno, Williams and Tzara. With the concerns of students in mind, each section is fully introduced and each piece of writing summarized in the notes.

Contents

288pp   0 335 09944 0 (Paperback)   0 335 09945 9 (Hardback)

DEBATING TEXTS
A READER IN TWENTIETH-CENTURY THEORY AND METHOD
Rick Rylance (ed.)

This anthology presents examples from a broad range of the most important theoretical schools of this century, from liberal humanism to contemporary feminism, from Russian Formalism to Marxism and post-structuralism, and includes writings by F.R. Leavis, Barthes, Derrida, Williams and Fish among others. The examples are arranged in seven self-contained sections, and each section is prefaced by a clear account of context and leading ideas and contains a guide to further reading. Three principles underlie the choice, organization and exposition of the essays and extracts included: firstly, the desire to make central primary texts more easily and widely accessible; secondly, an awareness of the need for a connection between literary theory and the actual practice of criticism, which has promoted the choice within each section of an example of the close application of theoretical principles to a piece of writing; and thirdly, the aim of providing readers with a sense of the development of literary theory and alerting them to the grounds of contemporary arguments. The reader is encouraged through guides to further reading to move confidently and with heightened curiosity beyond the selection contained here.

Literary theory engages fundamental questions about our activities as readers of and commentators on that body of material we call literature. Above all, this book is about debate.

304pp   0 335 09005 2 (Paperback)   0 335 09006 0 (Hardback)

ENGLISH ROMANTIC POETRY
AN INTRODUCTION TO THE HISTORICAL
CONTEXT AND THE LITERARY SCENE

Kelvin Everest

This new study presents a concise but comprehensive introduction to the political, social and literary contexts of English Romantic poetry. The significant movements and events of the momentous historical epoch in which the major English Romantic poets lived and worked – which stretched from the American War of Independence to the Great Reform Bill – are presented in careful outline. The life and career of each of these poets – Blake, Wordsworth, Coleridge, Shelley, Keats and Byron – is then described and placed in detailed relation to the larger historical forces and circumstances of the period, and to the literary culture within and against which they worked and published.

The book includes a detailed historical and literary chronology of the period and bibliograhpies on the historical and literary context and on works by and about the six poets featured.

Contents
Part 1: The historical context – Years of revolution: 1775–93 – Years of reaction: 1793–1815 – The post-war period: after 1815 – Part 2: The social relations of the Romantic poets – Blake, Wordsworth, Coleridge – Keats, Shelley, Byron – Part 3: The literary scene – Conclusion – Chronology – Bibliography – Index.

128pp   0 335 09297 7 (Paperback)   0 335 09298 5 (Hardback)

REVOLUTION IN WRITING
BRITISH LITERARY RESPONSES TO THE FRENCH REVOLUTION

Kelvin Everest (ed.)

The bicentenary of the French Revolution gave rise to immense interest, both popular and academic, into the historical, political and cultural legacies of the events of 1789. This innovative volume forms a broad-ranging investigation into the British literary reponses to this monumental upheaval. Mary Wollstonecraft, Edmund Burke, and Tom Paine of course provide a recurring central focus of attention, but there are also searching considerations of the impact of the Revolution on the romantic poets, and on such relatively neglected figures as Hannah More, who here for the first time receives constructive analysis from More, who here for the first time receives constructive analysis from a feminist perspective. Theoretical issues are also a major interest in this volume, including both the Revolutionary period's own attempts to theorize its experience, and our contemporary struggle to establish a mode of literary-historical analysis which can mediate between text, history, and theory.

Contents

Contributors

Kelvin Everest, Tom Furniss, Harriet Devine Jump, Philip W. Martin, Michael Rossington, Kathryn Sutherland, John Whale.

176pp   0 335 09756 1 (Paperback)